Introduction to engineering measurements

Consulting editor:

C. T. Butler, B.Sc.(Eng.), C.Eng., F.I.Mech.E., F.I.Prod.E.

Head of Department of
Mechanical and Production Engineering,
Trent Polytechnic, Nottingham

Also in the series:

Introduction to engineering measurements

H. G. Bass

McGRAW-HILL

New York · St. Louis · San Francisco · Düsseldorf ·
Johannesburg · Kuala Lumpur · Mexico · Montreal ·
New Delhi · Panama · Rio de Janeiro · Singapore ·
Sydney · Toronto

Published by
McGRAW-HILL Publishing Company Limited
MAIDENHEAD · BERKSHIRE · ENGLAND

07 094146 7

PRINTED AND BOUND IN GREAT BRITAIN

Preface

The need to make measurements of an increasing number of physical variables, coupled with the speed and accuracy of measurement which is now being demanded, have led to an increasing sophistication of measuring equipment and techniques. The effects of this are now being felt in all branches of engineering.

Measuring equipment has become not only more sophisticated, but also more varied; this variety has meant that practising engineers and technicians have had to acquire the ability to select critically from the wide range of available equipment. Selection is not so much a matter of knowing what is 'good' and what is 'bad', but rather of deciding what is appropriate to the particular measurement problem on hand.

Besides being able to select, those concerned must be competent to handle measuring equipment correctly, and to gauge the reliability of the results obtained from it. Measurement, like design, differs from many other engineering activities in that the existence and consequences of error may not immediately be apparent. A series of measurements taken in the course of development may not be seen to be invalid until a later date—possibly not until final design and manufacture have been completed. In such cases, measurement errors may prove expensive.

Informed selection and use of equipment, and an appreciation of the causes and magnitudes of errors, are more likely to be achieved if the operating principles of the equipment are understood. It is the aim of this book to set down these principles as simply as possible, primarily for those who are becoming involved with engineering measurements for the first time: it is not intended as a reference source for experts.

The need for education in measurement techniques was acknowledged when the Joint Committee for Higher National Certificates and Diplomas in Mechanical, Production and Aeronautical Engineering introduced the compulsory subject of Engineering Measurements into the HNC in Engineering. The requirement for a suitable textbook to cover the syllabus for the new subject, in a manner intelligible to students at the first-year HNC level, provided the prime motivation for writing the present book. The same syllabus has provided the guide lines determining the scope of the book.

It is hoped that, besides providing a satisfactory treatment of the subject for the course mentioned above, the book will be useful as preliminary reading for a number of more advanced courses. The aim has been to keep the content as practical as is consistent with these terms of reference, and to avoid, as far as possible, the encumbrances of abstruse physics and advanced mathematics. These aspects of the subject can be pursued by the would-be measurement specialist at a later date.

Because of its relation to the HNC Engineering Measurements syllabus, the book has been written primarily for readers with a 'mechanical' background. This has produced the problem of steering a satisfactory course through a subject which is both electrical and mechanical. The methods of dealing with electrical and electronic topics may seem unduly naïve to 'electrical' readers. To such readers, apologies are offered for the many electrical half-truths which the book undoubtedly contains. On the other hand, those mechanical engineers who regard all electricity as suspect will probably consider the content too electrical. One cannot, however, alter the nature of the subject. Some functional understanding of a limited number of electrical and electronic devices is now essential to an appreciation of measurement techniques. This understanding need not be deep, nor require a detailed knowledge of electrical theory. It is rather a question of appreciating the capabilities and limitations of the various electronic 'boxes' which now form an inevitable part of the measurement scene.

In spite of the wide variety of measurements with which engineers may now be concerned, there is a great deal of material which is relevant to many or all measuring systems, rather than specific to a particular system. For this reason, the book has been divided into three parts. Part 1 deals with the common background material; Part 2 with specific measurements, and Part 3 with performance. Although performance logically belongs to the 'common' section of the subject, it has been relegated to the final chapters so that concepts of performance could be related to equipment described in earlier chapters. The final chapter on dynamic performance should also provide a suitable lead-in to more advanced works.

I am indebted to a large number of industrial organizations, and colleagues both past and present, for assistance with various sections of the book. To attempt to list all these would be to risk offence by omission. I believe those concerned are aware of my gratitude. Where photographs or descriptions of equipment peculiar to a particular manufacturer have been included, the source has been acknowledged.

H. G. BASS

Contents

Contents

Contents

Part 1

General Background

1. Terminology

The act of making a measurement involves a comparison of an unknown quantity with a known quantity of similar kind. Thus a measurement of length with a metre scale is a comparison between the unknown length and a known length marked on the scale. The comparison may be indirect: a mechanical pressure gauge does not contain a series of reference pressures with which the measured pressure may be compared; but it has at some previous time been subjected to known pressures, and its scale marked off (or its mechanism adjusted) accordingly—i.e., it has been *calibrated*. If the known quantities used in the comparison process are known with sufficient accuracy, they may be referred to as *standards*. A particular standard may represent any number of the corresponding *units*, or a fraction of a unit. Units, standards, and calibration are discussed more fully in chapter 2.

Given some concept of the appropriate unit, the unaided human senses are capable of making estimated measurements of many physical variables; e.g., given the concept of a metre, estimates of length can be made. Such estimates are usually inaccurate. The general purpose of measuring equipment is to enable the user to make measurements with greater accuracy than could be achieved without it.

In using a metre scale, the comparison of the known and unknown lengths is made directly by eye. More commonly, the measuring process ends with a pointer moving relative to an instrument scale. An indicator of this kind is called an *analogue display*, meaning that the magnitude of the pointer displacement represents, or is analogous to, the measured value. The alternative to an analogue display is a *digital display*—a series of digits (figures) appearing on a screen, or printed on paper, so that the measurement is read directly as a number. A digital display requires less concentration on the part of the observer than does an analogue display, since interpolation between scale markings is not required.

1.1 Analysis of the measuring system

A simple instrument, such as a mercury thermometer, is a self-contained single unit. Although, as an academic exercise, it is possible to consider such instruments as being divided into different functional parts, there is little to

3

be gained in practice by doing so. On the other hand, more sophisticated measuring systems usually comprise a number of distinct functional elements; a better understanding of these systems can be acquired by considering these elements separately.

A measuring system commonly consists of: (a) a device to convert the measured value into a convenient form of *signal*; this signal is usually, but not necessarily, electrical; (b) a receiving instrument which interprets the signal to the user of the equipment; (c) a means of transmitting the signal from (a) to (b). Figure 1.1 represents a generalized measuring system of this kind. The accepted term for the converting device is the *transducer*; the other two

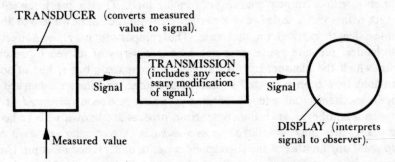

Figure 1.1 Generalized measuring system

sections of the system may conveniently be called the *display* and the *transmission* respectively. In some cases the transmission may consist of a simple electrical connection. In others, some modification of the transducer output may be necessary before it can operate the display. (The term 'transmission' has been used here to include any such modification, or *conditioning*, of the signal; this is a broader usage of the term than is customary in the field of telecommunications.) The three main functional elements are not necessarily physically separate units. It is quite common for signal-conditioning elements, such as amplifiers, to be combined with either the transducer or the display. The present trend, resulting from recent advances in microelectronics, is for miniature conditioning elements to be built into the transducer unit. (Where this is done, manufacturers almost invariably refer to the whole unit as the transducer.) Some authorities restrict the use of the word 'transducer' to devices with an electrical output; other terms, such as 'primary element' or 'measuring element' are then used for non-electrical devices performing the transducing function.

A distinction may be made between *primary* and *secondary* transducers. Consider the device shown schematically in Fig. 1.2, which is intended to convert force (the weight W) into an electrical potential. The force extends the spring S by an amount determined by the spring stiffness. Hence, S may be regarded as a primary transducer, converting force to displacement.

4

The lower end of S is mechanically connected to a sliding contact on the potential divider D, and the position of this contact determines the reading of the voltmeter V. The potential divider may therefore be called a secondary transducer in this application. (A particular type of transducer may perform a primary transducing function in some applications, and a secondary transducing function in others.)

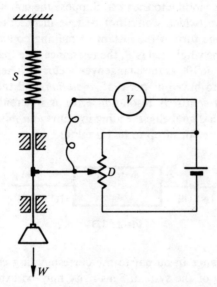

Figure 1.2 Schematic two-stage transducer

1.2 Performance

In discussing the performance of measuring systems in general terms, it is convenient to regard the system or part of a system under discussion a sa 'box' which receives a certain input, and produces a corresponding output (Fig. 1.3). The 'box' could represent one of the elements in the measuring chain shown in Fig. 1.1, or it could represent the whole system. If the whole system is being considered, the input is the quantity being measured (sometimes called the *measurand*), and the output is the observed response of the display.

In an ideal measuring system, the output would always bear a known relationship to the input, and would respond instantaneously to any change in input. Such ideal performance cannot be achieved in practice—there will always be some inaccuracy or *error* in the relationship. Error is usually expressed as a percentage of the full measuring range of the unit or system concerned. Thus, if an electrical indicator reading from 0 to 100 mA is specified as accurate to ± 2 per cent, it may exhibit errors of up to ± 2 mA anywhere within its range.

5

There are many possible causes of error—friction, temperature changes, faulty observation, and so on. Errors may also be inherent in the operating principle of the measuring device. Consider the sliding contact on the potential divider D in Fig. 1.2. If the resistance is in the form of a wire coil, it is virtually impossible to obtain 'smooth' changes in output as the contact slides along the coil, since the resistance must change by a finite amount as the contact moves from one turn of the winding to the next. Suppose the coil has 100 turns, and make the assumption (which would not be true in practice) that the slider loses contact with one turn at the instant of making contact with the next. If the resistance of the whole coil is R, the resistance on either side of the contact would 'jump' by $R/100$ as the changeover occurred. The potential divider would then be said to have one per cent *resolution*, and the resulting errors are called *resolution errors*. A resolution error is inherent in any form of digital display; e.g., a digital clock reading in hours and minutes is inevitably liable to a resolution error of up to half a minute.

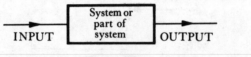

Figure 1.3

The ratio of a change in output to the corresponding change in input is called the *sensitivity* of the system. Sensitivity may be expressed in a wide variety of units, according to the instrument or system concerned. In the case of a mercury-in-glass thermometer, for instance, the input is a temperature change, and the output is the displacement of the end of the mercury column; sensitivity would therefore be expressed in mm/degC. Where input and output are of the same form, the ratio of output to input is referred to as *magnification* or *gain* rather than sensitivity. 'Magnification' is normally applied only to mechanical devices, whereas 'gain' may be applied to both electronic and mechanical equipment; thus an amplifier producing an output of 100 mV for an input of 2 mV is said to have a voltage gain of 50.

Sensitivity, magnification and gain are all expressions for the slope of a graph of output plotted against input. If this slope is constant, the device or system concerned is said to be *linear*. (More strictly, it should be said to have a 'linear response' or 'linear characteristic'.)

Where equipment is used to measure rapidly changing variables, it is necessary to distinguish between *static* and *dynamic* accuracy. Again considering a mercury-in-glass thermometer, it might be accurate within 0·2 per cent if tested by immersing it for a long period in a liquid bath maintained at a steady temperature. Any error found in a test of this kind would be *static error*. However, if it were transferred from a bath at 20°C to another bath at 100°C, it would not immediately indicate 100°C. After allowing for any static errors, the difference between the actual and 'true' readings at any instant after transfer would be *dynamic error*.

The magnitudes of the dynamic errors in a measuring system depend on the way in which the input changes; hence, if dynamic accuracy is to be specified, the nature of the input must also be specified. One method of doing this is to define the error in terms of the response to a sinusoidal input of stated frequency. A sinusoidal input will produce, in general, a sinusoidal output of 'incorrect' amplitude—i.e., there is an amplitude error, which usually increases with increasing frequency. The magnitude of this error at stated frequencies gives an indication of the dynamic performance of the system. This method of testing is known as *frequency-response* testing; it is discussed more fully in chapter 14.

1.3 Fields of measurement

Although the basic principles of measurement are common to all branches of engineering, the techniques used for measuring similar variables may vary according to application. The decision to use a particular technique may be based on considerations of cost, environment, accuracy and speed of measurement, physical size, or reliability.

In production engineering, most measurements are concerned with physical dimensions. The main requirement in this field is for high orders of accuracy, measurements correct to one part in 10^4 being commonplace. Often speed of measurement is of secondary importance, since, in the normal process of selective inspection, production samples are taken at intervals and inspected by manual methods. If automatic 'on-line' inspection is employed, however, high-speed measurement may be essential to avoid delaying the production process. Cost of inspection equipment is important, as it represents part of the production costs and must be justified on economic grounds. This particular field of measurement is usually known as *metrology*.

Measuring equipment associated with continuous industrial processes is known as *process instrumentation*. The object of the equipment in this case is to ensure proper control of the process. (Control may be the responsibility of the plant operators, acting on information provided by the instruments, or it may be initiated automatically by the instruments themselves.) Cost must again be justified on economic grounds, except where instruments are required for reasons of safety. In many applications, relatively slow speeds of response are acceptable, since the measured quantities themselves are incapable of rapid rates of change. Processes often run non-stop for long periods; long-term reliability with minimum maintenance is therefore important, particularly on automatically controlled plants. The measuring equipment must be robust, as environmental conditions are often unfavourable.

In contrast to the fields of metrology and process instrumentation, there are many measuring situations in such fields as research and the testing of machinery, where speed of response is of primary importance. If the measured quantity is of a transient or cyclic nature (e.g., the pressure in an internal-combustion engine cylinder) the equipment must be capable of 'following' the changes in the variable as they occur. A further requirement for measuring equipment in research applications is versatility. Whereas in other fields of measurement equipment is usually intended to make a specific measurement, (or, in the case of metrological instruments, measurements of a well-defined type) research equipment should be useful for more than one project. If sufficient versatility can be achieved, cost may not be a primary consideration.

A feature common to all measurement fields is the increasing usage of electronic equipment; the principal reasons for this are the very rapid speeds of response of electronic devices, and the ease with which electrical signals may be amplified and transmitted over large distances. Because of these advantages, there is a growing tendency to convert the measured value into an electrical signal at an early stage in the measurement process. Thus, although there is a large number of possible variables (displacement, temperature, pressure, etc.), the measurement problem ultimately becomes that of measuring an electrical quantity. Systems intended for fundamentally different measurements may therefore contain a number of similar electrical and electronic elements; some of the more common of these elements are discussed in chapters 4, 5, and 6.

Summary

Measurement is a process of comparison, which may be direct or indirect. The quantity with which the unknown value is compared may be called a standard; adjustment of the readings of a measuring system to standard input values is called calibration.

Most measuring systems may be regarded as a 'chain' comprising transducer, transmission, and display; transmission elements often have to condition the signal from the transducer to make it suitable for the operation of the display.

An error is a departure of the output of any part of the system from the value truly representing the input; errors are usually expressed as a percentage of the full measuring range. Errors caused by dynamic inputs may greatly exceed those associated with static inputs. The slope of the output–input graph may be called sensitivity, gain, or magnification.

2. Units and Standards

It is axiomatic that before anything can be measured, a unit appropriate to the measured quantity must be established. Two systems of units—the metric and imperial (or UK) systems respectively—have been of major international importance in recent years. Neither of these systems was uniquely defined; there have been variant forms of both in existence at the same time. A recent decision of most major countries to adopt a single system, known as the 'Système Internationale' or 'SI', has greatly simplified the situation. SI units are based on metric units, and are in many respects identical to those of the MKS system.† In the UK, the change to SI is intended to be virtually complete by 1975 (see ref. 1).

2.1 SI units

SI units are based on the kilogramme as the unit of mass, the metre as the unit of length, and the second as the unit of time. These are familiar metric units. It should be emphasized at the outset, however, that SI does not use the kilogramme as a unit of force, as some metric systems have done. The confusion between mass and weight, which was prevalent with many earlier systems of units, should therefore be eliminated. SI units are in fact *coherent*. This means that products and quotients of the units produce units of the resultant quantity. Thus, since the metre is the unit of length, and the square metre the unit of area, then these units are coherent, since $1 \text{ m} \times 1 \text{ m} = 1 \text{ m}^2$. Readers familiar with imperial units will recall that they were not coherent in all respects. In one variant of the imperial system, the pound was used as the mass unit, the foot and second as the length and time units respectively, and the pound-force as the force unit. The basic relation between force and mass being that 'force is equal to mass times acceleration', the unit of force coherent with the lb, ft, s, would be given by $1 \text{ lb} \times 1 \text{ ft/s}^2$. This is clearly not the lbf, since by definition 1 lbf gives a mass of 1 lb an acceleration of g ft/s^2 (approximately 32·2 ft/s^2 at the surface of the earth). The coherent unit of force in this system was therefore $(1/g) \times 1$ lbf (the poundal).

The SI unit of force is the newton, defined as the force required to give a mass of 1 kg an acceleration of 1 m/s^2. By definition, this is a coherent unit.

† The MKS system is one of the more recent variants of the metric system; it was adopted by many branches of the UK electrical industry.

2.1.1   Basic units. In any system, certain units are referred to as *basic*, meaning that they are defined, as opposed to being derived from other units. A certain minimum number of units must be defined in this way, though the choice of just *which* units are defined is theoretically open. Length, mass, and time are customarily chosen as basic units. As stated above, in SI these are the metre, the kilogramme, and the second respectively. The remaining mechanical units may be derived from these basic units. Further basic units are required to deal with thermodynamic, electrical, and optical quantities. These basic units are the kelvin (temperature), the ampère (electric current) and the candela (luminous intensity).

2.1.2   Primary standards. Basic units must be defined in such a way that they can be reproduced to an acceptable degree of accuracy. To ensure this, there must be some form of ultimate *standard* for the unit to which all can refer, either directly or indirectly. This standard is known as the *primary* standard for the quantity concerned; its nature necessarily depends on the nature of the quantity to be measured. In the case of mass, the primary standard is a stable mass of metal which is internationally recognized as being the standard kilogramme; it is kept at the Bureau International des Poids et Mésures, at Sèvres, France. The standard metre was formerly defined in an analogous manner (i.e., by a physical object), but it is now defined in terms of the wavelength of light from a specified source. Similarly, the ultimate time standard, which was originally defined in terms of the mean solar day, is now defined in terms of the frequency of a particular radiation from the atom of caesium.

These changes reflect the current preference for *reproducible* primary standards rather than *fixed* primary standards. A reproducible standard is one which, in principle, can be established locally as required. (In practice, the nature of the equipment and expertise required to reproduce primary standards is such that the operation is outside the capabilities of anything but a highly specialized laboratory.) A fixed standard, in contrast, is a unique physical object; the standard kilogramme referred to above is the only remaining fixed primary standard. The 'non-mechanical' basic units—i.e., the ampère, kelvin,† and candela, are also defined in terms of reproducible standards (see ref. 2).

2.1.3   Multiple and Submultiple units. Multiples and submultiples of SI units are expressed by the addition of standard prefixes to the nominal unit.‡ Many of the prefixes are already familiar from their usage in former metric systems. The more commonly encountered prefixes, with their abbreviations and meanings, are given in Table 2.1.

† The kelvin (K) is identical to the degree Celsius (°C, formerly called Centigrade) but is used for temperatures measured relative to the absolute zero ($-273 \cdot 15°C$).

‡ The term 'nominal unit' is used here to mean the metre, gramme, second or ampère, as opposed to the SI *basic* units (metre, *kilo*gramme, second and ampère).

Although there is no theoretical objection to the use of any of the prefixes of Table 2.1 with any SI unit, restricted use of the prefixes is recommended (see ref. 3). The principles of the recommended restrictions are firstly that only units which are commonly required should be employed, and, secondly, preference should be given to units for which the power of 10 in the third

Table 2.1   SI unit prefixes

(Preferred prefixes are in bold type)

Prefix	Symbol	Meaning
giga	G	Nominal unit $\times 10^9$
mega	M	Nominal unit $\times 10^6$
kilo	k	Nominal unit $\times 10^3$
hecto	h	Nominal unit $\times 10^2$
deca	da	Nominal unit $\times 10$
deci	d	Nominal unit $\times 10^{-1}$
centi	c	Nominal unit $\times 10^{-2}$
milli	m	Nominal unit $\times 10^{-3}$
micro	μ	Nominal unit $\times 10^{-6}$
nano	n	Nominal unit $\times 10^{-9}$
pico	p	Nominal unit $\times 10^{-12}$

Table 2.2   Preferred multiples of basic units

Basic unit	Recommended multiple and submultiple units							Remarks
metre (m)		km		mm	μm	nm		μm also known as *micron*
kilogramme (kg)	Mg		g	mg	μg			Mg also known as *tonne*
second (s)		ks		ms	μs	ns		Use of min, hour, day also approved
ampère (A)		kA		mA	μA	nA	pA	
kelvin (K)								Multiples not used
Nominal unit multiplier	10^6	10^3	10^0	10^{-3}	10^{-6}	10^{-9}	10^{-12}	

column of Table 2.1 is divisible by 3. Recommended multiple and submultiple units for the basic quantities are given in Table 2.2.

2.1.4   Derived units. From the SI basic units, the remaining units required in the various branches of engineering may be derived. Individual derived units will be discussed in more detail in the course of this book as the subject matter of the chapters requires. A selection of derived units is given in Table

11

2.3, with their respective recommended multiples and submultiples. It will be noted that some of these units are given special names.

2.1.5   Conversion factors. Imperial units will inevitably be used in some branches of industry for a number of years after the official adoption of SI units. Conversions between the two systems will therefore be necessary. Some of the more frequently required conversion factors are given in the Appendix.

Table 2.3   Derived units

Quantity	Name	Abbreviation	Recommended multiples and submultiples						
Force	newton	N (kg m/s²)			kN	mN	µN		
Work (and energy)	joule	J (Nm)	GJ	MJ	kJ	mJ			
Power	watt	W (Nm/s)	GW	MW	kW	mW	µW	nW	pW
Pressure†		N/m²	GN/m²	MN/m²	kN/m²				
Velocity		m/s			km/s				
Electrical potential	volt	V		MV	kV	mV	µV		
Electrical resistance	ohm	Ω		MΩ	kΩ				

† The *bar* (10^5 N/m²) is also used.

Fuller information on conversion factors, and on the nature and use of SI units, may be obtained from ref. 3.

2.2   Calibration

An indication has been given of the nature of SI units, and of the primary standards on which they are based. Such standards are not accessible for the purpose of checking industrial measuring equipment. In the case of a fixed standard, this inaccessibility is due partly to geographical inconvenience, and partly to the deterioration of the primary standard which would result from frequent handling. Similar arguments apply to reproducible standards, except that in this case it is the equipment required to reproduce the standards which must be safeguarded. Such equipment is invariably complex and expensive, and requires properly trained operators.

Thus, whether the primary standard is in the fixed or reproducible class, more practical forms of standard are required for the routine checking of industrial measuring equipment. Practical standards are required also for a number of derived quantities for which there is no primary standard. The standards used for these purposes are variously described as *reference*, *laboratory*, or *working* standards. Unfortunately, the relationship between the several terms used to describe the quality of standards is not precisely defined, except in certain specialized fields. Thus, the term *laboratory standard*, which is usually applied to the highest-grade standard in a particular laboratory, does not define the grade of the standard in any absolute sense. The laboratory standard in one organization might be of the same quality as the working standard in a better-equipped organization.

Any valid system of standards must conform to the principle of *traceability*. This means that any particular standard must at some time have been checked against a standard of higher grade, which must itself have been checked against the next higher grade, and so on, the process eventually being *traceable* back to the primary standard. The frequency at which these various checking processes are carried out depends on the nature of the standards concerned. A standard may take the form of a single piece of material (such as a bar employed as a length standard) which is subject only to slow deterioration through wear; or it may be in the form of a relatively complex instrument, for which there are several possible causes of error.

The process of checking a measuring system against a standard, or a standard against a higher-grade standard, is called *calibration*. If errors are found during calibration, they may be taken into account in subsequent use; an alternative course in the case of a measuring system is to adjust the responses of the system—i.e., to *recalibrate* it. The course chosen will depend on the nature of the equipment and the use to which it is put. Recalibration of, say, a micrometer screw gauge is scarcely practicable (apart from resetting the zero). On the other hand, more sophisticated measuring devices usually incorporate a number of calibration adjustments.

2.2.1 Calibration adjustments. If equipment is intended to be recalibrated by the user, the manufacturer's instruction book will specify the correct procedure. Whatever the details of the calibration process, the main adjustments for the majority of instruments are functionally similar. Two basic adjustments which are almost always provided are for zero and sensitivity respectively. *Zero adjustment* is universal on measuring devices having moving parts; *sensitivity adjustment* (also called *gain, range* or *span* adjustment), though not invariably provided, is customary where mechanical linkages or electronic amplifiers are incorporated. The zero adjustment adds or subtracts an equal amount from all the indications of the system,† whereas the sensitivity adjustment expands or contracts the response over the whole measuring range (i.e., it adds or subtracts an equal *percentage* of all indications of the system).

As an example of sensitivity and zero adjustments, consider the hypothetical spring balance shown in Fig. 2.1. The principle of the instrument is that a load attached at A produces a rotation of the beam about the pivot B, the rotation being resisted by the restraining torque of the spring S. If it is assumed that the centre of gravity of the unloaded system is at the pivot point

† This will be only approximately true in systems for which the relation between the input and the response is not linear.

13

B, then the relation between the measured weight *W* and the deflection (found by taking moments about *B*) is

$$Wl\cos\theta = K\theta, \qquad \text{or} \qquad \frac{\theta}{\cos\theta} = \frac{l}{K}W, \tag{2.1}$$

where *K* is the torsional stiffness of the spring, and the other symbols are as shown in the diagram. It will be noted that the input–output relationship is not precisely linear: it is approximately linear if θ is small. Suppose now the spring *S* is replaced by a nominally identical spring, which in fact has a slightly different torsional stiffness $(K+\Delta K)$. This will produce an error in the

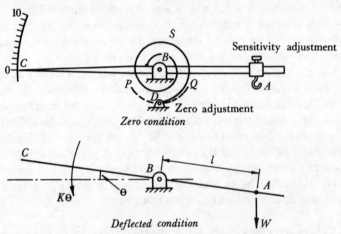

Figure 2.1   Calibration adjustments

readings which increases with the deflection. (If the springs are truly geometrically identical, it will produce no zero error.) The error in the reading could be corrected by moving the fixture *A* to increase the length *l* by Δl, where $\Delta l/l = \Delta K/K$. The relationship between *W* and θ is then restored to that represented by eq. (2.1), since $(l+\Delta l)/(K+\Delta K)$ is equal to l/K. This is a sensitivity adjustment, since it produces an equal percentage change in all the readings.

If we now assume that the unstrained length of the replacement spring differs from that of its predecessor, the position of the pointer at zero load will be offset from the zero mark on the scale, i.e., there will be a zero error. This can be corrected by relocating the fixed end *D* of the spring. A zero adjustment could therefore be provided by arranging for the point *D* to be set in any required position on the circular arc *PDQ*. Thus on this particular instrument, the zero adjustment may be provided at *D*, and the sensitivity adjustment is provided at *A*. A closer investigation of the statics of the mechanism shows that the two adjustments are not entirely independent. The fixture *A* cannot be weightless; its movement along the beam will therefore

14

alter the position of the centre of gravity, which was assumed to be at the pivot point, and this will produce a zero error.

Although complete independence of calibration adjustments is desirable in measuring equipment, it is seldom achieved. Any recalibration procedure, therefore, usually involves a series of alternate settings of the sensitivity and zero adjustments.

2.2.2 Frequency of checking. Reasons for measuring systems 'losing' their calibration are many: they include accidental damage, abuse, wear of moving parts, ageing of electronic components, and changes in the environmental conditions. No general rule can therefore be laid down for the frequency at which calibration checks should be carried out. A decision must be made for each measuring system, taking into account the likelihood of errors developing and the accuracy required. This applies equally to routine measuring equipment and to instruments used as standards. As the likelihood of errors developing in instruments generally increases with increasing complexity, many standard instruments are of relatively simple design, even though this simplicity may mean that complex manual procedures are necessary to obtain readings from them.

2.3 Functions of the NPL and BCS

Industrial users must be able to determine the accuracy of their measuring equipment, in order to maintain the efficiency of their own internal processes, and to operate successfully in the framework of national and international trade. They must therefore have access to the appropriate standards. These standards may be in the hands of the user organization itself, or, more frequently, in the hands of the suppliers of the measuring equipment. In either case the standards employed must be traceable back to the appropriate primary standards. However, the nature of primary standards is such that, even though they may be reproducible, it is seldom feasible for the user of the equipment, or the supplier, to have direct access to them. Consequently the process of checking against higher-grade standards must stop short of the primary standard, unless the cooperation of the custodian of the appropriate primary standard is obtained.

In the UK, the main authority charged with the care and maintenance of primary standards (and of the national standard in the case of the kilogramme) is the *National Physical Laboratory* (NPL), and one of the functions of this organization is to carry out calibration checking against primary standards. A great deal of calibration work at lower levels was also formerly done by the NPL, but much of this is now being handled by the *British Calibration Service* (BCS). The BCS was inaugurated by the Ministry of Technology in 1966, and is in a state of continuous development. Its aim is to make the calibration facilities of existing industrial measurement laboratories available to industry as a whole, under the general surveillance of the BCS headquarters. Laboratories may apply to the BCS for approval to offer calibration services for certain types of equipment to specified accuracies; if approval is granted, the laboratory may carry out calibration services of the appropriate types, and issue BCS calibration certificates. Lists of approved laboratories, with details of the services they are able to offer, are available from the BCS.† It is intended that eventually the BCS should relieve the NPL of most of its routine calibration duties, though the first few approved laboratories are concerned only with dimensional measurements, or with the measurement of electrical quantities.

Apart from its remaining activities in the field of calibration, and its wider research activities not specifically concerned with measurement, the NPL maintains an Advisory Secretariat which gives advice on measurement problems.‡ The object of this Secretariat is to give relevant information, if this is available within the NPL, or, if not, to suggest where such information might be obtained.

Summary

SI units are the internationally accepted units for engineering quantities. They are based on the metre, kilogramme, second, kelvin, ampère, and candela. Other units are derived from these basic units. Some derived units have special names—notably the newton, watt, joule, volt, and ohm.

The primary standards for the basic units are all reproducible, except for the mass standard, which is fixed. Primary standards, even when reproducible, are not accessible for the routine checking of measuring equipment. Lower-grade standards are used for this purpose. Any lower-grade standard must be 'traceable' to the corresponding primary standard.

Multiples and submultiples of SI units may be formed by means of standard prefixes. Not all of these prefixes are in general use. The preferred prefixes are mega, kilo, milli, micro, nano, and pico.

The process of comparing the responses of any measuring system with standard input values is called calibration. The calibration of all measuring devices should be checked from time to time, but no general rule for the frequency of such checks can be laid down.

UK national standards are maintained by the National Physical Laboratory, which carries out calibrations against primary standards, and some other specialized types of calibration. Much routine calibration is being transferred from the NPL to approved laboratories of the British Calibration Service.

† British Calibration Service, Stuart House, 23–25 Soho Square, London, W1V 5FJ.
‡ The Advisory Secretariat, Metrology Centre, National Physical Laboratory, Teddington, Middlesex.

References

1 *Change to the Metric System in the United Kingdom*, HMSO.
2 Pamela Anderton and P. H. Bigg, *Changing to the Metric System*, HMSO.
3 *The Use of SI Units*, British Standards Publication PD 5686.

3. Electrical fundamentals

Because of the rapid growth of electrical and electronic instrumentation, a basic functional appreciation of electrical principles is essential to an understanding of measurement techniques. The purpose of this chapter is to summarize, in practical terms, some of the more important electrical concepts. The notes given here are not comprehensive, and are given solely for the benefit of those readers who may be out of touch with electrical technology. No attempt is made to extend electrical knowledge beyond the minimum necessary for the understanding of subsequent chapters. Prior acquaintance with the basic concepts of current, e.m.f., and potential difference is assumed. Following the usual—though strictly incorrect—practice, the word 'voltage' will be used to denote potential difference (p.d.) when it is convenient to do so.

3.1 Alternating and direct current

A voltage, and the resulting current, may be either *direct* (unidirectional) or *alternating* (continually reversing, usually sinusoidally). A direct voltage is specified by giving its amplitude only, in V, mV, or μV; an alternating voltage is specified by its magnitude plus its frequency in hertz (the hertz, abbreviated to Hz, is one cycle per second; the multiple units kHz and MHz are also common). Similarly, currents are expressed in A, mA, or μA, with a statement of the frequency in the case of alternating currents. The stated magnitude of alternating voltage or current is assumed to be the *root mean square* (r.m.s.) value unless otherwise stated. This is the magnitude of the equivalent direct quantity, in terms of power dissipation. It is occasionally necessary to specify the maximum value, or amplitude, of an alternating quantity. The term *amplitude* can be ambiguous. Where doubt could exist, care should be taken to specify whether the *peak* (i.e., mean-to-peak) value or the *peak-to-peak* value is intended. The abbreviations 'a.c.' and 'd.c.' are used to mean 'alternating' and 'direct' respectively when convenient; e.g., the term 'a.c. voltage' is generally accepted, though strictly the 'c', standing for current, is redundant. The process of converting an alternating quantity to the corresponding direct quantity is called *rectification*; it is a comparatively simple electronic technique.

3.2 Component characteristics

Electrical circuit components possess one or more of the qualities of resistance, inductance, and capacitance. The meanings of these terms, and that of the related term *impedance*, are discussed briefly below.

3.2.1 Resistance. The resistance of a conductor in a d.c. circuit is defined as the ratio of the voltage across it to the current flowing through it; or, in conventional symbols, $R = V/I$. The resistance of a metallic conductor is constant at constant temperature, provided that the conductor is not subjected to varying strain. For most metals, resistance increases with (a) temperature, and (b) positive strain in the direction of current flow. Changes of resistance with strain are small; they are of little significance in general engineering, but they provide a useful method for measuring strain. The resistance of a given material (as opposed to that of a conductor of a particular form) is specified by giving its *resistivity*, which is defined as the resistance between opposite faces of a 10 mm cube of the material.

The resistances of semiconductors also depend on temperature and strain; the rates of change of resistance with respect to both temperature and strain are substantially greater than the corresponding rates for metallic conductors. In general, the resistances of semiconductors decrease with increasing temperature.

If two resistances, R_1 and R_2, are connected in series, the net resistance is $R_1 + R_2$; if they are connected in parallel, the net resistance is $R_1 R_2/(R_1 + R_2)$.

3.2.2 Inductance. Within the scope of the present book, the concept of inductance is of importance only in connection with alternating or pulsating currents. In this context, the inductance of a conductor, which in practice is usually in the form of a wire-wound coil, may be regarded as a measure of its ability to generate an alternating e.m.f. when placed in an alternating magnetic field. If this field is caused by a current in the conductor itself, the generated or *induced* e.m.f. opposes the e.m.f. which is producing the current. For this reason it is referred to as a 'back' e.m.f., and its effect is to reduce the current due to the applied e.m.f. Thus an inductive coil (or *inductor*) in an a.c. circuit is analogous to a resistance, in so far as it produces a reduction in the current. This analogous effect is called the *reactance* of the conductor. If it were possible to produce a coil having inductance but no resistance, it would offer no opposition to current flow when placed in a d.c. circuit; in an a.c. circuit, its reactance would be V/I, where V is the voltage across it, and I the current through it. In practice, a coil must possess some resistance, though it may be negligibly small compared with its reactance.

The reactance of a coil is not constant. It depends on the rate of change of the magnetic field associated with the coil—i.e., on the frequency of the current producing the field. For an air-cored coil, the reactance is directly proportional to frequency. For iron-cored coils, the relationship is not linear. The effect of introducing iron, or other ferrous material, into the magnetic field associated with the coil is to increase its inductance, and consequently its reactance.

3.2.3 Capacitance. A capacitor presents a theoretically infinite resistance to d.c., but will pass an alternating current if an alternating voltage is applied across it. (Strictly, an alternating current does not 'pass through' a capacitor, but for practical purposes it may be regarded as doing so.) For a given applied voltage, the magnitude of the current depends on the frequency of the supply and the value of the capacitance. As for an inductor, the ratio V/I is called the reactance of the capacitor; in this case, it is inversely proportional to frequency.

A conventional capacitor consists of two parallel plates of conducting material separated by an insulating dielectric. When a potential V is applied across the capacitor, the plates acquire an electric charge Q which is related to the capacitance C by the relation $Q = CV$. The capacitance of two capacitors connected in parallel is equal to the sum of the individual capacitances.

3.2.4 Impedance. Impedance is defined as the value of V/I for any circuit or part of a circuit, at a stated frequency. In a d.c. circuit, impedance is synonymous with resistance. For a pure inductance or pure capacitance in an a.c. circuit, it is synonymous with reactance. Usually, a.c. circuits contain both resistances and reactances, both contributing to the impedance of the circuit.

The current and voltage in a reactive circuit are not in phase with each other. It is not essential for the purposes of this book to be able to calculate phase relationships in reactive circuits, but it will occasionally be necessary to remember that these phase differences exist. Impedance, being the ratio of volts to ampères, is measured in ohms, like resistance. It is denoted by the letter Z.

3.3 Electromagnetism

Any electrical phenomenon which results from the presence of a magnetic field can be classed as electromagnetic. Thus inductance, discussed in section 3.2.2, is an electromagnetic effect. Other electromagnetic effects which play an important part in measuring equipment are outlined below.

3.3.1 Reluctance. The reluctance of a magnetic flux path is analogous to the resistance of an electrical circuit. Like electrical resistance, it depends on the length and cross-sectional area of the path, and on the nature of the material or materials through which the path passes. The reluctance of a path through iron, or other ferrous material, is very small compared with the reluctance of a path of similar dimensions in air.

3.3.2   Transformer action. The magnetic field due to an alternating current in a coil (the *primary*) will induce an alternating e.m.f. in a neighbouring coil (the *secondary*). For efficient operation, good magnetic coupling is required between the two coils; i.e., a low-reluctance path in the form of an iron core is required to ensure that a dense magnetic flux is produced by a given primary current, and that this flux passes through the secondary.

3.3.3   Motor and generator effects. A conductor moving so that it cuts a magnetic field has an e.m.f. induced in it. By suitable arrangement of a number of conductors on a rotor turning in a magnetic field, a number of induced e.m.f.s may be added; this is the principle of a generator.

A current-carrying conductor placed perpendicular to a magnetic field experiences a force, which will cause it to move unless it is restrained. The direction of the force depends on the direction of the current. This is the motor principle; again, by suitable arrangement of conductors on a rotor, the forces may be added to produce a useful turning moment.

The motor and generator effects interact. As soon as a conductor in a motor moves through the field, an e.m.f. is induced in it, opposing the applied voltage which is causing the motion. Similarly, the conductors of a generator, if it is supplying current, experience forces due to the currents they are carrying. These forces are in opposition to the mechanical forces applied to drive the conductors through the field.

3.3.4   Eddy currents. In a conventional generator, the conductors are organized on the rotor so that the induced e.m.f.s are additive, and the net e.m.f. can be used to supply current in an external circuit. There are no short-circuit paths between the conductors inside the machine. Hence no current flows in the conductors when no external electrical load is connected to the output terminals; under these circumstances the retarding forces referred to in section 3.3.3 are not experienced.

Suppose now the rotor of the generator were replaced by a hollow cylinder of conducting (but non-magnetic) material (Fig. 3.1). The upper part of the cylinder, which is passing under one of the poles of the field magnet, has an e.m.f. induced in it, as would any other form of conductor. However, in the case of the cylinder, immediate short-circuit paths are provided by those parts of the cylinder not in the field. Currents, called *eddy currents*, consequently flow round these paths.

The exact pattern of the current paths is of no importance. The important point is that because they flow, forces will be exerted on the cylinder to oppose its motion. Similar effects will be experienced in any situation where a conductor of substantial area moves relative to a magnetic field.

3.4 Comparator circuits

There are two basic types of circuit which measure electrical quantities by methods of direct comparison: *bridge circuits* and *potentiometers*. These circuits compare the quantity to be measured with a known quantity of similar type. In this respect they differ from simple deflection instruments: an ammeter, for example, measures current by comparing a torque derived from it with a torque derived from a spring; it does not directly compare the current with another current.

Comparator measuring circuits do not fit readily into the generalized

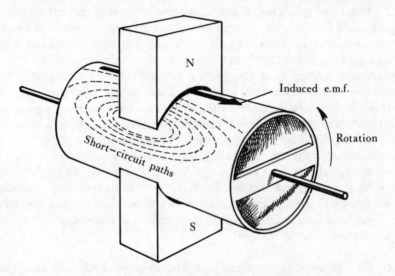

Figure 3.1 Formation of eddy currents

'transducer–transmission–display' measuring system proposed in section 1.1. Physically, comparator circuits may form part of the transducer, or they may be built into the display; they may also take the form of an intermediate unit, which might be regarded as a transmission element. It is, therefore, not possible to deal with comparator circuits in terms of the generalized system. However, in discussing a particular system in which the physical location of the comparator circuit is known, it may still be useful to employ the terminology of the generalized scheme.

3.4.1 D.C. potentiometer. Figure 3.2a shows a d.c. potentiometer in its simplest form. Current from a dry cell E flows through a uniform long resistance S, called the *slidewire*. The purpose of the circuit is to measure the d.c. potential v, which is applied between the points j and h as shown. The sliding contact Y is adjusted until the galvanometer D_1 shows no deflection. (A galvanometer is a sensitive meter which responds to current flow in either direction.) This can occur only if the p.d. across the portion *fg* of the slide-wire is equal to *v*: if these two quantities were unequal, current would flow through the circuit *fjhg*, and cause deflection of the galvanometer. If the terminal p.d. of the cell *E* is *V*, then $v = (x/l)V$, where *x* and *l* are the lengths indicated on the diagram. (This may be proved simply by Ohm's law.)

The arrangement of Fig. 3.2a is of limited practical use, principally because it is restricted to a single voltage range (the terminal p.d. of the cell), the value

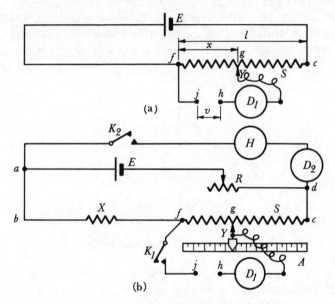

Figure 3.2   Simple potentiometer circuits

of which will change as the cell runs down. Figure 3.2b shows how the circuit may be modified to overcome this objection. Current from the dry cell *E* now flows in a series circuit comprising the slidewire *S*, the variable resistance *R*, and the fixed resistance *X*. The purpose of *R* is to provide an adjustment to compensate for changes in the output of the dry cell. The relative values of resistances *X* and *S* determine the potential drop across *S*, i.e., the measuring range of the potentiometer. The calibrated scale *A* has been added alongside the slidewire, so that the unknown p.d. can be read off directly, after balance has been obtained.

The relation between the length *fg* and the p.d. across it will be constant only if the current through the slidewire is kept constant. This may be checked periodically by comparing the p.d. between the points *b* and *c* with the e.m.f. of the standard cell *H*. (The essential feature of a standard cell is that it maintains its e.m.f. at a constant value, within very close limits, provided that no appreciable current is taken from it; this limitation prevents it from being used to power the potentiometer, in place of the cell E.) To check the p.d. between b and c, switch K_1 is opened and K_2 closed. A second galvanometer D_2 will indicate any unbalance between the p.d. being checked and the e.m.f. of the standard cell. Balance may be restored by adjustment of R. This operation is referred to as *standardizing* the potentiometer. Practical potentiometer circuits use only one galvanometer in place of D_1 and D_2, with a single multiple-contact switch which rearranges the circuit for standardizing.

The simple circuit of Fig. 3.2b differs in many ways from those of commercial potentiometers, but serves to illustrate their essential characteristics. Of these, the most important is that no current is drawn from the source of the unknown p.d. when the circuit is balanced. Consequently, a potentiometer

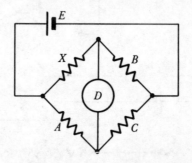

Figure 3.3   Basic Wheatstone bridge

measures p.d.s without introducing 'loading errors' which are inevitable in voltage measurement if the measuring device takes current (section 5.1.1). The second point of importance is that potentiometers powered by dry cells require standardizing at regular intervals if they are to retain their accuracy.

Commercial potentiometers fall into two categories: manually balanced bench instruments, and self-balancing potentiometric recorders. Manually balanced types are usually powered by dry cells and manually standardized. Self-balancing recorders are standardized automatically (section 5.4).

3.4.2   Wheatstone bridge. Four resistors, a detector, and a potential source connected as in Fig. 3.3 constitute a Wheatstone bridge. The resistances A, B, C have known values, and X is a resistance to be measured. If the bridge is d.c. energized, the detector D may be a sensitive galvanometer.

There are two basic methods of using the bridge, shown in Figs. 3.4a and 3.4b respectively. In the *balanced* bridge (Fig. 3.4a), A is a calibrated variable resistance, which is adjusted until the detector shows that there is no p.d. between the points q and s. Application of Ohm's law to the circuit shows that under these circumstances the values of the resistances must be such that $X/A = B/C$. X may therefore be found if A, B and C are known.

An advantage of the balanced method of use is that the result is virtually independent of the supply voltage. The source E may be an ordinary dry cell, and the variations in its output voltage during the course of its life will be unimportant. The resistor S in Fig. 3.4a is not essential to the functioning of the circuit. It is frequently included as a current-limiting device, to restrict the self-heating of the resistors. (Self-heating can cause errors, due to the changes in resistance it produces.) The value of S will affect the sensitivity of the circuit, and it could be used for this purpose if a variable resistor were employed, though it is more usual to adjust the sensitivity of the detector itself.

The manually balanced Wheatstone bridge is primarily useful as a general-purpose laboratory instrument. *Unbalanced* bridges (Fig. 3.4b) usually form

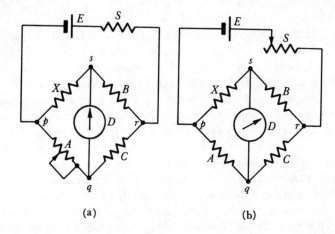

(a)   (b)

Figure 3.4   Wheatstone bridges: (a) balanced; (b) unbalanced

part of a measuring system designed for a specific purpose, one arm of the bridge being some form of transducer which produces changes in resistance in response to changes in the measured variable. Most unbalanced bridges are equi-armed—i.e., the three fixed resistances are equal to the resistance of the transducer under certain specified conditions. (The transducer might be a resistance thermometer, which measures temperatures by measuring the change in resistance of a metallic coil. If the resistance of this coil were 100 Ω at 0°C, the other three bridge resistances might also be 100 Ω; balance would then be obtained at 0°C.) Subsequent changes in the transducer resistance cause a p.d. to be developed across the detector D.

If the resistance of the detector is assumed to be infinite, it may easily be shown that the unbalance p.d. across it varies very nearly linearly with the change in the value of X. Suppose the resistances are all initially equal to R, and that the value of X is then increased to $(R+\Delta R)$, producing a voltage v between the points q and s. Since the detector has been assumed to be of infinite resistance, no current flows through it. The current along the path *pqr* must therefore be constant, and equal to $V/2R$, where V is the voltage applied between the points p and r. Similarly, the current along the path *psr* is $V/(2R+\Delta R)$. The p.d. between s and r is therefore $VR/(2R+\Delta R)$, and the p.d. between q and r is $VR/2R$, or $V/2$. The p.d. between q and s is given by

$$v = (\text{p.d. across } qr) - (\text{p.d. across } sr)$$
$$= V/2 - VR/(2R+\Delta R)$$
$$= V\Delta R/(4R+2\Delta R).$$

This does not represent an exactly linear relationship between v and ΔR. However, if ΔR is very small compared with R, as is often the case in practice, the expression reduces to

$$v \simeq \frac{V}{4} \cdot \frac{\Delta R}{R},$$

(3.1)

which is a linear relationship. In practice, detectors do not have infinite resistance, though some have resistances which are sufficiently high to be regarded as infinite compared with the resistances in the bridge arms. Often the detector is a simple low-resistance galvanometer, in which case the analysis above does not apply. However, a more complex analysis, using Thévenin's theorem, shows that even in the low-resistance case the deflection of the detector will be very nearly proportional to ΔR, provided ΔR is small. The near-linearity of the relationship can be shown very simply in practice, using a calibrated variable resistor in place of X.

The main advantage of the unbalanced form of the bridge over the balanced form is that a reading is obtained automatically on the detector, without the necessity for manual operations. Its disadvantage is that it lacks the inherent accuracy of a 'null-balance' method. In particular, the reading of the detector depends on the value of the bridge voltage V. This must be kept constant, unless it is intended to calibrate the bridge each time it is used. S is shown as a variable resistance in Fig. 3.4b to indicate that, if a dry-cell supply is used, a means of adjusting the bridge voltage V is required.

3.4.3 A.C. bridges. A Wheatstone bridge may be a.c. energized, without altering its principle; such bridges are in fact frequently used. This, however, is not what is usually meant by the term *a.c. bridge*. An a.c. bridge (or *impedance bridge*) is one which, besides being supplied from an a.c. source, has arms which are wholly or partly made up of reactive components (inductors and capacitors).

Figure 3.5 shows a generalized a.c. bridge, the arms having impedances Z_1, Z_2, Z_3, and Z_4 respectively. If the bridge is balanced, it can be shown, by considering the voltages at the points b and d, that the numerical values of these impedances must be such that $Z_1/Z_2 = Z_3/Z_4$. Although this is a necessary condition for balance, it is not all that is required; if the impedances are in this ratio, the *magnitudes* of the voltages at b and d will be equal. However, they could be equal but out of phase, in which case the detector (which must be an instrument sensitive to a.c., not a simple galvanometer) would indicate a state of unbalance.

Because of this complication, the balancing of an a.c. bridge is a relatively complicated business. Most a.c. bridges used for industrial measurements are therefore used in the 'unbalanced' mode, and calibrated empirically. Like the unbalanced Wheatstone bridge, they are used for specific applications, rather than for general-purpose measurements.

The subject of a.c. bridges is a complex one, and readers requiring further information should consult a suitable electrical text (e.g., ref. 1). For the purposes of this book, it will be sufficient to remember the following points: (a) the components in the arms of an a.c. bridge do not have to be of the

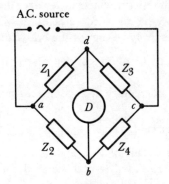

Figure 3.5 Basic impedance bridge

same type; bridges comprising two resistors and two inductors are common; (b) an a.c. bridge is sensitive to changes in the frequency of the supply, since the impedances of the reactive components change with frequency; (c) for a number of reasons, including (b) above, a.c. bridges tend to be less stable than simple d.c. bridges, and calibration checks may therefore have to be made more frequently.

Summary

Electrical circuit components possess one or more of the qualities of resistance, inductance, and capacitance. Inductance does not affect d.c., but capacitance 'blocks' it. Both inductive and capacitive components present impedance to a.c., the value of this impedance depending on frequency.

Conductors moving relative to magnetic fields have e.m.f.s induced in them. Current-carrying conductors in magnetic fields experience forces; this applies whatever the cause of the current—it may be the result of an induced e.m.f., or of an externally applied voltage. The force on a conductor carrying an induced current resists the movement producing the current; this is true for conductors carrying eddy currents, as well as for conductors in 'organized' circuits.

Two basic measuring circuits are: (a) the potentiometer, for precise measurements of d.c. voltage; (b) bridges, which may measure resistance, inductance, or capacitance. Resistance bridges may be either d.c. or a.c. energized, and may be used in either the balanced or unbalanced mode. Impedance bridges used for engineering measurements are normally used in the unbalanced mode.

Examples

1. An unbalanced Wheatstone bridge consists of three fixed resistances of 100 Ω each, and a fourth resistor which varies over the range 100 Ω to 105 Ω. The detector, which may be regarded as being of infinite impedance, reads directly in mV, and the supply voltage at the bridge terminals is 4 V.

(a) What is the sensitivity of the bridge at balance point, expressed in mV/Ω?
(b) What is the total percentage change in sensitivity over the measuring range?

(Ans.: 10 mV/Ω; 4·7 per cent.)

2. The potentiometer circuit of Fig. 3.2b is to be used to measure p.d.s from 0 to 50 mV. A 10 Ω slidewire is to be used, and the p.d. between the points *b* and *c* is to be standardized at 1·1 V.

(a) Find the value of the resistance *X*.
(b) If the e.m.f. of the cell *E* may vary from 1·55 V to 1·35 V, find the corresponding values of the variable resistance *R*. (Neglect the internal resistance of the cell.)

(Ans.: 210 Ω; 90 Ω, 50 Ω.)

Reference

1 C. T. Baldwin, *Fundamentals of Electrical Measurements*, Harrap, 1961.

4. Multi-purpose transducers

The concept of a transducer, as a device for converting the measured value into some convenient form of signal, was introduced in section 1.1. The transducers described in this chapter have been selected because each has a number of possible applications, and will be referred to several times in subsequent chapters. There are many other transducers, both electrical and non-electrical. These will be described as necessary in the course of the book, in the contexts of their particular applications. Those described here convert a mechanical signal (a force, strain, or displacement) into an electrical signal of some kind. Transducers are named according to the nature of the input: thus a displacement transducer converts a displacement into a signal of some other kind, such as voltage.

4.1 Variable potential divider

The variable potential divider, which has already been encountered as the secondary transducer in Fig. 1.2, converts displacement to voltage. A relatively long resistor R (Fig. 4.1) is connected across a constant-voltage source. The output voltage v is obtained between the sliding contact D and one end of the resistor. If resistor is uniform, the output is given by

$$v = (x/l)V. \tag{4.1}$$

The similarity between this circuit and that of the potentiometer (section 3.4.1) is evident. For this reason, the potential divider is often called a potentiometer. (Strictly, this is incorrect: a potentiometer is an instrument for measuring electrical potential, whereas a potential divider is a device for dividing a potential in a ratio determined by the position of a sliding contact. However, the name 'potentiometer' or 'pot' is almost universally used for this class of transducer.)

As a displacement transducer, the potential divider has several inherent weaknesses. Equation (4.1) is true only if the resistance between the output points A and B is infinite. If an electrical load is connected between these points, the output voltage will be less than that predicted by eq. (4.1). The error, which is referred to as 'loading error', is caused by the net resistance between the points D and F being reduced by the presence of the new current path between A and B.

Other objections to the potential divider arise from its use of a sliding contact, or 'wiper'. Sliding contacts must cause friction and eventual wear, and may prove unreliable in some applications, due to corrosion and dirt at the contact point. Also, if the resistance is in the form of a wire coil, the resolution is limited. (This is the most usual form for the resistance; continuous tracks of carbon and plastic materials are also used.) In spite of these limitations, variable potential dividers are widely used. They are simple and inexpensive, and require only a low-voltage d.c. supply; they may be used to measure angular displacements, by arranging the coil in the form of a circular

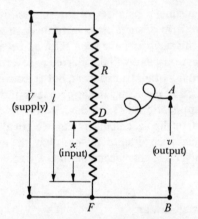

Figure 4.1   Variable potential divider

arc. A number of practical problems of design make potential dividers unsuitable for the measurement of very small displacements; a maximum wiper travel of 10 mm or so is necessary for acceptable results in most applications.

4.2   Electrical-resistance strain gauge

The electrical-resistance strain gauge converts strain (i.e., longitudinal displacement of one end of the gauge relative to the other) into a change of electrical resistance. It is common practice to refer to these devices merely as 'strain gauges'; this practice will be followed here, though strictly the abbreviated term could be used for any means of measuring strain.

4.2.1   Bonded-foil gauges. The commonest form of strain gauge is shown in Fig. 4.2. It consists of a strip of thin metallic foil which is bonded to the member in which the strain is to be measured; the bond ensures that both gauge and member experience the same strain. The nature of the bond must be such that the gauge is electrically insulated from the material to which it is attached. A typical size for a strain gauge of this type would be 5 mm × 20 mm, though gauges as small as 2 mm × 2 mm are available.

The increase in resistance obtained by straining the gauge may be partly explained by the normal dimensional behaviour of elastic materials. If a strip of elastic material is positively strained (extended), it will suffer a reduction in its lateral dimensions. This may easily be demonstrated with a strip of rubber. So when a strain gauge is extended longitudinally, its lateral dimensions, and consequently its cross-sectional area, must decrease. Since the resistance of a conductor is proportional to its length and inversely proportional to the area of its cross-section, the resistance of the gauge would be expected to increase with positive strain. Although this explanation appears to justify the increased resistance in principle, it does not give good quantitative results. The changes in length and cross-sectional area for a given strain may be calculated, and the expected increase in resistance found. In general, the calculated figures do not entirely account for the changes in resistance

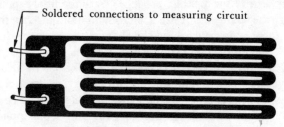

Soldered connections to measuring circuit

Figure 4.2   Foil-type strain gauge

obtained in practice. Further, one particular metal which is sometimes used for strain gauges (nickel) suffers a *decrease* in resistance with increasing strain. It would therefore appear that some internal change takes place in the structure of the material, which affects its resistivity.

Some of the necessary characteristics of a practical strain gauge have already been mentioned. It must be rigidly fixed to the strained member, and electrically insulated from it. Further, it must be of small cross-sectional area, so that its presence does not significantly affect the stress in the strained member, and it must be sufficiently sensitive to produce a measurable output. The metal of which it is made should have a high elastic limit, so that it can be used over a wide range of strain without suffering permanent deformation.

These requirements are reflected in the design of the gauges. The foil of which they are formed is approximately 0·02 mm thick, and they are mounted on a plastic backing which provides the insulation, and facilitates bonding. Sensitivity is determined by the material of the gauge. The relation between the strain, ε, and the corresponding change in resistance, ΔR, is given by

$$\Delta R/R = F\varepsilon \tag{4.2}$$

where R is the unstrained resistance of the gauge, and F is the *gauge factor*, which is constant for a particular gauge. The value of R, for most commercial gauges, is in the range 50–1000 Ω, and F is usually about 2. In use, the gauge may well be required to detect a change in strain of 5×10^{-6} (or 5 *microstrain*). Putting $F = 2$, and substituting this value for ε in equation (4.2), shows that this requirement is equivalent to detecting a change in resistance of 1 part in 10^5. A high value of F is therefore desirable in the interests of increasing sensitivity. The value quoted above is typical for copper–nickel alloys, which are commonly used for strain gauges. There are other materials which will give higher gauge factors, but practical considerations often prevent their use. Some of the points which have to be considered in selecting a strain gauge material are its coefficient of thermal expansion, its temperature co-efficient of resistance, and the ease with which it can be joined to copper leads.

Temperature effects constitute an inherent difficulty in the use of strain gauges. A coefficient of thermal expansion different from that of the test piece will cause errors due to strain produced by differential expansion. More serious still are the changes in resistance brought about directly by change of temperature; these can easily exceed the changes in resistance due to strain. It is essential, therefore, that strain-gauge systems should be designed to eliminate temperature effects. Where possible, this is done by incorporating a second *temperature-compensating* gauge in the circuit, as described in section 4.3. This method requires that the compensating gauge should be maintained at the same temperature as the measuring gauge. In some applications this may not be possible. An alternative is to use *self temperature-compensating* measuring gauges; these may be of composite construction, or specially thermally processed, to be virtually unaffected by temperature over some stated range. It is important to note that a particular temperature-compensated gauge is manufactured for bonding to a material with a specified co-efficient of expansion. If, therefore, the self-compensating qualities of the gauge are being relied on, care must be taken to ensure that the correct gauges are used.

A theoretical objection to the use of bonded strain gauges is that, in most applications, it is impossible to check the accuracy of the readings obtained from them. Once bonded in position, the gauge cannot be removed and resited in a calibration situation—e.g., it cannot be rebonded to a standard test piece of which the characteristics are accurately known. Strain gauges are often used in situations where no other form of strain measurement is possible. As no check on performance can be made, the value of the gauge factor given by the manufacturer has to be accepted. Factors are usually quoted with a tolerance of ± 1 per cent or less. Where a batch of similar gauges is obtained, tests may be carried out on a representative sample, but this does not guarantee the performance of any individual gauge in another situation. However, the quality and uniformity of most modern gauges is such that this objection is not so serious as might first appear.

4.2.2 *Gauge bonding.* Like other bonding operations, successful strain-gauge bonding depends on careful surface preparation and the use of the correct bonding agent. The bond has to be formed between the surface to be strained and the plastic backing material on which the gauge is mounted by the manufacturer. It is important that the adhesive should be suited to this backing; various materials are used for backings, requiring different adhesives. Choice of adhesive is also influenced by the required life of the installation, and by the working conditions. Gauge suppliers normally supply the appropriate adhesives, and will also give detailed instructions on the correct bonding procedures.

Non-corrosive fluxes must be used when connecting the leads to the gauge, and overheating of the gauge must be avoided. After bonding and soldering, the gauge installation is coated with a protective lacquer to prevent damage to the gauge or bond due to the ingress of moisture.

4.2.3 Other types of strain gauge. The bonded-foil gauge, described in section 4.2.1, is the most commonly encountered type of gauge. Early strain gauges were made from fine wire, but these gauges have now been virtually superseded by foil gauges. For applications where a foil gauge would be

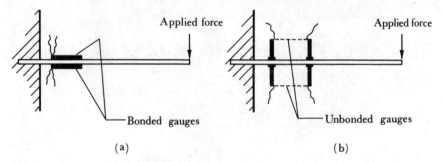

Figure 4.3 Bonded and unbonded strain gauges: force transducer using (a) bonded gauges; (b) unbonded gauges

insufficiently sensitive, *semiconductor strain gauges* (also called piezo-resistive elements) may be employed. Semiconductor strain gauges have higher temperature coefficients of resistance than metal gauges, and generally tend to be less stable; metal foil therefore remains the preferred material for most applications.

Strain gauges are used extensively as primary transducers, principally for measuring strains in locations where other methods would be impracticable. They are also used as secondary transducers for measuring force, pressure, and acceleration. In these applications, deformation of an elastic member is derived from the variable being measured, the resulting strain in the member being detected by strain gauges. Some of the difficulties inherent in the use of strain gauges as primary transducers are no longer encountered when they are used in a 'secondary' capacity. Since knowledge of the actual strain in the deformed member is of no interest, the precise value of the gauge factor is unimportant, and calibration is simplified. (The transducers will be calibrated by comparison with known values of the appropriate measured variable— e.g., pressure, force, or acceleration.) There is also more freedom in the choice of method of attachment of the gauges to the strained member. *Unbonded* strain gauges are often employed. These are fine resistance wires suspended between rigid supports, the support usually being linked or attached in some

Figure 4.4 Unbonded strain gauges (approximately six times actual-size). The arrangement shown is incorporated in a number of transducers; basically, the gauges respond to forces applied to the centre of the cross-member on which they are mounted. (*Photo by courtesy of Bell & Howell Ltd.*)

way to an elastic member. Such designs generally give greater sensitivity than would be obtained from a comparable design using bonded gauges. Figure 4.3 shows how a simple force transducer might be made, incorporating either bonded or unbonded gauges. In both arrangements gauges are attached above and below the cantilever spring, sensing positive and negative strains respectively. It will be apparent that where unbonded gauges are required to measure negative strains, the gauges must be prestressed during the assembly of the transducer. Figure 4.4 shows an established form of mounting for unbonded strain gauges.

An alternative form of construction which is being increasingly used in transducers is to form the gauge as an integral part of the elastic member. The techniques used to do this are similar to those used in the manufacture of miniature integrated and thin-film circuits respectively. Using the integrated circuit technique, miniature elastic members may be produced from silicon, the strain gauges being formed by chemical treatment of the required portions of the surface. In the thin-film process, the gauges are formed by depositing a film of gauge material on to the surface of the member. Both methods produce transducer elements which are smaller than similar elements employing bonded gauges, and may prove to give better long-term reliability.

4.3 Strain-gauge bridges

Strain gauges are almost invariably connected into a Wheatstone bridge (section 3.4.2) in order to obtain a measurable output. Since no output can be

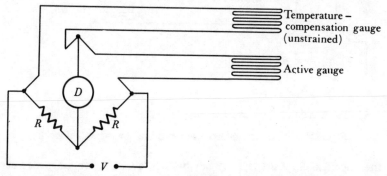

Figure 4.5 Temperature compensation of strain-gauge bridge

obtained from the strain gauge without the bridge, it is often convenient to regard the bridge as part of the transducer. Where strain gauges are performing a secondary transducing function, this is in fact a realistic assumption— e.g., in the force transducer of Fig. 4.3, the bridge would normally comprise four strain gauges, all mounted on the cantilever spring.

The equal-armed, unbalanced form of Wheatstone bridge is almost always used for strain-gauge work. For the small changes of resistance obtained, the output of a bridge of this kind may be considered to be directly proportional to the change in resistance—i.e., proportional to strain. It has already been stated that two of the difficulties associated with strain-gauge work are: (a) the small changes in resistance which have to be measured, and (b) spurious changes in resistance due to temperature changes. The problem of temperature sensitivity may be overcome in most cases by arranging for the balancing arm of the bridge to consist of a second strain gauge identical to the measuring gauge, and subject to the same changes in temperature, as in Fig. 4.5. The compensating gauge should be attached to an unstrained piece of material similar to that on which measurements are being made, and placed close to it. If close agreement between the temperatures of the two gauges cannot be guaranteed, *self-compensating* gauges should be employed.

In certain applications, where equal and opposite strains are known to exist, it is possible to attach two gauges to the strained material in such a way that one experiences a positive strain, and the other experiences an equal negative strain. In this way, not only is reliable temperature compensation achieved, but the sensitivity of the measuring system is increased. A case in which this technique may be applied is that of making strain measurements on the surfaces of beams, where it is known that equal and opposite strains are experienced at corresponding points on the upper and lower surfaces.

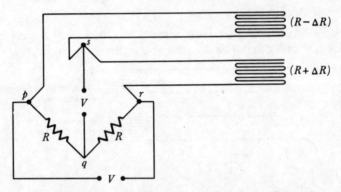

Figure 4.6   Gauges subjected to equal and opposite strains

A further increase in sensitivity may be obtained by using two gauges on each surface, the four gauges used being the four arms of the bridge.

The sensitivity of the measuring bridge in these arrangements is directly proportional to the number of *active* (or strained) gauge elements. It was shown in section 3.4.2 that in the case of a change ΔR in the resistance R of one arm of an equal-armed bridge, the resulting out-of-balance voltage across an 'infinite-impedance' detector is given by

$$v = \frac{V}{4} \cdot \frac{\Delta R}{R} \tag{4.3}$$

Now consider the case where two active gauges are used, experiencing equal and opposite changes in R (Fig. 4.6). Applying arguments similar to those of p. 26, the voltage between points s and q is given by

$$v = \frac{V(R+\Delta R)}{2R} - \frac{V}{2} = \frac{V}{4} \cdot \frac{2\Delta R}{R}, \tag{4.4}$$

i.e., twice the output obtained with a single active gauge, for a given value of R. It may similarly be shown that the values of v for a four-active-arm bridge is $(V/4)(4\Delta R/R)$. Since the sensitivity is proportional to the number of active gauges, this number is sometimes referred to as the *bridge factor*. Four-active-arm bridges are extensively employed when strain gauges are used as secondary transducers, as in Fig. 4.3, to give maximum sensitivity combined with full temperature compensation. The effect of increasing the number of active gauges is the same if a low-impedance detector is used, even though the simple theory given above no longer applies.

A strain-gauge bridge may be made up by the user, or may be purchased as a 'package' requiring only connection to the required number of active gauges, and to a source of power, unless internal batteries are used. Packaged strain-gauge equipment usually incorporates amplification of the bridge output.

4.3.1   Calibration. Reference has been made, on p. 32, to the basic problem of calibrating bonded-gauge systems for strain measurement, namely, that the

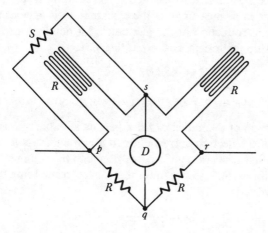

Figure 4.7   Calibration of strain-gauge bridge

gauges are fixed to the structure under test, in which it is not generally possible to induce known strains. It is therefore necessary to establish the relationship between strain and the bridge-indicator reading, on the assumption that the gauge factor given by the gauge manufacturer is correct. In principle, this relationship could be established by calculation, but a practical procedure eliminates many possible sources of error.

Simple strain-gauge bridges often employ indicators having scales marked in arbitrary units. The object of the calibration in this case is to determine the relation between these arbitrary units and the measured strain. More sophisticated commercial equipments incorporate provision for adjusting the bridge calibration, using an indicator reading directly in terms of strain. Calibration then involves making the necessary adjustments to obtain the correct scale readings. The technique employed in either case is to produce a known change in the resistance of one of the bridge arms to simulate a particular value of strain. The value of the change in resistance required for this purpose may be calculated if the unstrained resistance of the gauge, and the gauge factor, are known.

Bearing in mind the magnitudes of the changes in R which are produced in a strain gauge (typically about $0\cdot1\ \Omega$ in $100\ \Omega$, the measurement of the *change* being required to an accuracy of, say, one per cent), it will be apparent that the 'simulated' strain cannot be satisfactorily produced by introducing another resistance in series with the active gauge. Apart from the difficulty of making such a low-value resistor to the required degree of accuracy, variations in contact resistance could well invalidate results. Instead, the required change in resistance is produced by connecting a large resistance in parallel with one of the gauges (Fig. 4.7).

To calibrate the bridge, it is necessary to select one or more values of S which will produce a change in resistance corresponding to a strain within the range of strains to be measured. If the change in resistance of the arm *ps* resulting from the introduction of the resistance S is defined as ΔR, then the standard relationship for resistances in parallel gives

$$R - \Delta R = RS/(R+S),$$

or

$$\Delta R = R - RS/(R+S) = R^2/(R+S). \tag{4.5}$$

Thus, if the deflection of the indicator for a particular value of S is observed, it is known that this deflection corresponds to a particular value of ΔR. It is now necessary to find what value of ε corresponds to this value of ΔR. Combining eq. (4.2) with eq. (4.5) shows that the strain corresponding to a parallel resistance S is given by

$$F\varepsilon = \frac{R}{(R+S)}, \tag{4.6}$$

or

$$S = \frac{R(1-F\varepsilon)}{F\varepsilon}. \tag{4.7}$$

In practice, since $F\varepsilon \ll 1$, the term $F\varepsilon$ in the numerator in eq. (4.7) can usually be neglected without introducing significant error.

The value of ε represented by a particular value of S, or the values of S required to simulate particular values of ε, may therefore be determined from eqs. (4.6) and (4.7) respectively. If a linear relationship between indicator deflection and strain is assumed, only one value of S is required to establish the calibration; this value should be chosen to give an indicator reading at or near full-scale deflection.

A bridge with n active arms may be calibrated in a similar manner. The strain represented by a given value of S is then $1/n$ (approximately) of the strain predicted by eq. (4.6). In practice, this calibration procedure is seldom required for bridges with more than one active arm, since these are encountered mainly in composite transducers measuring some variable other than strain. (Overall calibration in terms of the measured variable is used in these cases.)

4.3.2   Practical bridge details. In practice, any form of strain-gauge bridge requires a bridge-zeroing adjustment. This is necessary because of the virtual impossibility of making strain gauges, or bridge resistors, with resistances which are equal within the very close tolerances demanded by the sensitivity of the bridge. A simple way of introducing a zero control is shown in Fig. 4.8; the small resistance Z is adjusted to achieve initial balance. It should be noted

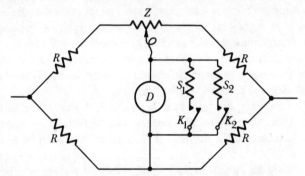

Figure 4.8   Zero and sensitivity adjustments

that the resistance of the sliding contact is in the detector line, not in one of the measuring arms, so that small variations in this resistance will have no significant effect on the indicator readings. A further requirement in any general-purpose strain-measuring system is a means of changing the sensitivity of the bridge. If the indicator is a simple d.c. galvanometer, this may be achieved by means of a number of shunt resistors (S_1, S_2,), which may be switched in as required. In many commercial galvanometers, shunt resistors are built into the instrument for this purpose. If the bridge output is amplified, sensitivity may be adjusted by varying the gain of the amplifier.

In stress-analysis work it is normally possible to incorporate only one active gauge in the bridge, and it is common practice to have the remaining bridge resistors built into a compact bridge unit. Since the bridge unit will not necessarily be at the same temperature as the measuring gauge, it is essential in this case to use a self-temperature-compensating active gauge 'matched' to the material of the structure under investigation. Where this technique is adopted, compensation for resistance changes with temperature in the gauge *leads* is also required. In a bridge where active and compensating gauges are juxtaposed, and connected to the bridge by leads of similar length, this difficulty is not encountered; in this case the leads in the two arms experience the same changes in temperature. For the case where no true compensating gauge is provided, lead compensation may be effected by the 'three-wire' technique described on p. 153 in connection with resistance thermometers.

4.4 Piezo-electric crystals

The piezo-electric effect, though known for many years, has only recently been applied to routine measurements. The effect is peculiar to the crystals of a small number of substances, of which quartz is the best known. If crystals, or sections of crystals, of these substances are subjected to mechanical strain, complementary electrostatic charges appear on pairs of opposite faces. A familiar application of this effect is the crystal pickoff used in record players.

The magnitude of the piezo-electric charge is proportional to the mechanical strain in the crystal; since this strain must result from an applied force or pressure, the charge may be used as a basis for measuring the force or pressure respectively. Unfortunately, the charge is very small; for this reason, transducers often employ a number of crystal sections in the form of a stack, connected so that the charges will be additive.

Piezo transducers require no power supply, which may be an advantage in some applications, but there are quite serious electrical problems on the output side. The basic difficulty is that the charge is developed as a result of the *application* of a load to the crystal. If the charge is removed, it will not be regenerated by an existing steady load. No new charge will be obtained until there is a further *change* in the state of strain in the crystal. The problem is therefore to measure the charge without removing it; this problem is considered in section 6.1.2. It should be noted that, even if no attempt is made to measure the charge, it will always leak away eventually, because of the imperfect insulation properties of the crystal itself. The rate at which this occurs is accelerated by leakage through the insulation of any other equipment electrically connected to the crystal, since no known material is a perfect insulator.

Piezo transducers are therefore unsuitable for 'static' measurements, since they are sensitive to changes in the applied load, rather than to the absolute value of the load. Their applications lie in the field of dynamic measurement, where the measured variable is changing rapidly enough to make the effects of charge leakage negligible. The time taken for serious leakage to occur depends on the quality of the components used in the complete measuring system. With high-grade equipment, a reading may be held for a few minutes without a significant drop.

The inability of piezo transducers to measure absolute values may not necessarily be a serious disadvantage. Often the absolute values may be deduced by other means. Piezo transducers are commonly used to measure pressure variations in the cylinders of internal-combustion engines. In this case, it is known that the pressure must be atmospheric at a particular time during the cycle; using this point as a reference, the absolute pressures at other points in the cycle may be deduced from the indications of the system. Piezo transducers are used mainly for measurements of pressure and acceleration. (For acceleration measurement, the force required to accelerate a known mass is applied to the crystal.) Their outstanding characteristic is the ability to respond to very rapid changes in the value of the measured variable. This ability results from the absence of moving parts, and the negligibly small compression of the crystal under load. Transducers can be made to very small dimensions, and can withstand relatively high temperatures without producing serious errors. A two per cent change in output for 100°C rise in temperature would be typical, and a temperature limit of 250°C. Temperature limits are important where combustion pressures are being measured, since

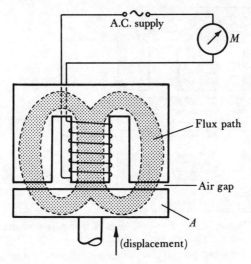

Figure 4.9 Inductive displacement transducer

the transducer must be mounted close to the combustion process if its fast response is to be exploited.

Reference has been made above to the use of quartz for piezo-electric crystals. The main characteristics of quartz are good stability, relatively poor sensitivity, and ability to withstand high temperatures. Some other piezo-electric materials are more sensitive than quartz; these materials are generally less stable, and lose their charge more quickly due to their poorer insulation properties. The low outputs of quartz transducers put more stringent demands on the signal-conditioning equipment, with a consequent increase in the cost of the complete system.

4.5 Inductive devices

The inductance of a coil may be changed substantially by altering the reluctance of the magnetic flux path associated with it. This effect is particularly apparent when the majority of the flux path passes through iron; if there is only a small air gap in the flux path, the inductance of the coil is very sensitive to changes in the width of the gap. This sensitivity may be exploited as a method of measuring displacement.

A typical arrangement for an inductive (or *variable-reluctance*) displacement transducer is shown in Fig. 4.9. A coil is wound on the centre limb of an *E*-shaped iron former, and is energized from an a.c. supply. The flux follows the path indicated on the diagram, passing through the small air gap between the core, which is fixed, and tne movable iron plate *A*. Small vertical movements of the plate (often called the *armature*) produce changes in the inductance of the coil. The changes in inductance produce changes in reactance,

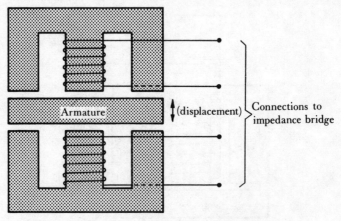

Figure 4.10   Two-coil form of inductive transducer

which may be detected by the simple circuit shown in the diagram. The a.c. meter *M* detects the current variations which result from the changes in reactance.

The device of Fig. 4.9 has the disadvantage that the displacement–current relationship is very non-linear. A substantial improvement may be obtained by using two coils, as in Fig. 4.10, with the armature between them. The output in this case would be taken from an impedance bridge, in which the transducer coils would form two variable arms. Although linearity is much improved by using two coils in this way, the useful range is limited to a few mm.

4.5.1 Differential transformer. If linearity over a substantial range is important, a more satisfactory type of displacement transducer is the differential transformer, shown schematically in Fig. 4.11. The primary winding *A* is fed from a source of alternating voltage. The resulting magnetic field cuts the identical secondary windings, *B* and *C*, and induces alternating e.m.f.s in them. If the movable iron core *D* is in its central position, the e.m.f.s induced in the two coils will be equal. Since B and C are connected in 'series opposi-tion', there will be no resultant p.d. between the output terminals X and Y. A movement of the core towards B increases the iron in the flux path linking A and B, thus increasing the e.m.f. induced in B. At the same time, the induced e.m.f. in C is reduced. There will now be a resultant e.m.f. between X and Y, equal to the difference between the e.m.f.s induced in B and C respectively. The magnitude of the resultant e.m.f. depends on the magnitude of the core displacement, and its phase relationship to the supply voltage depends on the direction of displacement.

For a certain range of core displacement, the input–output relation for a differential transformer is linear within very close tolerances. For this reason,

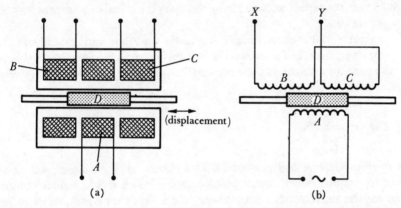

Figure 4.11 Differential transformer: (a) physical layout; (b) electrical schematic

the device is sometimes called a *linear variable differential transformer*, or LVDT. The extent of the linear range depends on the dimensions and physical layout of the coils; it is typically about 10 per cent of the total length of the transducer, and may represent virtually any displacement from 0·2 mm upwards. The output obtained for a given displacement depends not only on the physical design of the transducer but also on the supply voltage and frequency. It is convenient to express the sensitivity at a given supply fre-quency in mV/mm for a one-volt supply; expressed in this way a sensitivity of 50 mV/mm would be typical. As for other inductive devices, sensitivity improves with increasing frequency, but the relationship is not linear. The choice of supply frequency (or *carrier* frequency, as it is normally called) is not governed entirely by considerations of sensitivity. If high-frequency mechanical vibrations of the core are to be measured, it is essential that the supply frequency should be substantially higher than the highest likely frequency of the mechanical input.

The output of a differential transformer is not greatly affected by tempera-ture changes, provided that the temperature of the whole transducer is uniform. On the other hand, temperature gradients in the transducer can cause serious errors. Maximum working temperatures are limited by the materials of construction, and are usually in the region of 200°C.

4.6 Capacitive devices

The principle of varying capacitance may be employed for displacement transducers. A capacitor, in its simplest form, comprises two parallel metallic plates separated by a non-conducting material (the dielectric). In capacitance transducers, this non-conducting material is usually air. Capacitance is directly proportional to the effective area of the plates, and inversely proportional to the distance between them. A displacement input can therefore be made to vary the capacitance either by changing the effective plate area, or the plate separation.

In general, variable capacitance is less convenient than variable inductance as a working principle for displacement transducers. One reason for this is that the need for a sufficient plate area makes capacitive transducers relatively large.

4.7 Digital pickoffs

An inductive device much used in digital measuring systems is the *inductive pickoff* (Fig. 4.12). A coil is wound over a permanent bar magnet, and connected to circuitry which counts voltage pulses. Pulses will be induced in the coil if any ferrous material moves through the field of the magnet, temporarily changing the reluctance of the flux path. Pickoffs of this kind are frequently mounted adjacent to toothed wheels, to count the number of teeth passing, and hence deduce the number of revolutions of the wheel. The inductive pickoff differs from the inductive devices previously described in that it requires no power supply.

The magnitude of the voltage pulse depends on the clearance between the moving part and the magnet, and on the speed of the moving part. If greater sensitivity is required, the coil may be wound on an *E*-shaped magnet, giving a layout similar to that of Fig. 4.9. Other arrangements are possible—e.g., the magnet may be mounted on the moving part, if this is non-ferrous, instead of inside the pickoff coil.

An alternative means of generating voltage pulses, which is less sensitive to the speed of the moving object, is a photo-electric pickoff. Photo-cells and photo-transistors are devices which change their electrical characteristics with changes in the intensity of the light falling on them. The type most commonly encountered is classed as photo-conductive, meaning that the change which takes place is a change in electrical resistance (or conductivity). Though devices of this kind can be used for analogue measurements, they are more frequently used to generate pulse signals to mark the occurrence of a particular event. Figure 4.13 shows the principle of an arrangement for generating a voltage signal corresponding with the arrival of the object *A* in the path of the light beam between the source *L* and the photo-cell *P*. Suppose that the resistance of the cell is *r* when the light beam is falling on it, and that the resistor *B*, which is connected in series with it across the voltage source *E*, has resistance *R*. The output voltage *v* is then equal to a proportion $R/(R+r)$ of the supply voltage. (This may be shown by a simple application of Ohm's

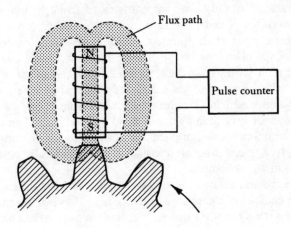

Figure 4.12   Inductive pickoff

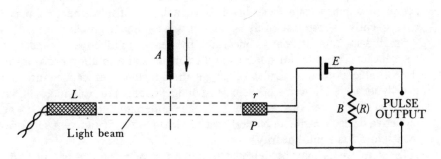

Figure 4.13   Photo-electric pickoff

law.) When the light beam is interrupted by the arrival of *A*, the resistance of *P* changes to some value *r'*, where $r' > r$. There is consequently a drop in the output voltage. If *A* continues to move and passes out of the light beam, the output voltage is restored to its original value. Thus, electrical signals corresponding to the arrival and departure of *A* are obtained. Practical circuits may be more complex than that shown, with a view to obtaining a better-defined output pulse.

Summary

There is a number of transducers which may be regarded as general-purpose devices. These convert a mechanical quantity, such as displacement, into an electrical signal.

Variable potential dividers convert displacement to voltage. They have linear characteristics only if no current is taken from the output. Reliability may be adversely affected by wear or dirt at the sliding contact.

Strain gauges convert strain into a change in resistance, which is measured by means of a Wheatstone bridge. The bridge may contain one, two, or four active gauges; it must always be compensated for the effects of temperature. If strain measurements are to be made, the gauges are bonded to the strained member; gauges used in transducers for measuring other variables may be bonded, unbonded, or manufactured as an integral part of an elastic sensing device. In strain-measuring applications, calibration of the bridge by strain-simulation techniques is necessary, since it is not generally possible to apply known strains to the gauges.

Piezo-electric transducers respond to pressure or force inputs by producing an electric charge; if the charge is dissipated, it is not regenerated by the presence of a steady input. Further, the charge slowly leaks away through the piezo crystals themselves, and through the insulation of any equipment connected to them. Piezo transducers are therefore suitable only for dynamic measurements. Measurement of the charge without dissipating it presents difficulties, and calls for sophisticated signal-conditioning equipment. The action of a piezo transducer involves virtually no displacement of mass; consequently its response to dynamic inputs is extremely good.

Small displacements may be measured by means of inductive or capacitive transducers. These do not suffer from the contact and resolution problems of the variable potential divider. Changes in inductance or capacitance are usually measured in terms of the corresponding changes in reactance, so that a.c. measuring methods are required. The differential transformer is an inductive device which can be designed to measure a wide range of displacements, and has good linearity.

Discrete events may be detected by inductive or photo-electric pickoffs. These are digital rather than analogue devices; they are used principally in counting and timing applications.

Examples

1. A variable potential divider (Fig. 4.1) has a total resistance of 2 kΩ and is fed from a 10 V supply. The output is connected into a load resistance of 5 kΩ. Determine the loading error for the slider positions corresponding to $x = l/4, l/2$, and $3l/4$. (Loading error is defined as the difference in output volt-

ages obtained when on open-circuit and on load respectively.) Use the results to plot a rough graph of loading error against x/l.

(Ans.: 0·17, 0·46, and 0·53 V.)

2. A strain-gauge bridge comprises two fixed 120 Ω resistors, one active gauge, and one unstrained temperature-compensation gauge. The two gauges are of unstrained resistance 120 Ω and gauge factor 2·2. Find the bridge output voltage (with the output open-circuited) for a supply voltage of 3 V, when the active gauge is subjected to 600 microstrain.

(Ans.: 0·99 mV.)

3. For the bridge of example 2, find the strain which would be represented by a 100 kΩ calibration resistance shunting one arm of the bridge.

(Ans.: 546×10^{-6}.)

Suggestions for further reading

1 H. K. P. Neubert, *Strain Gauges, Kinds and Uses*, Macmillan, London, 1967.
2 C. C. Perry and H. R. Lissner, *The Strain Gage Primer*, McGraw-Hill, 1962.
3 *Notes on Linear Variable Differential Transformers*, Schaevitz Engineering Technical Bulletin AA-1b.
4 H. K. P. Neubert, *Instrument Transducers*, Oxford University Press, 1963.

5. Electrical Displays

It was suggested in section 1.1 that a typical measuring system could be regarded as a 'chain' comprising transducer, transmission, and display. The purpose of this chapter is to consider the displays with which the transducers described in chapter 4 may be associated. Chapter 6 will then deal with the question of adapting the transducer outputs to suit the input requirements of the display.

5.1 Direct-deflection meters

A direct-deflection meter is an analogue current indicator which draws all the power required to operate it from the signal being measured. Apart from a few special-purpose instruments, almost all modern direct-deflection instruments work on the moving-coil principle. The coil (Fig. 5.1), which carries the current to be measured, is suspended in a permanent magnetic field. As the current flows in opposite directions in the two sides of the coil, the resulting forces on the coil (section 3.3.3) form a turning moment, the magnitude of which is proportional to the current. This turning moment displaces the coil until an equal and opposite turning moment is developed by the hairspring attached to the coil. It must be emphasized that, whatever the units of the scale calibration, the deflection of a particular meter movement is determined solely by the current in the moving coil.

Moving-coil meters may be adapted to measure various current or voltage ranges by the use of suitable shunt and series resistances. Suppose the meter is required to give f.s.d. (full-scale deflection) for some current I, which is greater than the f.s.d. current i of the movement (i.e., the current which, when flowing through the meter coil, will produce full-scale deflection). The resistance X (Fig. 5.2) must be chosen so that, when the total current flowing from A to B is I, the current passing through the meter coil is only i. Similarly, to use the meter as a voltmeter of range V volts, the resistance Y (Fig. 5.2b) must be chosen so that a voltage V applied between C and D produces a current i through the coil.

The method described for changing the current range of a meter by shunting is applicable only if the required range I is greater than the f.s.d. current i. This imposes a limitation on the use of moving-coil meters for current measurement, as the f.s.d. current *i* cannot be reduced indefinitely. The lower the value of *i*, the less robust the movement becomes, the ultimate limit depending on the use to which it is to be put. For a general-purpose bench instrument, the limit is about 50 μA. Lower values, down to about 1 μA, are

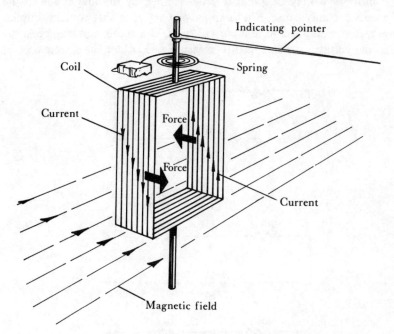

Figure 5.1   Principle of moving-coil meter

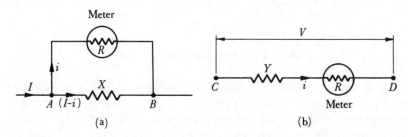

Figure 5.2   Range setting of moving-coil meter: (a) current ranges; (b) voltage ranges

possible for instruments which can be protected effectively from shock and abuse. A further drawback of movements designed for low f.s.d. currents is that the coil resistance is substantial. To obtain the necessary torque from a small current, many turns of fine wire have to be used, producing an inevitable increase in resistance. The coil of a 50 μA f.s.d. movement may have a resistance of several kΩ. In many current-measuring applications this will be unacceptable, because of the reduction in circuit current caused by the meter resistance.

5.1.1 Loading error. The lower limit on the useful voltage range for which a given movement may be adapted is determined by the magnitude of the *loading errors* it may cause. The term *loading error*, in this context, implies that the meter is taking sufficient current to make a significant change in the value of the voltage it is intended to measure.† Consider the simple case of

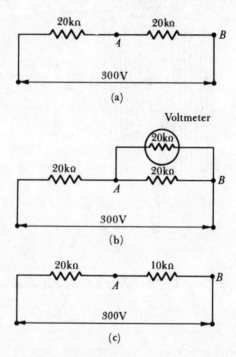

Figure 5.3   Loading effect of voltmeter

Fig. 5.3, in which the voltage between the points *A* and *B* is to be measured by a meter having a total resistance (i.e., meter coil + series resistor) of 20 kΩ. From inspection of the circuit before the meter is applied (or by Ohm's law) it is evident that the measured value ought to be 150 V. However, when the meter is applied (Fig. 5.3b), there are two 20 kΩ resistors in parallel between *A* and *B*, making a net resistance of 10 kΩ, as shown in Fig. 5.3c. Again, inspection or Ohm's law shows that the actual potential between *A* and *B* will now be 100 V, assuming that the supply voltage has not changed. The meter will therefore read 100 V, so that although it is reading the voltage existing

† The term *loading error* may be used more generally, to refer to any change in a measured quantity caused by a measuring device. It could, for instance, be used to refer to the effect of ammeter resistance mentioned in the previous paragraph.

in the circuit after it has been connected, it is 33·3 per cent in error with respect to the voltage it was intended to measure. This class of error *must* occur when a voltage is measured by any meter which takes current. It can be made negligibly small only if the total meter resistance is very high compared to the resistances in the circuit in which the measurements are being made. The loading problem has been illustrated here by means of a simple d.c. example. The difficulty occurs equally in a.c. circuits, the only difference being that impedances, rather than resistances, have to be considered.

5.1.2 Multimeters. Direct-deflection meters may be single-range, single-function instruments, or they may incorporate a number of shunt and series resistors, providing various voltage and current ranges. Portable meters of this type are known as *multimeters*, or, more frequently, by the name of a leading manufacturer. Most multimeters will measure alternating currents and voltages, and resistance, in addition to direct currents and voltages. The a.c. quantities are first rectified, so that they can be measured by the moving-coil meter. Readings on a.c. ranges are r.m.s. values, and are correct for sinusoidal waveforms only; serious errors may arise if measurements are attempted on other waveforms. There will also be restrictions on the frequency range over which the meter may be used. Resistance is measured by applying a p.d. from a dry cell (contained in the meter) to the unknown resistance and measuring the resulting current. The accuracy of this method is relatively poor. A bridge circuit (section 3.4.2) should be used in preference to a multimeter if a precise value of resistance is required.

It will be apparent from the above discussion of loading error that discretion is needed in the selection and use of direct-deflection meters for test or experimental purposes, particularly for voltage measurements in high-resistance circuits. (Where meters are part of permanent installations, loading errors can be allowed for in calibration.) The criterion for judging a meter in this respect is the f.s.d. current of the movement, as this has a direct bearing on the magnitude of the loading error. A small f.s.d. current means a high total resistance when the meter is applied to voltage measurement, and the higher this resistance, the smaller the loading errors will be. Meter specifications usually give either the f.s.d. current, or the 'ohms per volt' at f.s.d. These two methods of specifying the movement sensitivity give the same information. Consider a movement of resistance R with a series resistance Y. If V volts applied to the meter terminals produce f.s.d., then the f.s.d. current must be $V/(R+Y)$. But the 'ohms per volt' is by definition $(R+Y)/V$, i.e. it is the reciprocal of the f.s.d. current. A typical multimeter might have a 50 μA f.s.d. movement; it could equally well be described as being a '20 000 ohms per volt' meter.

In the example of Fig. 5.3, if we assume that the voltmeter range was 200 V, the 'ohms per volt' of the meter was 20 000/200, or 100. The f.s.d. current was, therefore, $\frac{1}{100}$ A, or 10 mA. This would be a very high figure for a modern

51

multimeter. If a 50 μA movement had been used, the resulting error would have been approximately 0·3 per cent, which would be acceptable under most circumstances.

The criterion for assessing the suitability of a meter for current measurement is its resistance, which should be as low as possible. For a multimeter on its lowest range, this will normally be the resistance of the meter coil. When making a current measurement, the net meter resistance is added to that of the circuit in which the measurement is being made. It will reduce the current to $R_c/(R_m + R_c)$ of its former value, where R_c is the original circuit resistance,

Figure 5.4   Multi-channel u.v. recorder (*Photo by courtesy of Bell & Howell Ltd.*)

and R_m is the net meter resistance. (This reduction may be of no consequence, if the value of the actual current is required, rather than that of the current before the meter was introduced.) Meter resistances are often expressed in terms of the millivolt drops they cause across the meter at specified currents. Where a number of ranges is obtained by shunting, the millivolt drop at f.s.d. is constant for all ranges, since it is equal to the product of the f.s.d. current and the resistance of the moving coil.

5.1.3   Galvanometers. A certain type of moving-coil meter is referred to as a galvanometer. There is no difference in principle between a galvanometer and other moving-coil meters. They are usually uncalibrated, centre-zero instruments with sensitive movements, employing filament suspensions for the coil in place of the conventional jewelled bearings and torsion spring. One of their chief applications is for 'null detection' in comparator circuits—i.e., the detection of the condition of zero current in the circuit. Galvanometers are often provided with a selection of shunt resistors, which may be switched across the coil to lower its sensitivity when required.

An important development of the galvanometer is the *u.v. recorder*, 'u.v.' standing for 'ultra-violet'. (The same instrument is sometimes called an *oscillograph*.) This is a form of galvanometer which produces a record of its deflections by means of an ultra-violet light beam reflected from a small mirror attached to the moving coil. The light beam records on a paper chart which is sensitive to strong u.v. light, but virtually unaffected by normal daylight. Before the advent of the u.v. recorder, the problem of obtaining a record from a moving-coil instrument was not satisfactorily solved, as the torque developed by movements of this type is seldom adequate to cope with the friction of other methods of recording.

The use of miniature galvanometer coils and light-beam recording makes very high speeds of response possible. A typical coil for a u.v. galvanometer is about 10 mm × 1 mm. Unfortunately, the reduction in coil dimensions also reduces sensitivity; movements designed for very rapid response may have f.s.d. currents of around 200 mA. It is normal practice for manufacturers of u.v. recorders to supply ranges of interchangeable galvanometers, with characteristics varying from high speed with low sensitivity to low speed with high sensitivity. Satisfactory response at signal frequencies up to several kHz may be obtained. Instruments of this type are normally 'multi-channel', i.e. several galvanometers are mounted in the same recorder, providing simultaneous records on a single chart (Fig. 5.4). Chart speeds are invariably adjustable, up to a maximum of about 2 m/s.

5.1.4   *Galvanometer damping.* All instruments intended for making dynamic measurements require to be correctly damped. Damping torques are applied to meter movements to prevent excessive oscillation in use. (A meter movement is analogous to a torsional pendulum, and, if undamped, will oscillate when disturbed from its neutral position.) Suitable damping is incorporated in single-function instruments by the manufacturer, but in the case of a multi-purpose galvanometer, damping depends on the circuit in which it is used.

The ideal damping torque is proportional to the angular velocity of the movement; it may be produced either by viscous friction, or by electrical means. Most galvanometers, except some very high-speed types, use electrical damping, which is produced by the generator effect (section 3.3.3). E.m.f.s proportional to velocity are induced in the coil due to its motion; the retarding forces on the coil, however, are proportional to the *currents* resulting from these induced e.m.f.s. (The current in the coil at any instant is the vector sum of the deflecting current and the induced current; it is convenient in discussing the behaviour of the coil, however, to consider the two currents as being independent.) The magnitude of the induced current produced by a given induced e.m.f. depends on the resistance of the circuit to which the galvanometer is connected. This is referred to as the *external resistance* of the galvanometer. Galvanometer suppliers usually quote the value of the external resistance required to give the correct damping. To obtain optimum dynamic performance, the circuit resistance must be adjusted to this value, by the use of additional resistors. Referring to Fig. 5.5a it can be seen that the external resistance consists initially of the resistance of the signal source, plus any other circuit resistance R_c which is already in series with it. If the total resistance is not equal to the recommended value, it should be increased or

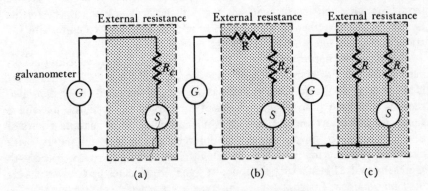

Figure 5.5 Galvanometer damping

decreased by the addition of the series or parallel resistance R as required (Figs. 5.4b and 5.4c respectively).

The adjustment of damping by parallel resistors inevitably affects the sensitivity of the galvanometer. The situation is analogous to that of changing the range of a current meter by shunting it, as described on p. 48. If, therefore, the circuit resistance is adjusted by means of a parallel resistor, calibration of the galvanometer must be carried out after this adjustment has been made. Similarly, the damping of any precalibrated electrical indicator cannot be adjusted in this way if the original calibration is to be retained.

5.2 Amplifying meters

The usefulness of direct-deflection meters is limited by the minimum practicable f.s.d. current, and the consequent limitation on the total meter resistance for voltage applications. Amplifying meters, in the form of the valve voltmeter (or VVM) were originally introduced primarily to overcome this resistance limitation, and the associated problem of loading error. Meters of this class are now available in multimeter form, and frequently employ transistor circuits in place of the original valve circuits. In spite of these developments, they are still often referred to as 'VVMs'. From the user's point of view, there is no basic difference between valve and transistor types, except that transistorized multimeters are often powered by internal batteries, and therefore require no external supply.

An amplifying meter consists of an electronic amplifier plus a moving-coil meter of the type already discussed. The circuitry employed is outside the scope of this book, but it may assist readers familiar with the simple triode amplifier to regard it as an amplifier of this type combined with a moving-coil meter. Voltage measurements could be made with this combination by applying the unknown voltage (or a known proportion of it) between grid and cathode, and measuring the resulting change in the anode current with the meter. This simple arrangement would have many practical drawbacks, but it serves to illustrate two important points about amplifying meters. Firstly, they respond to a voltage input rather than a current input; for current measurements, a proportional voltage is developed from the current (e.g., by passing it through a known resistor inside the meter). Secondly, they have very high input impedances, compared with direct-deflection meters. Even in the simple circuit described above, the input impedance could be several MΩ (it would be virtually equal to the grid-leak resistance of the triode). This high impedance is the most important characteristic of amplifying meters, as voltage measurements on high-resistance circuits can consequently be made without serious loading errors.

5.3 Oscilloscopes

The action of a cathode-ray oscilloscope (or CRO) depends on the deflection of a high-velocity electron beam. The importance of this fact is that, for the class of measurements with which this book is concerned, the deflecting mechanism may be regarded as having zero inertia. In its normal mode of operation, the oscilloscope shows how a voltage signal applied to its input terminals is varying with respect to time.

Figure 5.6 shows the essentials of a simple oscilloscope. The electron beam is formed inside a cathode-ray tube, and is directed at the fluorescent end of the tube, or *screen*. The system which produces the beam is sometimes called an *electron gun*. If the beam is stationary, a spot of light will be seen on the screen. There are four essential controls associated with the formation and initial positioning of the beam: *brightness*, which is self-explanatory; *focus*, which adjusts the definition of the beam; *X-shift* and *Y-shift*, which move the beam horizontally and vertically respectively. It is usually necessary to adjust some or all of these controls when first setting up the oscilloscope. After this initial adjustment, subsequent motion of the light spot depends on the voltages applied between the two pairs of plates X_1, X_2 and Y_1, Y_2. In the normal mode of operation, a *saw-tooth* waveform is applied across the *X*-plates; this is a voltage which increases linearly with respect to time up to a certain

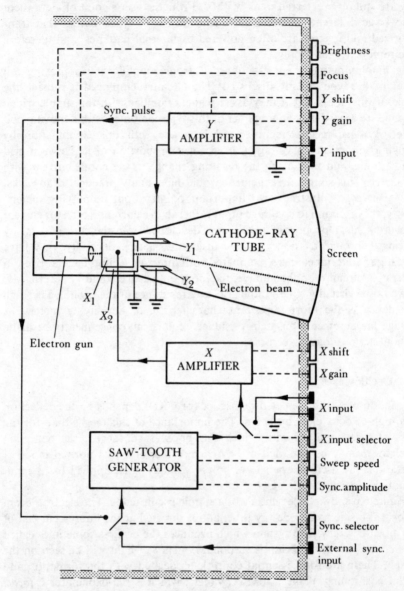

Figure 5.6 Oscilloscope controls

maximum value, then returns virtually instantaneously to its initial value, as shown in Fig. 5.7.

The path of the electron beam is deflected by an electric field. Consequently, when the saw-tooth voltage is applied across the *X*-plates, the light spot moves across the screen at constant velocity during the *ramp* (or inclined) portion of the wave, and returns very rapidly during the *step* (or vertical) portion. At the frequencies of the saw-tooth wave normally employed, the image of the spot persists on the screen sufficiently long for it to appear as a continuous line. During the step, or return, portion of the wave, the electron beam is cut off; the horizontal line seen on the screen, which is referred to as the *time base*, is therefore produced by the ramp portion of the waveform only.

The production of the time base requires two electronic units inside the oscilloscope, each with its external control: a variable-frequency time-base generator, to produce the saw-tooth waveform, and a variable-gain amplifier (the *X*-amplifier). The frequency of the time base must be variable, so that the horizontal velocity of the light spot (the *sweep speed*) can be adjusted to suit

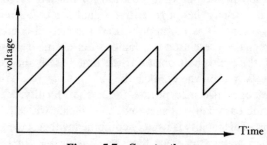

Figure 5.7   Saw-tooth wave

the frequency of the signal which is to be examined. Usually, two external controls are provided for this, giving coarse and fine control. The '*X*-gain' control is normally set so that the time base occupies the full width of the screen. On many oscilloscopes the sweep-speed controls are calibrated, permitting measurements of the signal frequency to be made.

With the time base in operation, the oscilloscope will give a 'picture' of any voltage applied across the *Y*-plates, provided that this voltage is sufficient to produce a visible shift of the electron beam. The voltage necessary to do this is relatively large, so another variable-gain amplifier (the *Y*-amplifier) is incorporated between the signal-input terminals and the *Y*-plates. The gain adjustment of this amplifier may be continuous, but on oscilloscopes intended for voltage measurement it is controlled by a multi-position switch. Each position of the switch is marked with the sensitivity it represents, usually in V/cm or mV/cm. The V or mV refers to the amplitude of the input signal, and the cm to the corresponding vertical shift obtained on the screen. A centimetre grid is normally marked on the screen as an aid to measurement. To obtain a satisfactory picture, or 'trace', of a voltage waveform, the time-base frequency must be set accurately to the frequency of the waveform, or to a submultiple of that frequency. If this is not done, a stationary trace will not be obtained, as successive sweeps of the time base will start at different points on the wave.

It is virtually impossible to obtain a stationary trace merely by manual adjustment of the coarse and fine time-base frequency controls, without the assistance of an internal *synchronization* or *triggering* pulse (abbreviated to 'sync' and 'trig' respectively). This is a signal, having the same frequency as the input signal, taken from the Y-amplifier to the time-base generator. Provided the settings of the manual frequency controls are approximately correct, this internal signal will hold the picture stationary. A sync signal is always provided, its amplitude usually being adjusted by an external control. The adjustment routine differs from one oscilloscope to another; in general, the sync amplitude should be set to the lowest value which will satisfactorily hold the trace.

Provision is often made for the sync signal to be taken from an external source if required. A selector switch for 'internal' or 'external' sync is then fitted, which is left in the 'internal' position for normal usage. The external sync connection is used when a repetitive signal has to be related to some other recurring event. It is commonly used in internal-combustion engine work, when a signal representing the combustion-chamber pressure has to be correlated with the crankshaft position; the time base is then triggered from a cam-operated switch on the crankshaft.

Some oscilloscopes also incorporate a 'one-shot' facility, whereby a single sweep of the time base can be generated, to coincide with the occurrence of a transient event. This facility is usually combined with a screen having longer 'persistence' than usual; the trace then remains visible for long enough to allow it to be examined. 'Storage' oscilloscopes, in which a trace can be stored and redisplayed after a substantial time interval, are also available.

Normally it is possible to inject an external signal into the X-amplifier, in place of the internally generated time base. This is used when the relation between two voltages is to be examined, instead of between one voltage and time.

A further facility found on many oscilloscopes is an a.c.–d.c. selector for the Y-input. This switch may be used to separate the a.c. 'ripple' from a signal made up from both a.c. and d.c. components. Electrically, the switch may merely introduce a capacitor into the input line to 'block' the d.c. component, though some oscilloscopes employ separate Y-amplifiers for the a.c. and d.c. positions of the selector. The use of the terms 'a.c.' and 'd.c.' in this connection may be slightly confusing. In the d.c. position, both a.c. and d.c. inputs will be accepted, but the d.c. will be blocked when a.c. is selected. Where separate amplifiers are provided, the a.c. amplifier is usually capable of responding to higher frequencies than is the d.c. amplifier, and/or of giving increased vertical sensitivity. The range of frequencies which a general-purpose oscilloscope will handle satisfactorily (its *bandwidth*) is usually from d.c. to several kHz or even MHz. Some less expensive instruments are suitable for a.c. signals only; these are referred to as being *a.c.-coupled*, as opposed to the more usual *d.c.-coupled* (or *direct coupled*) arrangement.

The main advantages of the oscilloscope as a measuring instrument are its 'zero-inertia' response and high input impedance. Its disadvantages are low sensitivity, relatively low reading accuracy, and inability to provide a permanent record, unless special cameras are used to photograph the trace. If a record is required, a u.v. recorder is often more convenient, provided the signal frequency is not too high. In comparing the suitability of these two instruments for a particular application, it should be remembered that the oscilloscope is a high-impedance (voltage-sensitive) device, whereas the u.v. recorder is a low-impedance (current-sensitive) device. Different input arrangements will therefore be required in the two cases.

5.4 Comparator instruments

There are a number of display instruments which work on the comparator principle, rather than on the deflection principle which is used in the moving-coil meter. These instruments are generally capable of better accuracy and

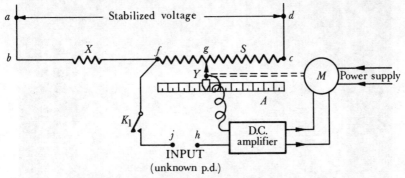

Figure 5.8 Principle of self-balancing potentiometer

repeatability than deflection instruments, particularly under arduous environmental conditions. Most are based on potentiometer or balanced-bridge circuits (sections 3.4.1 and 3.4.2 respectively) and incorporate servo-operated self-balancing mechanisms. In principle, the servo system takes the place of the human operator: it senses an unbalanced condition in the circuit, and takes the necessary action to restore the balance.

Figure 5.8 shows schematically how the d.c. potentiometer circuit of Fig. 3.2b must be modified to make it self-balancing. Any difference between the unknown p.d. and that across the portion fg of the slidewire is fed to a d.c. power amplifier; the amplifier output controls the reversible servo motor M which drives the sliding contact Y back to balance point. The drive will continue until there is no input to the amplifier—i.e., until the correct balance point is reached. A similar principle may be applied to resistance bridges, the amplifier taking the place of the bridge detector.

A significant advantage of the self-balancing principle over the deflection principle is that it provides ample power to drive recording pens and/or control mechanisms. Self-balancing instruments are very robust, and are widely used for the continuous recording of process variables. Figure 5.9 shows a typical industrial example, recording a single variable. Multi-channel and multi-range versions are also available. Recorders of this type are not designed for a very high speed of response. They are usually classified in this respect by the time required for the balancing mechanism to drive the pen through the full measuring range, which is typically about 2 s. Potentiometric

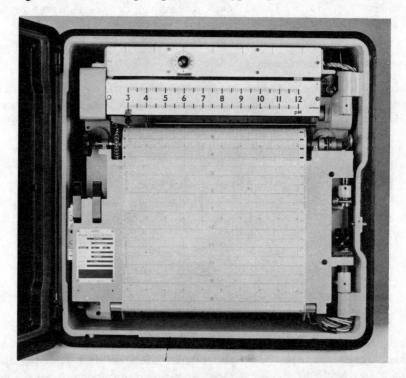

Figure 5.9 Industrial self-balancing potentiometer. (*Photo by courtesy of Kent Instruments Ltd.*)

recorders employing battery-powered measuring circuits require standardizing, like their manually balanced equivalents. Most modern self-balancing recorders use zener-diode† sources in place of batteries. Standardizing may then be dispensed with, the reference voltage from the zener diode being sufficiently stable.

A comparator principle electrically similar to that of the d.c. potentiometer

† A zener diode is a solid-state electronic device. Its special feature is that it 'breaks down' at a specific voltage—i.e., it presents high impedance until this voltage is reached, then passes current readily. The break-down effect can be utilized conveniently as a basis for a constant-voltage source.

is used in *digital voltmeters*. These instruments combine the inherent accuracy of the potentiometric method with the advantages of digital display and a very high input impedance. Digital voltmeters are available in multimeter form; their overall performance is generally better than that of other types of multimeter, but prices are correspondingly higher.

5.5 Counter–timers

The number of occurrences of a particular event may be counted by mechanical cyclometer-type counters, provided the count rate is relatively low, and a mechanical impulse can be derived from each occurrence. The application of mechanical counters may be extended to include the counting of electrical pulses, by adding a relay mechanism to make the necessary electro-mechanical

Figure 5.10 Digital counter–timer–frequency-meter. (*Photo by courtesy of Dawe Instruments Ltd.*)

conversion of the input. The maximum count rate of instruments of this class is a few tens of counts per second.

Electronic counters (Fig. 5.10) are much more versatile. They respond to voltage pulses over a wide range of frequency and amplitude. In addition to the counting function, they are usually capable of measuring time and frequency. Large digital displays are employed, which are more easily read than those of the majority of mechanical counters.

The frequency range of electronic counters is wider than is likely to be required for pulses originating from a mechanical source; 100 kHz is a typical maximum counting frequency. The amplitude of the operating pulse may vary from a fraction of a volt up to several hundred volts. This feature is useful when the counter is used in conjunction with an inductive pickoff of the type shown in Fig. 4.12, as the amplitude of the output pulse from the pickoff varies with the speed of the moving body which initiates it. Simplified block diagrams of a counter–timer–frequency-meter are shown in Fig.

5.11. To appreciate the principle of operation of this instrument, it is necessary to accept the functions of the four main electronic 'blocks', which are as follows:

(a) The *oscillator*, which produces a stable high-frequency signal.

(b) The *divider*, which will divide the frequency of any input signal it receives by 10, 10^2, 10^3, etc., according to the position of selector switches.

(c) The *gate*, which has two signal inputs; a 'main' input and a 'control' input. The main input is either passed directly through to the output, or blocked, according to the signals received from the control input. Successive pulses on the control input 'open' and 'shut' the gate respectively, passing the main signal during the interval, which is known as the *gating period*.

(d) The *pulse counter*, which counts every pulse it receives and registers the total.

The three modes of operation may be seen from Fig. 5.11. For time measurement, the oscillator output is fed to the divider, which is set to select a suitable

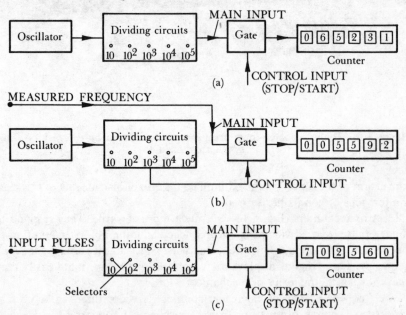

Figure 5.11 Modes of operation of a digital counter—timer—frequency-meter: (a) time measurement (b) frequency measurement (c) counting.

counting unit; e.g., if the oscillator frequency is 100 kHz, selection of 'divide by 10^5' will produce a divider output of one pulse per second, and the final reading of the display will then be in seconds. These pulses are registered by the counter for a period determined by the 'start' and 'stop' pulses, representing the limits of the time interval being measured. The start and stop pulses may be initiated either manually or automatically, according to the nature of the application.

For frequency measurement, the measured signal becomes the main input to the gate, and the gating period is determined by the oscillator and divider. Thus, for a 100 kHz oscillator and the selector in the 'divide by 10^4' position, a 0·1 s gating period would be obtained; a reading of 1234 on the display therefore means that 1234 pulses are received in 0·1 s, so that the measured frequency is 12340 Hz. Care must be taken to ensure that the first significant figure has not been 'lost': if the instrument in the above case had a four-digit readout, the same result would be obtained with an input frequency of, say, 512·34 kHz, assuming the instrument to be capable of counting at this speed. Errors of this kind may be avoided by carrying out checks using shorter gating periods; thus, in the two cases quoted, selection of 'divide by 10' in place of 'divide by 10^4' should give readings of 0001 and 0051 respectively. The shorter gating period should be used only as a check on the first significant figure; to minimize the resolution error inherent in any form of digital readout, the maximum number of digits should be employed when obtaining a reading.

In counting applications (Fig. 5.11c), the oscillator is not used. The pulses to be measured, divided as necessary, provide the main input to the gate, and external start–stop signals, if required, provide the control input.

Summary

The simplest form of analogue electrical display is the moving-coil meter. Whatever its nominal function, the deflection depends only on the current through the moving coil. A particular movement may be adapted for different current and voltage ranges by means of shunt and series resistors respectively. The lower limit on the current which can be measured is fixed by the f.s.d. current of the movement. The usefulness of moving-coil meters for voltage measurement in high-resistance circuits is restricted by the possibility of loading errors.

'Electronic' or 'amplifying' meters have the advantages of higher input resistance on voltage ranges, and the ability to operate on current ranges below the f.s.d. current of the indicator.

U.V. recorders are high-speed instruments based on galvanometers. They can record alternating inputs with frequencies up to several kHz, but the sensitivities of galvanometers capable of this performance are low. U.V. recorders are relatively low-resistance devices.

Oscilloscopes have very high speeds of response, and high input impedance. Their primary function is to display the variations of a rapidly changing input voltage with respect to time. They may be calibrated on the vertical axis to measure voltage, and on the horizontal axis to measure time or frequency.

Self-balancing potentiometers and bridges work on the comparator principle. They are generally more accurate than direct-deflection meters, and have ample power to drive recording pens. Their responses are slow compared with those of u.v. recorders. Digital voltmeters also employ comparator principles. They are capable of better accuracies than analogue voltmeters, and have very high input impedances.

Electronic counter–timers give a digital display representing the number of input pulses received, or the time between 'start' and 'stop' signals. Most can also measure frequency, by counting the number of input pulses in a very short 'gating period'.

Examples

1. A meter coil has a resistance of 500 Ω and requires a current of 100 μA to produce full-scale deflection. Find the values of the resistors required to adapt this meter to read (a) 0–1 mA; (b) 0–1 V. State the overall resistance of the modified meter in each case.

(Ans.: 55·55 Ω shunt; 9·5 kΩ series; 50 Ω, 10 kΩ.)

2. Three 10 kΩ resistors are connected in series across a 6 V supply. A multimeter on a 0–5 V range is used to check the voltage across one of the resistors. What should be the minimum ohm-per-volt rating of the meter if the loading error is not to exceed 5 per cent?

(Ans.: 26 kΩ/V.)

3. Gating-periods of 1 ms, 10 ms, 100 ms, 1 s, and 10 s are provided on a digital counter–timer–frequency-meter having a 3-digit display. A gating period of 10 ms is selected to measure an unknown frequency, and a reading of 034 is obtained. What is the likely value of the frequency? What steps should be taken (a) to check the validity of the result; (b) to obtain a more accurate result?

(Ans.: 3·4 kHz; (a) select 1 ms gating period; (b) select 100 ms gating period.)

Suggestions for further reading

1   Sol D. Prensky, *Electronic Instrumentation*, Prentice-Hall, 1963.
2   T. D. Towers, *Electronic Laboratory Instrument Practice*, Iliffe Books, 1967, for *Wireless World.*
3   A. P. Malvino, *Electronic Instrumentation Fundamentals*, McGraw-Hill, 1967.

6. Transmission and signal conditioning

Some of the more common electrical transducers and displays have been described in chapters 4 and 5 respectively. It now remains to consider what ancillary equipment may be necessary to adapt the transducer output to the input requirements of the display. In some cases direct connection between transducer and display is possible. More frequently, some electrical modification of the signal is required, before it can be accepted by the display. The nature of this modification, and the equipment to produce it, are discussed in this chapter.

6.1 Amplification

A feature common to many electrical transducers is that they are insufficiently sensitive, i.e., the change in electrical output for a given change in mechanical input is too small to give an acceptable change in the indication of the display. In other words, there is a need for amplification of the signal. In chapter 5, it was pointed out that many displays—such as oscilloscopes and amplifying meters—already contain a signal-amplifying stage. So the problem may be solved in some cases merely by the selection of a display with sufficient built-in amplification. In others, it may be necessary to incorporate a separate amplifier, sometimes referred to as a *pre-amplifier*. Since it is to be included in a measuring system, any amplifier used in this way must have stable characteristics. Its gain (ratio of output to input) should remain constant, and its zero should not 'drift' (i.e., it should always give zero output for a zero-input signal).

An amplifier usually amplifies voltage. This type of amplifier may be called a voltage amplifier, but the prefix 'voltage' is often omitted. Some applications call for amplifiers which will amplify current or power; these are more frequently referred to by their full titles, as *current amplifiers* or *power amplifiers* respectively. There are also amplifiers which are useful for their impedance characteristics, rather than for any amplification they may produce.

Amplifiers are further classified as 'a.c.' or 'd.c.'. It has already been pointed out in connection with oscilloscopes that d.c. amplifiers accept a.c. inputs whereas a.c. amplifiers 'block' d.c. inputs. A further practical difference is that equipment employing a.c. amplifiers is less prone to zero-drift, which is often experienced with d.c. amplifiers.

6.1.1 Carrier amplifiers. A special type of amplifier which will be met mainly in conjunction with inductive transducers is the *carrier-frequency amplifier*. Commercial carrier-frequency amplifiers usually perform other functions in addition to that of amplification. Before discussing these other functions, the term 'carrier frequency' will be clarified. The term is used where the value of a measured quantity is represented by the amplitude of an alternating current or voltage of fixed frequency. The alternating quantity is then referred to as the *carrier*, and its frequency as the *carrier frequency*.

Consider the differential transformer of Fig. 4.11. It was mentioned in

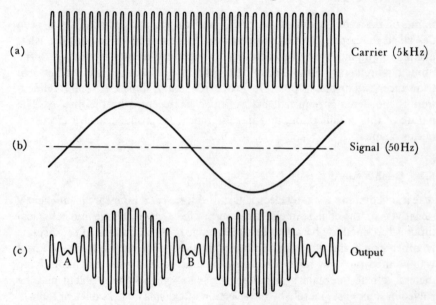

Figure 6.1   Amplitude modulation

section 4.5.1 that differential transformers are usually supplied from a high-frequency source. Suppose this frequency to be 5 kHz; then any output from the secondary windings due to displacement of the core will necessarily be at the same frequency. The core displacement determines the amplitude of the output signal, but does not affect its frequency. The carrier frequency in this case is 5 kHz. Suppose now that the core were displaced sinusoidally about its central position with a frequency of 50 Hz. The resulting output signal would be of the form shown in Fig. 6.1. A signal of this form is said to be *amplitude* modulated (abbreviated to A.M.).

Before the output signal is fed to the display it must be restored to the form of the original displacement; i.e., in this case, the 50 Hz signal has to be extracted from the amplitude-modulated wave. The electronic circuit which does this is called a *demodulator*. From consideration of Figs. 4.11 and 6.1, it will be apparent that the demodulator requires to be phase sensitive, i.e., it must be able to determine the phase of the transducer output relative to that of the supply. (Suppose the output wave between A and B in Fig. 6.1c is in phase with the supply to the primary winding. The point B corresponds to the instant when the core passes through its central position, which produces a 180° phase change in the carrier output. If this is not detected by the demodulator, it will not be possible to determine the direction of the original displacement.) It is therefore necessary for the demodulator to receive a phase-reference signal from the oscillator which supplies the 5 kHz power for the transducer. This interdependence of oscillator and demodulator is the principal reason for combining the signal-conditioning elements with the supply in a single unit. This unit is commonly called the carrier-frequency

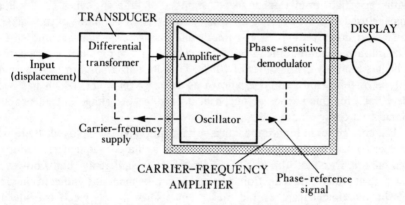

Figure 6.2   Functions of a carrier-frequency amplifier

amplifier, or simply the carrier amplifier, though amplification is only one of its functions. Figure 6.2 illustrates the essential components of a carrier amplifier. Sometimes a further signal-amplifying stage is added following the demodulator.

Besides being used for inductive transducers, A.M. carrier-frequency systems are often used with strain-gauge bridges. Where it is intended to amplify the bridge output, a.c. energization is sometimes preferred to the more traditional d.c., to avoid the problems of zero-drift associated with d.c. amplifiers.

An alternative to amplitude modulation which may be used for inductive and capacitive transducers is *frequency modulation* (F.M.). The circuits of electronic oscillators contain both capacitance and inductance, which together determine the frequency of the oscillator. If either of these quantities is provided by a transducer, and is consequently variable, the frequency of the oscillator will be controlled by the transducer. The change in frequency is approximately linear with respect to the change in inductance or capacitance over a small frequency range—perhaps ±5 per cent of the carrier frequency. Electronic techniques are available for converting this change to an analogue voltage signal. Like the A.M. carrier amplifier, a commercial 'F.M. amplifier' is often a composite unit, not merely an amplifier; it may contain the oscillator and the frequency–voltage conversion circuits (also known as the *discriminator*).

6.1.2 *Amplifiers for piezo transducers.* The basic problem of measuring piezo transducer outputs is that the voltage output results from a static charge. If current is taken from the transducer, the charge is dissipated, and the voltage signal is lost.

There are two approaches to the problem of 'conditioning' piezo transducer outputs. The first is to feed the output to a conventional voltage amplifier with very high input impedance. A number of different types of amplifier may be used in this way; they are often referred to by the name of the particular circuit employed—such as *cathode-follower*, *emitter-follower*, and so on. The important common feature of these circuits is the high input impedance, which is typically of the order of 10^8 Ω. The alternative solution is to employ a type of following amplifier, known as a *charge amplifier*, which has been developed for this particular purpose; it produces a voltage output proportional to a charge input.

If a conventional high-impedance voltage amplifier is employed, there will still be some current drain on the transducer and a consequent reduction in the charge. Provided the amplifier impedance is sufficiently high, however, the rate at which this reduction takes place can be made insignificant, in view of the dynamic nature of the measurements for which piezo transducers are used. In addition to the current drain, the amplifier and its connecting cable will impose a *capacitive* loading on the transducer. A piezo transducer has capacitance, and behaves like a capacitor as far as the relationship between charge and voltage is concerned. Thus, if its capacitance is C_p, and the charge developed as a result of the application of a particular input is Q, the open-circuit voltage V_o across the transducer will be given by $V_o = Q/C_p$. If now the transducer is connected to a cable and amplifier of combined capacitance C_c, the two capacitances will be additive and the new voltage corresponding to the same charge is given by $V = Q/(C_p + C_c)$. Clearly V is less than V_o—i.e., the sensitivity of the measuring system has been reduced; in general, this is an undesirable result. Further, the calibration will be affected by any change in the external circuit, such as a change in the type or length of cable.

The cable used to connect a piezo transducer to a conventional amplifier should, therefore, have low capacitance. It should also have high insulation resistance, to reduce the effects of charge-leakage. Piezo systems of this kind are usually supplied complete with the necessary cable, and calibrated accordingly.

Since the value of the charge Q corresponding to a certain input to the transducer is unaffected by the external capacitance, the performance of systems using charge amplifiers is little affected by cable length. High insulation resistance is, however, still required. Charge amplifiers are generally to be preferred to conventional amplifiers for piezo outputs, but are more expensive. A recent solution to the piezo output problem, which avoids any difficulty of cable characteristics, is to incorporate a miniature voltage amplifier in the transducer body. The only connections then required are to the output side of the amplifier, which is a low-impedance voltage source.

6.2 Impedance matching

The term *impedance matching* means the arrangement of successive elements in a measuring system so that the output impedance of one stage is suited to the input impedance of the next stage. The need for this may be seen by considering a hypothetical high-impedance transducer with a voltage output.

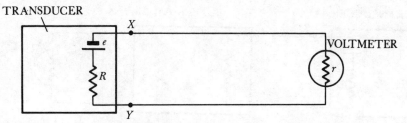

Figure 6.3   High-impedance transducer with low-impedance display

For a particular input value, the transducer may conveniently be regarded as a small cell of e.m.f. e in series with a large resistance R (Fig. 6.3). The quantity which is characteristic of the transducer for this particular input value is the e.m.f. e, so ideally this is the quantity which should be measured. Suppose now a voltmeter of relatively low resistance r is connected to terminals X and Y to measure the transducer output. A current of magnitude $e/(R+r)$ will flow round the circuit which has been completed by the meter. The voltage measured by the meter will therefore be

$$e - iR = e - \frac{eR}{R+r} = \frac{e}{1+R/r} \tag{6.1}$$

and the error in the measurement is

$$iR = \frac{eR}{R+r} = \frac{e}{1+r/R} \tag{6.2}$$

This is, in fact, another example of loading error, which was discussed in section 5.1.1.

Thus, instead of finding e, the nominal output of the transducer, the voltage $e/(1 + R/r)$ has been measured. Although meter M could be calibrated to allow for this error, there are objections to this approach. The most serious objection is that the sensitivity of the system has been reduced, perhaps seriously if R/r is large. Another objection is that there may be calibration figures for the transducer, relating the output e to values of the input. It would be preferable to be able to apply these figures directly to the readings of the voltmeter, without having to apply a correction involving knowledge of r and R. (This objection may be overcome only by making r so much greater than R that the loading error becomes negligible, or by using a comparator-type instrument, which takes no current from the source when balanced.)

The situation may be much improved by interposing a suitable high-impedance amplifier between the transducer and the display.† An amplifier used in this way is sometimes called a *buffer* amplifier; its main characteristics are high input impedance and low output impedance. Figure 6.4 shows the arrangement with the amplifier included, S and s being its input and output impedances respectively. The effect of the modification can be seen by using

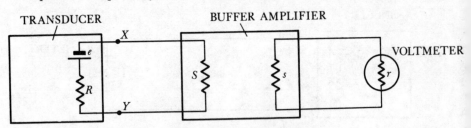

Figure 6.4   Use of buffer amplifier

numerical values for R, S, r and s. Let $R = 1$ MΩ, $S = 500$ MΩ, $r = 10$ kΩ, $s = 200$ Ω. These are feasible values, though a large value of R/r has deliber-ately been chosen to illustrate the effect of the amplifier. Using the expres-sion (6.2) for the first stage of the transmission (but putting S in place of r) shows that there will be an 'error' in the input to the amplifier of $e/(1 + 500/1)$, or approximately 0·2 per cent. A similar calculation for the second stage, from the amplifier to the display, gives a further error of about 2 per cent. This result should be compared with the attenuation which would occur in the absence of the amplifier. In this case, the attenuation of the signal would be $e/(1 + 10/1000)$, or about 99 per cent. In this simple example, the gain of the amplifier has been neglected. In principle, the amplifier could be designed to have any required gain. Many simple buffer amplifiers in fact have a voltage gain of slightly less than unity; they nevertheless perform the function of pre-venting serious 'loss' of signal amplitude.

The example above illustrates the importance of relating the input im-pedance of any stage of the measuring system to the output impedance of the previous stage. In electrical engineering, the object of impedance matching is

---

† The use of a high-impedance amplifier with a piezo transducer (described above) can be regarded as a case of impedance matching. It is, however, a non-typical case, because of the transient nature of the piezo output signal.

often to transmit maximum *power* to the next stage; it can be shown that this is achieved if the output impedance of the source is equal to the input impedance of the receiver. In measurements, the transmission of maximum power is of less importance than limiting the attenuation of the signal. For a voltage signal, this is best achieved by making the input impedance of the receiving device as high as possible.

6.3   Direct transmission

Although amplification and/or impedance matching may be essential for certain transducers, others are of sufficiently low impedance and high sensitivity to be connected directly to the display. Some transducers of intermediate sensitivity may be used either with or without amplification. Strain-gauge bridges come into this category. In the 'direct' arrangement, the bridge is d.c.-energized, and the output is measured by a sensitive galvanometer. If greater sensitivity is required, or greater power output (e.g. to drive a u.v. recorder), a d.c. amplifier may be incorporated; alternatively, the bridge may be energized with a suitable carrier frequency, in order to take advantage of the better zero stability of an a.c. amplifier on the output side. The bridge output is then taken to the display via an amplifier–demodulator (section 6.1.1).

6.4   Inter-unit connections

The type of cable used to connect the elements of an electronic measuring system may be of importance, particularly if high frequencies and/or high impedances are involved. Though there are laboratory situations in which simple p.v.c.-covered flex and crocodile clips may be adequate, such connections should not be used indiscriminately.

An ever-present danger in electronic measuring systems is that of *pick-up* in the signal lines. This term is used to describe spurious signals produced either by electro-magnetic induction, or by capacitive 'leakage'. A cable in an alternating magnetic field will have e.m.f.s induced in it, just like any other conductor. These e.m.f.s and the corresponding currents are referred to as *inductive pick-up*; it may be severe in the proximity of electro-magnetic devices, such as transformers, and near mains cables. *Capacitive pick-up* is caused by the ability of a.c. to 'pass' through a capacitance. Any two conductors separated by an insulator have capacitance. For cables, this capacitance is normally small, since the area of the 'plates' of the capacitor is small, but it can be significant under certain conditions. Capacitive reactance is inversely proportional to frequency; it is, therefore, large at low frequencies, so that leakage is small. The leakage may become serious either if the frequency is very high, or if other circuit impedances are high, so that the capacitive reactance of the cable is of comparable magnitude.

71

Techniques used to combat pick-up are: (a) the twisting together of lead-pairs; this presents a configuration of conductors such that any e.m.f. induced in one lead is cancelled by the e.m.f. induced in the other; (b) screening, the screens being at or near earth potential. Connections between the various units in a measuring system are often made with screened cable. The centre core is then used to connect the 'live' output terminals, and the screen is used to connect the 'common' terminals; the latter are usually connected internally to the chassis, or frame, of the equipment. Special-purpose electronic equipment is often supplied with its own interconnecting cables. Where these are supplied, it is good practice to use them. The importance of this in the case of piezo-electric transducers has already been stressed. Small spurious signals are also generated internally in electronic components. These signals become troublesome when high-gain amplifiers are used, since they are, in general, amplified to the same extent as the 'wanted' signal. Although techniques exist for separating wanted from unwanted signals, these cannot be successful for all frequencies, and the existence of unwanted signals sets an ultimate limit to the amplification which can be usefully employed. *Noise* is the general term used for all spurious signals, whether internally or externally generated.

6.4.1 Long connecting lines. If long transmission distances are involved, as in process instrumentation, new factors have to be considered which would be of little consequence in a laboratory. These factors include initial cost, the effect of line-resistance on transducer output (and of changes in line-resistance with ambient temperature), and stronger pick-up signals due to numbers of long cables being run together. These problems, coupled with the advantages of using standardized display equipment, have led to the introduction of standard signal-ranges for process measurements. It is now normal practice in this field to convert transducer outputs to a d.c. signal before transmission to the display, a signal range of 4–20 mA being typical. The converters used to produce this signal give a current output which is unaffected by variations in line resistance within wide limits. The low values of current used require only small, economical conductors. As all signals, after the converter, are d.c., they will not cause pick-up, and will not be much affected by pick-up from other sources (since d.c. receiving equipment does not respond readily to a.c.). A current in the range quoted can conveniently be displayed on a moving-coil indicator; alternatively, it can be recorded on a d.c. potentiometer, the input to the potentiometer being the voltage drop across a fixed resistor through which the signal current passes.

With the introduction of data processing and computer control in the industrial process field, it is possible that in future the transmitted signal will be of digital rather than analogue form. This would obviate the further signal conversion (from analogue to digital) which is at present necessary for data-processing equipment working with conventional industrial instruments.

Where even longer distances are involved, or where measurements have to be made in a missile or moving vehicle, it may be necessary to use radio techniques to transmit signals. This form of transmission is usually called *telemetry*. Telemetry is outside the sphere of general engineering measurements, and will not be discussed in this book. Reference 1 deals with telemetry in a measurement context.

Summary

Many transducers have to be followed by an amplifier, either to amplify the signal, or to provide a high-impedance load.

Amplifiers may be classed as either a.c. or d.c. An a.c. amplifier blocks d.c., but a d.c. amplifier will accept a.c.; d.c. amplifiers are prone to zero drift. Carrier amplifiers are used with transducers requiring high-frequency supplies; the so-called amplifier in an A.M. system is usually a unit comprising oscillator, amplifier, and demodulator. Similarly, a commercial F.M. amplifier may comprise oscillator, amplifier, and discriminator.

Piezo transducers must be followed either by a charge amplifier or by a conventional amplifier of high input impedance. Any transducer with a voltage output and high internal impedance should be followed by a high-impedance amplifier.

In process instrumentation, transmission distances are relatively large, and standard d.c. signal ranges are employed; this permits the use of standardized display equipment, and reduces pick-up problems.

Reference

1 R. H. Cerni and L. E. Foster, *Instrumentation for Engineering Measurement*, Wiley, 1962.

Part 2

Specific Measurements

7. Dimension, angle, and strain

The measurement of length and angle, which is the main subject of this chapter, belongs to the field traditionally known as metrology. This field is well covered by a number of well-known texts (e.g., refs. 1, 2 and 3), and only an outline will be given here. The measurement of linear strain, which has already been discussed in section 4.2 in connection with electrical-resistance strain gauges, is considered in this chapter in more general terms. The link between strain and length is that measurements of both are commonly made by measuring displacement.

Some types of displacement transducer were described in chapter 4 under the heading of 'multi-purpose transducers'. The more sensitive of these transducers, and a number of other less versatile displacement-sensitive devices, are extensively used for the measurement of length by comparative methods.

7.1 Length standards

The unit of length, the metre, is a basic SI unit. It is defined in terms of the wavelength of light emitted by the atoms of krypton-86 under specified conditions. The primary standard of length is thus reproducible, though the equipment and expertise required make its reproduction impracticable as a routine industrial procedure. Lower-grade length standards are normally in the form either of engraved scales, or of metal blocks or bars of specified length. A basic objection to such standards is their dependence on temperature, since all materials which can conveniently be used for their manufacture expand with an increase in temperature. In using a metallic length standard for accurate work, therefore, temperature effects have to be taken into account. Sometimes this is not so troublesome as might first appear; if the standard and the object to be measured are of similar material, they can be assumed to have expanded (or contracted) equally, provided they are known to be at the same temperature when the measurement is made. Since temperature affects the dimensions of standards of this kind, it is necessary to define the temperature at which the standard should be used. By international agreement, the nominal values of length standards correspond to a temperature of 20°C.

7.1.1 Line and end standards. Length standards in the form of blocks or bars, with two faces or ends at a defined distance apart, are known as *end standards*; those for which the nominal length is indicated by lines engraved on a bar or scale are called *line standards*. The term 'line standard' was originally used for a bar with only two lines engraved on it, representing a specified length. (The former imperial yard was a standard of this type.) Accurately engraved scales are now also commonly referred to as line standards. The distinction between a line standard and a scale is an arbitrary one; normally, only the highest-grade scales are referred to as 'standards'. An engineer's steel rule would not usually be classified as a line standard, but there is no reason in principle why it should not be.

Both end standards and line standards have their applications. Much routine dimensional inspection work in production engineering is done by means of end standards, using comparators, i.e., instruments which measure a dimension by comparing it with the length of the standard. Some less routine measurements, on the other hand, may be made more conveniently by instruments incorporating line standards.

7.1.2 Gauge blocks. Practical end standards for lengths up to about 200 mm are provided by *gauge blocks* (also known as *slip gauges*). A gauge block is a rectangular hardened-steel block with two opposite faces at a defined distance

Table 7.1 Contents of 112-piece gauge-block set

Size (mm)	Increment (mm)	No. of pieces
1·0005	—	1
1·001–1·009	0·001	9
1·01–1·49	0·01	49
0·5–24·5	0·5	49
25–100	25	4

apart, these faces being ground and lapped to make them flat and parallel within fine limits. The blocks are produced in sets with which it is possible to build up a 'stack' of any required height, the flatness and finish of the surfaces of the blocks being such that they can be made to adhere to each other sufficiently strongly to keep the stack together during normal use. The process of making the blocks adhere is referred to as *wringing*: it involves a combination of pressure normal to the surface to be joined with sliding motion of one surface over the other.

British Standard 4311: 1968 (*Specification for metric gauge blocks*) lists the pieces for a number of sets of gauge blocks, with up to 112 pieces in a set. A typical 112-piece set comprises the blocks listed in Table 7.1.

Gauge blocks are produced in a number of different grades, depending on the use for which they are intended. The principal difference between grades lies in the permissible tolerances for length, parallelism, and flatness. Grades intended for general use normally include two 2 mm *protector blocks* for use at the ends of the stack, to reduce wear on the remainder of the set; these blocks may be harder material than the other blocks, or may be of similar material, but replaced at more frequent intervals. The effects of wear on the sizes of blocks may be taken into account if periodic checks are made against higher-grade sets, the highest-grade sets being calibrated by inter-ferometric methods (section 7.4).

The procedure for selecting blocks to make up a specified length is as follows: first subtract 4 mm from the required length to allow for the pro-tector blocks, assuming that these are to be used; then select blocks to give the *least* significant figures, and work towards the most significant figure. Sup-pose, for example, that a length of 57·1125 mm is to be made up from the blocks listed in Table 7.1. Subtracting 4 mm for the protector blocks leaves 53·1125 mm; the least significant figure can be accounted for only by the use of the 1·0005 mm block, leaving 52·112 mm; the 0·002 mm can be removed by the use of the 1·002 mm block, leaving 51·11 mm, which can be made up from the 1·11 mm and 50 mm blocks respectively.

7.1.3 Length bars. For lengths greater than about 200 mm gauge blocks become unwieldy, and the self-adhesion of the 'wrung' blocks cannot be relied upon to keep the stack together. End standards for greater lengths are therefore made in the form of round bars, known as *length bars*. Like gauge blocks they are made in several grades. The lower-grade bars have drilled and tapped ends, so that they may be combined by means of studs. A typical set comprises 11 bars, from 25 mm to 200 mm in 25 mm steps, plus bars of 375, 575 and 775 mm respectively. For lengths not exactly divisible by 25 mm, com-binations of end bars and gauge blocks are used. Details of end bars and their tolerances may be found in B.S. 1790/1961: (*Length bars and their accessories*).†

7.2 Comparators

The process of determining length involves the comparison of the unknown length with one of the forms of standard described in section 7.1. When a line standard is employed, it usually forms an integral part of a measuring instrument. End standards, on the other hand, are not built into measuring instruments. (To do so would restrict the range over which the instrument could be used.) The normal method of using end standards is to calibrate an instrument by means of the standards, then use the instrument to measure the unknown dimension. Instruments used in this way are known as comparators.

---

† At the time of writing, this British Standard is still in Imperial units; it is to be revised in SI units.

The purpose of a comparator is to detect and display very small differences between a measured dimension and the length of a standard, the difference being detected as a displacement of a sensing probe. The essential function of the instrument is thus to *magnify* a small input displacement, so that it is represented by a displacement sufficiently large to be seen clearly on an analogue scale. Magnification may be obtained mechanically or optically, or by means of electrical or pneumatic transducers. Though many ingenious mechanical systems have been devised, there are limits to the magnification which may be satisfactorily obtained in this way. A further disadvantage of mechanical comparators is that it is difficult to incorporate adjustment of the magnification. Consequently electrical and pneumatic transducers are being increasingly used in general-purpose comparators, where adjustment of the magnification over a wide range is desirable.

7.2.1 Mechanical magnification.

In the field of general mechanical engineering, the normal methods of obtaining high magnifications are by the use of levers or gears respectively. These methods are not suitable, in their conventional forms, for use in comparators. The special requirements of comparators are, briefly: (a) very high magnification, usually greater than 1000 : 1; (b) a completely predictable input–output relation, unaffected by reversals in the direction of the input; backlash and friction in the movement must therefore be avoided; (c) low input force: this must be such that the contact pressure between the sensing probe and the component being measured is insufficient to cause significant deformation of the component surface.

Requirements (b) and (c) above preclude the use of gears,† and requirement (b) also precludes the use of conventional pivots.

A very simple mechanical comparator could be made as shown in Fig. 7.1. The standard or the component to be measured is represented by *A*. The plunger *B* is supported by the split washers *C* (Fig. 7.1b), which ensure its correct location, without imposing too great a load on *A*. The indicating pointer *D* is made in the form of a single cranked lever, mounted on the flexible strip *F*, and operated directly by *B*. (The use of flexible strip mountings rather than pivots is normal practice in comparators, to avoid the play which is inevitable in a conventional pivot.)

The magnification obtainable from this simple mechanism depends on the length of pointer which can be tolerated, but is unlikely to exceed 100 : 1. At least one further magnifying stage must be added to obtain magnifications of the order required in routine inspection work in production engineering. Figure 7.2 shows a possible development using a further mechanical–optical

† The common workshop dial indicator, which is basically a plunger-operated magnifying gear train, may be used as a simple comparator. Dial indicators may have sensitivities of up to about 0·1 mm/rev, corresponding to an overall magnification of approximately 1500 : 1. This represents about the practical limit for magnification by a gear train in a device of this kind.

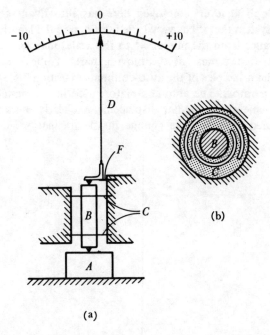

Figure 7.1   (a) Simple mechanical comparator; (b) split washer

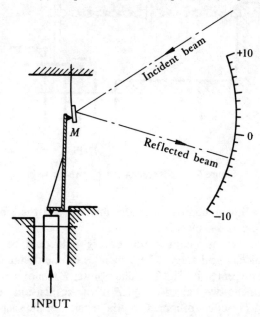

Figure 7.2   Addition of optical magnifying stage to simple comparator

stage. The 'optical lever' employed here has the advantage over a purely mechanical system that it has very little inertia, and the length of the 'pointer' (i.e. the distance from the mirror M to the scale) may be increased without any addition to the mass of the moving parts. Optical magnifying stages employing the principles of the auto-collimator (section 7.5.3) have also been used in comparators. The auto-collimator, used in the manner described on p. 93, in fact measures angular displacement. Clearly the angular displacement measured could be the change in the inclination of a lever in the

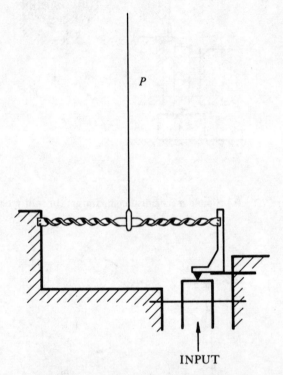

P

INPUT

Figure 7.3   Magnification by twisted strip

mechanism of a linear comparator; the method can therefore be used to measure small linear displacements.

Alternatively, the basic comparator of Fig. 7.1 could be followed by a second purely mechanical stage. The principles of one design (C. E. Johannson Ltd.) are represented in Fig. 7.3. The pointer P is mounted on a twisted-strip suspension, the two halves A and B of the suspension being twisted in opposite senses. The effect of increasing the tension in the suspensions is that they tend to 'unwind', turning the pointer P, which moves in a plane perpendicular to the plane of the diagram. Overall magnifications of the order of 5000 : 1 are claimed for this mechanism.

Dimension, Angle, and Strain

7.2.2 *Electrical magnification.* Numerous electrical transducers are available which will magnify small displacements; the more common of these have already been described in chapter 4. Those employed in comparators are normally based on the principle of variable inductance, and incorporate an amplifier in the transmission stage to provide further magnification. A variable-gain control on the amplifier provides a convenient means of varying the sensitivity.

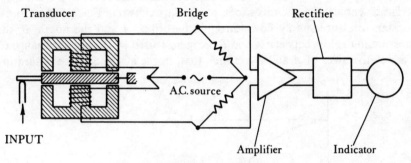

Figure 7.4   Electrical comparator

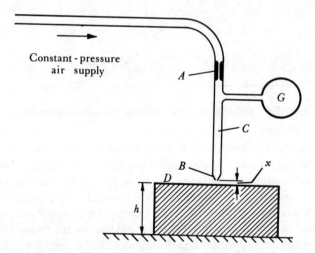

Figure 7.5   Pneumatic comparator

The linearized form of inductive transducer (Fig. 4.10), has been used successfully in comparators. Figure 7.4 shows the schematic layout of the complete system, comprising inductive transducer, bridge, amplifier, rectifier and indicator. Overall magnifications as high as 50 000 : 1 have been obtained with electrical comparators.

7.2.3 *Pneumatic magnification.* The principle of the obturated nozzle, widely used in other branches of instrumentation where a sensitive non-electrical

83

displacement transducer is required, may be used as the basis for a compara-tor. Pneumatic comparators share most of the advantages of electrical com-parators, but require a supply of clean compressed air, which is usually less readily available than an electrical supply. They have certain further advantages in some specialized applications, e.g., they can operate without mechanical contact with the measure component, and may be adapted rela-tively easily for the measurement of internal diameters.

The essentials of a pneumatic comparator are shown in Fig. 7.5. Air from a constant-pressure supply flows through the orifice A and the nozzle B, the pressure in the line between A and B being measured by the pressure gauge G. The relative sizes of A and B are such that, in the absence of the obturating

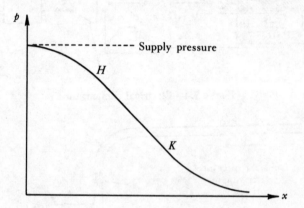

Figure 7.6   Relation between pressure and nozzle-clearance

surface D, B offers less restriction to the air flow than does A. Under these circumstances, the pressure, p, in part C of the line will be very nearly equal to that of the surrounding atmosphere. The pressure gauge G therefore registers approximately zero. If now the surface D is brought into contact with B so that it completely seals off the exit, p will rise until it equals the supply pres-sure. The point which is of interest is the behaviour of the pressure p as the surface D approaches the nozzle, i.e., the relationship between p and the clear-ance x. The nature of this relationship is shown in Fig. 7.6. It will be noted that over a substantial portion of the curve, between H and K, the relation between p and x is very nearly linear. The indicated pressure p may therefore be used as a measure of x, and differences in p will represent differences in the height of components (or gauge-block stacks) introduced successively under the nozzle.

The rate of change of p with x depends on the pressure of the air supply, and on the ratio of the areas of the cross-sections of the nozzle and orifice respectively. Variation of this ratio provides a convenient method of adjusting the magnification. If the orifice A is replaced by a variable restriction, such as a needle valve, continuous adjustment of the magnification is provided.

7.2.4 Comparator calibration. Comparators are general-purpose instruments which have to be calibrated, or 'set-up', against end standards for each particular application; calibration follows the general principles laid down in section 2.2.1. 'Coarse' and 'fine' zero adjustments are usually provided. The coarse adjustment consists in mounting the whole body of the comparator at a suitable height above the measured component; fine adjustment may be the same in principle, using a fine screw movement, or it may be incorporated in the operating mechanism of the comparator. Sensitivity is adjusted by using two stacks of gauge blocks corresponding to the required readings at (or near) the two ends of the scale. The usual procedure of alternate adjustment of the sensitivity and 'zero' settings must then be carried out, treating one end of the scale as the zero.

7.3 Line-standard instruments

The primary advantage of line-standard instruments is that, in their more elementary forms, they do not require calibration each time they are used. If only a small number of measurements of a given type is to be made, a line-standard instrument is often more convenient. For repeated measurements of components on production lines, however, comparators are preferred, since they require little manipulation and are easy to read.

Small linear dimensions are commonly measured either by the *micrometer screw gauge*, or by *vernier calipers*. These are both *line-standard* class instruments, and it is assumed that they are too well known to require description here. Measurements may be made with a micrometer to accuracies of the order of ± 10 microns, and with vernier calipers to perhaps ± 30 microns. These figures presuppose that checking has already been carried out against end standards of higher orders of accuracy, and that any errors found in the instruments during such checks are taken into account when making measurements.

7.3.1 Measuring machines. Instruments having a capacity for measuring lengths greater than about 200 mm are usually categorized as measuring machines. Most such machines incorporate built-in line standards and are based on the principle of the travelling microscope. The introduction of a component or standard causes a relative displacement, between the microscope and finely divided scale, equal to the length to be measured. Readings from the scale, on which the microscope is focused, are taken before and after displacement, thus giving the required length. Some machines of this type are capable of measuring along three perpendicular axes simultaneously. Further details of measuring machines and the techniques of using them may be found in refs. 2 and 3.

7.4 Interferometry

The use of light waves for length measurement has already been mentioned in connection with the primary length standard. As light waves can be used to establish a standard, it would be expected that the principle might have other applications in the field of length measurement.

The exact nature of light has not been established with certainty. However, the behaviour of light beams can be satisfactorily explained in the present context on the assumption that they are propagated as sinusoidal waves, the colour of the light being determined by its wavelength. If light waves are to be used for the purpose of accurate measurement, it is therefore necessary that light of a constant colour, known as *monochromatic light*, should be employed.

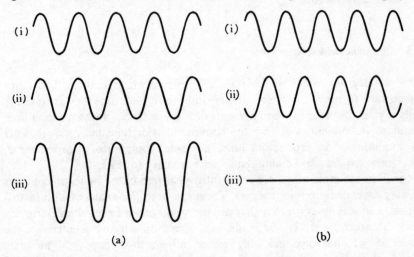

Figure 7.7   Interference: (a) waves in phase; (b) waves 180° out of phase

Certain heated elements, such as mercury vapour, cadmium, and krypton-86, make suitable sources of monochromatic light.

Apart from the provision of a source of monochromatic light, a basic difficulty in the use of light-wave techniques is that of 'counting' the number of wavelengths corresponding to the length to be measured. Wavelengths are very small—about 0·5 μm—and although this is advantageous from the standpoint of resolution, the problem of determining the number of wavelengths in a given length is a formidable one. The method used to establish lengths or displacements by means of light-waves is basically that of observing the *interference* of one wave with another.

7.4.1 Principle of interference. If the convention of representing light rays by sinusoidal waveforms is accepted, the phenomenon of interference may be simply explained. Referring to Fig. 7.7a, the waves (i) and (ii) are of the

86

same amplitude, wavelength and phase. A simple calculation (or graphical exercise) will ascertain that the result of adding or 'mixing' these two waves together will be a further sinusoidal wave, having the same wavelength as the two original waves, but double its amplitude, as shown by the trace (iii) in the diagram. In terms of light rays, this means that the result of mixing two rays, which are of the same frequency (i.e., of the same wavelength) and in phase, will be a ray of greater brightness than either of the two component rays. The converse applies in the case of the sinusoidal waves illustrated in Fig. 7.7b, where the waves (i) and (ii) are 180° out of phase. The resultant 'wave' in this case has zero amplitude, representing complete darkness. This phenomenon is referred to as interference, and its use for the purposes of measurement is called *interferometry*.

Further consideration of Fig. 7.7b suggests that if the wave (ii) arrived at its new position by being displaced slowly to the right (from its position in Fig. 7.7a) through a distance equal to half of its wavelength, the resultant brightness would diminish gradually from maximum to minimum. The fact that this diminution had occurred could therefore be used to deduce that the distance moved was, in fact, one half wavelength. This provides a basis for measurement of displacement by means of interference. There are two potential causes of error in the method: the first is that the change from brightness to darkness is a gradual one, and the positions of maximum brightness and darkness are therefore difficult to identify; the second (and more serious) possible cause of error is that the same result would occur if the waveform (ii) had been displaced to the right by one half wavelength *plus any number of whole wavelengths*. Thus the mere existence of darkness does not establish the extent of the displacement with certainty. The first of these difficulties is unimportant in some of the applications of interferometry, because of the small wavelengths involved. (An error of a small part of a wavelength is negligible in many contexts.) The second difficulty, that of determining the exact number of half wavelengths, is fundamental when the method is applied to absolute (as opposed to comparative) measurement of length.

7.4.2 Length measurement by interferometry. Interferometric methods are used for length measurement only when high orders of accuracy are required, as they are expensive both in terms of equipment and time. One of the chief applications is the absolute determination of the sizes of high-grade gauge blocks. The method may also be used for the comparison of gauge blocks. Figure 7.8a illustrates this application of the principle. A block of glass known as an *optical flat* is allowed to rest across the top of the two gauges to be compared. The special feature of an optical flat is that its lower surface is ground and polished to a very fine degree of flatness and finish. A vertical beam of monochromatic light of known wavelength is arranged to fall on the flat. Part of the beam passes through the glass, strikes the upper surfaces of the gauge blocks, and is reflected back upwards towards the source. However, the nature of the lower surface of the optical flat is such that some of the light will be *internally* reflected at this surface. Thus, an individual ray of light incident on the lower surface of the flat may be regarded as being split into two parts, one part being reflected at this surface, and the remainder passing through the optical flat and being reflected at the surface of the gauge block. This is shown schematically in Fig. 7.8b. In the interests of clarifying the diagram, an incident ray is shown inclined to the vertical, and certain liberties have been taken with the laws of optics (e.g., refraction has been ignored, and the two reflected rays have been drawn parallel to each other). These approximations may be justified in practical cases, where the incident ray is perpendicular to the surface of the block, and the inclination of the optical flat to the horizontal does not exceed about 2 minutes of arc. The important point about this

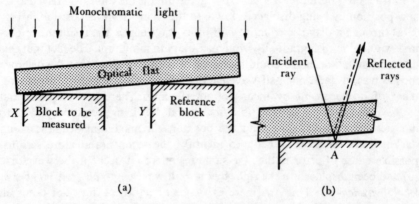

Figure 7.8 Comparative length measurement by interferometry

arrangement is that the reflected ray comprises two parts—that reflected at the block, and that internally reflected at the lower surface of the flat. These two parts have travelled different total distances, and are recombined after reflection.

It has been shown in Fig. 7.7 that the result of mixing two light waves of the same frequency depends on their phase relationship. In the case under consideration, the two rays must have the same wavelength, since they originate from the same source. They will therefore 'interfere' or 'reinforce' according to their phase relationship, which in turn depends on the relative distances travelled by the two waves. Consideration of Fig. 7.8b (again regarding both incident and reflected rays as vertical) indicates that the difference in the distances travelled by the two parts of the 'split' light wave is twice the separation between the optical flat and the block at the point A. Thus the two parts of the reflected wave will interfere if the separation at this point is one-quarter of the wavelength of the light (i.e., if the difference in the distances travelled by the two parts is half a wavelength). If the separation is denoted by δ, and the wavelength by λ, then a ray reflected at A will experience interference if $\delta = \lambda/4$; there will also be interference corresponding to points where the separation is equal to *any* odd number of quarter wavelengths, i.e., if $\delta = 3\lambda/4, 5\lambda/4, 7\lambda/4$, etc; in general, there will be interference if

$$\delta = (2n-1)\,(\lambda/4), \tag{7.1}$$

n being any positive integer. An observer viewing the gauge block from above will therefore see a series of dark lines, or 'interference fringes' corresponding to the points at which the separation of the two surfaces has one of the values given by eq. (7.1).

This state of affairs is illustrated in Fig. 7.9, in which all representation of light rays has been omitted for the sake of clarity. If L_1, L_2, etc., represent the positions of the fringes, then the lengths δ_1, δ_2, etc., may be found by putting the appropriate values of n in the expression $(2n-1)\,(\lambda/4)$. The

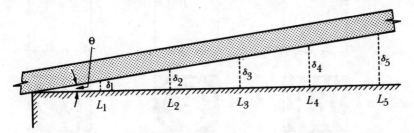

Figure 7.9   Relation between fringe spacing and surface separation

information which can be obtained from the fringes is, basically, the inclination of the optical flat to the top surfaces of the gauge blocks; from this information, the difference in the heights of the blocks may be calculated. First, the mean value of x, the fringe separation, is found; this is done by counting the number of fringes over the maximum possible distance in any particular case, to minimize the error caused by the poor definition of the fringes. Having determined the mean value of x, the value of the inclination θ is given by $\tan\theta = (\delta_2 - \delta_1)/x$. However, eq. (7.1) shows that the difference between any two consecutive values of δ is $\lambda/2$, so $\tan\theta$ is in fact equal to $\lambda/2x$. This value of $\tan\theta$ can be used to determine the difference in the heights of the blocks, provided that the distance between the faces X and Y (Fig. 7.8) is known. The interference principle may also be applied to the absolute (as opposed to comparative) determination of length, but the techniques involved are more complex than those described above (ref. 2).

The interferometric method of length measurement using conventional monochromatic light is satisfactory only if the difference in the path lengths of the two parts of the 'split' beam is less than about 200 mm. If the paths differ by more than this, it is difficult to obtain satisfactory fringes. The principle may be used over greater distances if laser beams are employed in place of conventional light. The advantage of a laser beam is that its wavelength is constant within very close limits. Although the light from the conventional sources used in interferometry is described as monochromatic, there are always slight variations in wavelength within a given beam. These variations do not cause serious applicational difficulties in the techniques which have been described here, but make the fringes less distinct as the path length increases. A further advantage of laser beams is that they are more readily formed into parallel beams than are conventional light rays. More information on the application of laser beams in this and other fields may be obtained from ref. 4.

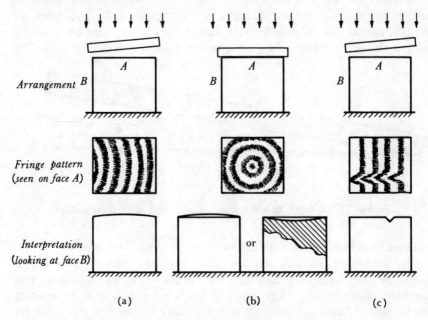

Arrangement

Fringe pattern
(seen on face A)

Interpretation
(looking at face B)

(a)   (b)   (c)

Figure 7.10   Interference patterns from surface defects

7.4.3   Surface imperfections. In the foregoing discussion of interference fringes, perfect flatness and finish of the surfaces concerned have been assumed. If the surface is imperfect in either of these respects, the resulting variations in the separation between the surface and the optical flat will cause corresponding irregularities in the interference fringes. It follows, therefore, that the principle may be used to measure imperfections of flatness and finish.

The nature of the information which may be obtained from interference fringes used in this way can be seen from the simple examples illustrated in Fig. 7.10. Bearing in mind the principle of fringe formation, it will be appreciated that the path of a particular fringe corresponds to points of equal separation of the two reflecting surfaces. In case (a) therefore, it follows that the top surface of the block must be convex, as shown. (A similar pattern would be obtained from a concave surface, if the optical flat were inclined in the opposite sense.) In case (b), the fringe pattern of a number of concentric rings, using an optical flat nominally parallel to the top face of the block, indicates that the surface under examination is either concave or convex, but does not determine which. If the pattern has been obtained merely by resting the flat on the block, as suggested in the diagram, the direction of curvature may be resolved either by applying very light downward pressure to one side of the flat, or by applying slightly heavier pressure to the flat at the point above the centre of the pattern. A convex surface will respond to the former test, as the flat will tip very readily, with the result that the area of contact (and therefore the centre of the fringe pattern) will move towards the point at which pressure was applied. Provided the pressure is very light, the pattern produced by a concave surface will not be significantly changed by this test. If, however, moderate pressure is applied at the centre of the pattern, a slight deformation of the flat in a downward direction will be produced if the surface is concave. This will cause a decrease in the separation of the surfaces, and the distance between fringes will be increased.

Case (c) in Fig. 7.10 shows the effect of a single 'trough' in the surface of the block. Since the distance between adjacent fringes corresponds to an increase in separation of the surfaces equal to $\lambda/2$, the depth of the defect in this case appears to be approximately 0·2 μm, if a wavelength of 0·5 μm is assumed. While a defect of this magnitude might be satisfactorily assessed without further complication of the apparatus, optical magnification of the fringe pattern is required if maximum information about the surface is to be obtained.

7.5 Measurement of angle

The unit of angle, the degree, has been unaffected by the introduction of SI units. It is subdivided into 60 minutes (60'), and each minute is subdivided into 60 seconds (60''). Readily defined and reproducible primary standards of angle are available. The standard may be taken either as the angle subtended by a circle at its centre (360°), or as the angle between two straight lines intersecting in a manner such that all four angles so formed are equal (90°).

As in length measurement, the measurement of an angle involves the comparison of the unknown angle with a known standard angle. The standard —again as in the case of length—may take the form of an engraved scale (a line standard), or of two surfaces known to be set at a particular angle to each other. The latter type would correspond to an end standard in the field of length measurement. Angle standards cannot logically be referred to as end standards; the term *face standard* will be used here to designate this type of standard.

7.5.1 Line-standard methods. A circular engraved scale used for angular measurements is referred to as a protractor. Those used for engineering purposes have an adjustable arm, often with a vernier scale attached, which may be set at any desired angle to a reference base-line. The vernier scale may usually be read to the nearest 5′, but the accuracy of measurement depends not only on the accuracy of the instrument itself but also on the method of use; there may be practical difficulties in making the comparison between the unknown angle and the angle set on the protractor.

Improved accuracy of comparison may be achieved by using a vernier protractor in conjunction with a spirit level. The combination of these two devices is called a *clinometer*. Basically, a clinometer is a protractor with a spirit level attached to the moving arm. The object to be measured is placed so that one face of the unknown angle is resting on a horizontal surface,

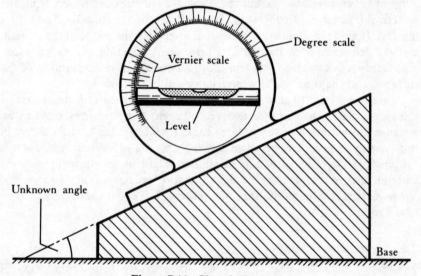

Figure 7.11   Use of clinometer

and the base of the clinometer is positioned along the line of greatest slope to the other face (Fig. 7.11). The moving arm of the instrument is then adjusted to the horizontal position by means of the spirit level, the scale reading then being equal to the unknown angle. In practice the base plate is unlikely to be precisely horizontal. A correction for this may conveniently be made by taking two successive readings, the first with the instrument in the position shown in Fig. 7.11, and the second with the instrument in the same vertical plane but resting on the base plate. The unknown angle is then equal to the algebraic difference of the two readings obtained.

7.5.2   *Face-standard methods*. There are two approaches to the problem of setting up two surfaces at a known inclination to each other. The first is to set up a triangle, by means of linear measurements, to contain the required angle; the second is to use blocks having faces machined and lapped to known angles (analogous to gauge blocks in length measurement) which may be combined to produce the required angle. The apparatus normally used for the first of these methods is called a *sine bar*. In use, the bar forms the hypotenuse of a right-angled triangle, the vertical side of which is determined by the height of a stack of gauge blocks. Any base angle, within the physical limitations of the arrangement, can be built up by this method, the value of the angle being calculated from its sine.

Angle gauge blocks (or angle slip gauges) provide a more convenient method of constructing standard angles. They are supplied in sets and may be wrung together in the same way as the gauge blocks used for length measurement. A conventional set comprises the following blocks:

90° square
41°, 27°, 9°, 3°, 1°
27′, 9′, 3′, 1′
27″, 9″, 3″

With this set, any angle may be built up, to the nearest 3″. At first, the number of blocks required to achieve this may appear small; this is because angle blocks have the advantage over linear gauge blocks that a block may be used to *subtract* its nominal value from the stack if required, instead of adding it. (This is achieved merely by reversing the positions of the ends of the block.)

7.5.3 Angle comparator (auto-collimator). If a face standard is to be used for angular measurement, a means of comparing the standard and the unknown angle is required. One approach to this problem is to combine the standard and the unknown angle in such a way that two nominally parallel faces are produced. These two faces may then be checked for parallelism, using established workshop techniques. An alternative, which gives a direct reading of the difference of the two angles, is to use an *auto-collimator*. The principle of this instrument is shown in Fig. 7.12. A parallel beam of light falling on the lens L is brought to focus in the focal plane FF of the lens. This remains true even if the beam is inclined to the axis of the lens, provided that the angle of inclination is not too large. If, therefore, a parallel beam of light derived from the point source S in the plane FF is incident on the reflecting surface AA, an image will be formed at some point I, again in the plane FF. The exact position of I depends on the angle, $\delta\theta$, between the reflecting surface and the normal to the incident beam. The angle between the incident and reflected beams will in fact be $2\delta\theta$. (This is a basic law of optics.) By considering the rays passing through the centre point P of the lens (which suffer no resultant deflection) and making the usual approximations for small angles, it can be seen that the relationship between the distance x and the angle $\delta\theta$ is given by

$$x = f \cdot 2\delta\theta \qquad (7.2)$$

where f is the focal length of the lens. Thus $\delta\theta$, the inclination of the reflecting surface to the plane of the lens, may be determined from a measurement of x.

In commercial instruments based on this principle, the displacement of the image is viewed through an optical magnifying system, and is seen superimposed on a scale calibrated directly in terms of $\delta\theta$. Equation (7.2) shows that the magnitude of x is independent of the distance D between the lens and the reflecting surface. There are practical limitations to the variations of D which can be tolerated—if D is too great, the reflected beam will not enter the lens. However, within these limitations, the instrument can be used without regard to the value of D.

To use the instrument, it is necessary to have a 'face' standard set up to within a few minutes of the unknown angle. (If the sensitivity is to be high the range of the x-scale seen through the optical system must be restricted;

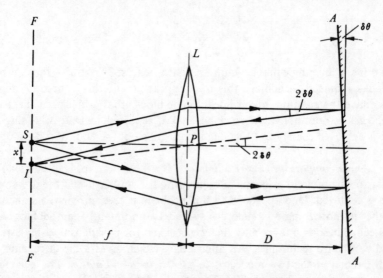

Figure 7.12   Auto-collimator principle

typically this range represents 30' of arc, and can be read satisfactorily to the nearest 0·5'.) The auto-collimator is set up over the angle standard, and is adjusted to give a convenient reading on the x-scale. A second scale reading is then obtained, with the standard replaced by the component to be measured. The difference in the readings then gives the difference between the standard and the unknown angle.

One practical drawback of this method of comparison is that a good reflecting surface is required. On newly finished components this will often, but not always, be available. If the surface does not have adequate reflecting power, the difficulty may often be overcome by placing (preferably wringing) a gauge block on the surface. Since gauge blocks are manufactured to close tolerances, no significant angular error will be introduced by the presence of the block.

7.5.4 Angular displacement. Relatively large angular displacements of stationary shafts may generally be measured with acceptable accuracy by means of circular engraved scales, with vernier attachments if necessary. The reading accuracy of such scales may be increased by increasing the scale diameter. If remote indication is required, displacement transducers similar in principle to those used for linear measurements may be employed—e.g., rotary potential dividers are suitable if high sensitivity is not required. The resistance winding of a potential divider may be made in the form of a helix, so that displacements of more than one revolution can be measured. Differential transformers for rotary motion are also available, giving linear output for angular displacements up to about 40°.

Measurements of torque in rotating shafts are often based on methods which require small angular displacements of one section of the shaft relative to another to be determined. Possible methods of making such measurements are discussed in section 12.2.2.

7.6 Linear strain

Strain is defined as the proportional change in dimension caused by stress in a material; e.g., if the stress in a material causes a dimension x to change by an amount of δx, the strain is $\delta x / x$. When δx represents an increase in x, the strain is regarded as positive, and the same sign convention is followed for the associated stress. If an elastic material is stressed in one direction only, stress and strain are connected by the relationship stress/strain $= E$, where E (the modulus of elasticity) is a constant for a particular material.

The most obvious application of strain measurement is in the field of materials testing, where the object is to discover the mechanical characteristics of the material. In this field, the work is usually carried out on specially made test pieces, and the measurement of strain is relatively uncomplicated. Strain measurement is also used as a means of calculating stresses in existing loaded structures. Although the stress–strain relationship becomes complex when a material is stressed in two or three dimensions simultaneously, it is still possible to determine stress from measurements of strain.

7.6.1 Methods of measurement. Measurement of strain may be regarded as the measurement of the displacement of one point on a body relative to another point on the same body. The displacements concerned are usually very small. It may be required to measure strains down to about 10 microstrain (1×10^{-5}), which, if measured over a length of 50 mm, would correspond to a relative displacement of only 0·5 μm.

Approached in this way, the problem of measuring strain becomes that of measuring small displacements. This problem has already been discussed in chapter 4 in connection with displacement transducers, and in section 7.2 in connection with comparators. The methods of magnification used for linear

95

comparators are, in principle, equally applicable to strain measurement, provided that suitable input arrangements can be devised to introduce the displacement into the magnifying device. This is generally quite straight-forward in the field of materials testing; a typical arrangement for measuring the strain in a test piece is shown schematically in Fig. 7.13. The lever mechanism *BCDAF* is clamped to the test-piece at the pivot points *A* and *B*, the distance *AB* being known. Any change in *AB*, due to straining of the specimen, causes a corresponding change in the dimension *CD*. This change forms the input of a displacement transducer, or of a mechanical or optical magnifying device. Strain-measuring devices used in this way are called *extensometers*. Often the displacement of *C* relative to *D* is measured with a dial gauge.

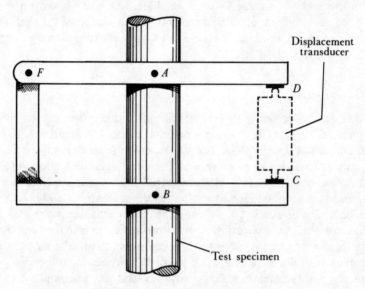

Figure 7.13   Basic extensometer

Extensometers are convenient in the field of routine materials testing, where measurements are usually taken under static conditions, and space is available in the neighbourhood of the test piece for a relatively cumbersome mechanism. They are not suitable for the majority of local measurements on existing structures, or for applications involving the measurement of rapidly varying strains. These local and dynamic strain measurements require a device having negligible mechanical inertia, and occupying minimum space —requirements which are met by bonded strain gauges, or, in some applications, photo-elastic methods (section 7.6.2).

The principles of bonded strain gauges were described in section 4.2. To analyse the stresses in complex structures, it is generally necessary to measure strain in three defined directions at a particular location on the structure. Multiple strain gauges are produced for this purpose (Fig. 7.14), comprising three gauges on a single mounting, and are known as *strain-gauge rosettes*. The profiles shown represent the approximate true size of typical general-purpose rosettes; configurations occupying much smaller surface areas are commercially available if required. (In practice, the use of miniature strain gauges is avoided if the application does not require them, as mounting is somewhat more difficult.) It will be apparent that the soldering terminals are relatively large compared to the 'grids', or active portions of the gauges, this not only simplifies the soldering operation, but reduces the magnitude of the small changes in gauge resistance which must inevitably be caused in making the joint. In use, a separate strain reading must be obtained from each of the three gauges; the method of calculating the stresses in the material from these readings may be found in books dealing with two-dimensional stress analysis.

The strain-gauge approach to stress analysis is generally satisfactory in cases where suitable plane surfaces exist on the structure for the attachment of the gauges. It is unsuitable for use at points where abrupt changes of contour occur. Such contour changes—notches, slots, etc.—do, in fact, cause stress concentrations, and are therefore likely to be of special interest in an analysis. Further drawbacks in the use of strain gauges for stress analysis are that only

 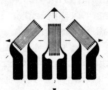

Figure 7.14   Strain-gauge rosettes (*Profiles by courtesy of Micro Measurements and Welwyn Electric Ltd.*)

surface strains can be measured, and that, for a comprehensive study, large numbers of gauges are required. Some of these difficulties may be avoided by the use of photo-elastic techniques.

7.6.2   Photo-elasticity. Photo-elastic measurements depend on the phenomenon of double refraction, which occurs when polarized light passes through strained transparent plastic materials (refs. 6 and 7). The effect of this double refraction is to produce fringes somewhat similar to those obtained in interferometry. Quantitative measurement on the fringes, from which strains in the plastic can be deduced, may be then made with instruments designed specifically for this purpose (polariscopes).

To obtain information about the stresses in a structure it is necessary that the photo-elastic material (the plastic) should be subjected to strains which are identical or analogous to those in the structure. There are two basic approaches to the problem of introducing these strains: either a plastic scale model of the structure may be made, and subjected to analogous loads, or an existing structure may be coated with the plastic, so that the plastic suffers the same strains as the structure.

If the model technique is used, information on stress concentrations and values may be obtained before the structure or component is made. Appropriate design changes can then be made before manufacture. This is particularly useful for large structures, where the cost of manufacture would be high, or for small components for which analysis by other methods would be impossible. In either case, the model would be scaled to a convenient size for exploitation of the photo-elastic technique. An extension of the straightforward model technique is to 'freeze' the stress pattern into the model for subsequent analysis. This is achieved by loading the model at an elevated temperature, and maintaining the load during cooling. The unique advantage of this procedure is that the model may subsequently be sectioned as required to investigate the internal stresses.

The coating technique, like strain gauging, gives information on surface strains only, but has the advantage over strain gauging that it provides an overall picture of the strain pattern. Strain gauges, however, are capable of greater accuracies: it is therefore common practice to make a general photo-elastic investigation, followed by strain-gauge measurements at points shown on the overall pattern to be of particular interest.

Coatings may be applied in liquid form, or by moulding and bonding of sheet material. The latter technique is preferred where possible, as it produces a coating of more uniform thickness. (Uniformity of thickness affects the accuracy of the results). As the polarized light has to be analysed after passing through the coating, a reflecting surface behind the coating is required. Reflection may be obtained from the surface of the structure itself, or from the adhesive used to bond the coating to the surface.

Summary

Lengths and displacements are measured in metres (or multiples or submultiples of metres), the metre being a basic SI unit. It is defined in terms of the wavelength of light from a specified source.

Lower-grade length standards are classified either as line standards (scales), or end standards. Length measurement involves the comparison of the unknown length with a standard of one of these two basic types. End standards are used for checking line-standard instruments and for the calibration of comparators. A comparator magnifies the difference between the measured dimension and the correct dimension, and displays the magnified difference to the operator.

Both absolute and comparative measurements of length may be made by methods based on the interference of light waves. Comparative measurements are relatively simple, and may be made by means of a single monochromatic light source and an optical flat. Fringes occur when the separation of the reflecting surfaces is equal to an odd number of quarter wavelengths of the incident light. The distance between adjacent fringes therefore corresponds to a change of one half wavelength in the separation of the reflecting surfaces.

Angles may be measured by line-standard or face-standard methods. Face standards are most commonly built up from angle block gauges; they may be compared with the unknown angle by means of an optical comparator

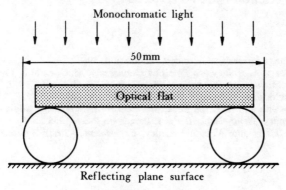

Figure 7.15

(auto-collimator). Angular displacements may be measured by methods similar in principle to those used for linear displacements.

In routine materials testing, strain may be measured with extensometers using methods of magnification similar to those used in comparators. Many strain measurements in other fields are made with bonded strain gauges. Strain gauges are particularly suited to measurements at specific points on loaded structures, and to dynamic strain measurements. Where an overall picture of strain conditions is required, photo-elastic methods are preferred.

Examples

1. The diameters of two rollers, each nominally 10 mm, are to be compared by means of interference fringes produced by an optical flat and monochromatic light of wavelength 0·6 μm (Fig. 7.15). Twelve fringes are seen in a length of 20 mm over the centre portion of the flat. Calculate the difference in the two diameters.

(Ans.: 7·2 μm.)

2. Select angle gauge blocks from those listed on p. 93 to construct 'stacks' as near as possible to the following angles:

(a) 17°40′39″; (b) 61°50′52″.

(Ans.: (a) +18°, 9′, 9″: −27′, 1′, 27″, 3″; (b) +90°, 3″: −27°, 1°, 9′, 9″.)

3. A clinometer has a zero error. When placed on a nominally horizontal

plane, a reading of +55′ is obtained. When turned through 180° about a vertical axis, the new reading with the measuring arm relevelled is −25′. (a) What is the magnitude of the zero error in the instrument? (b) What correction would have to be applied to an angle measured by the 'algebraic difference' method described on p. 92?

(Ans.: zero error of +15′; no correction.)

References

1   K. J. Hume, *Engineering Metrology*, Macdonald, 1963.
2   A. J. T. Scarr, *Metrology and Precision Engineering*, McGraw-Hill, 1967.
3   L. Miller, *Engineering Dimensional Metrology*, Edward Arnold, 1962.
4   David Fishlock (ed.), *A Guide to the Laser*, Macdonald, 1967.
5   T. G. Beckwith and N. Lewis Buck, *Mechanical Measurements*, Addison-Wesley, 1961.
6   A. W. Hendry, *Photo-elastic Analysis*, Pergamon Press, 1966.
7   James W. Dally and William F. Riley, *Experimental Stress Analysis*, McGraw-Hill, 1965.

8. Pressure

Pressure is defined as force per unit area; the fundamental SI unit of pressure is therefore the newton per square metre, also known as the *pascal*. Since pressure is a derived quantity it has no primary standard; various lower-grade standards are used for calibration purposes, some of which are described in section 8.10.

8.1 Practical pressure units

The N/m^2 is an inconveniently small unit for most practical purposes. There are conflicting views concerning the optimum unit for industrial use. The range of pressures normally encountered in industry can conveniently be expressed in kN/m^2, which is approximately one-seventh of the unit traditionally used in the imperial system, the lbf/in^2.

Low pressures are often expressed in mmH_2O (millimetres of water, or millimetres water gauge) or mmHg (millimetres of mercury). This is an abbreviated way of saying that the pressure is that which will support a liquid column of the stated height. In pressure calculations, is is important to note that these units are not true pressure units, as they do not have the dimensions of force/area.

8.2 Zero pressure

The theoretical zero of the pressure scale clearly corresponds to zero force per unit area. This is seldom the most convenient zero for practical purposes, since, at the surface of the earth, the atmosphere exerts a pressure of approximately 100 kN/m^2.† Although this pressure varies from place to place and from day to day, industrial pressures are usually measured relative to the prevailing atmospheric pressure, rather than relative to the true zero. Pressures measured in this way are referred to as *gauge* pressures, whereas those measured relative to the true zero are described as *absolute*. Industrially, pressures are assumed to be gauge pressures unless they are specifically stated to be absolute.

† 100 kN/m^2 is called a *bar*; the bar is sometimes used as the unit of pressure, particularly in meteorological work.

8.2.1 Negative pressure. When pressures are measured relative to atmospheric pressure, it is possible for them to be either positive or negative. (On the absolute scale, the concept of negative pressure has no physical meaning.) The word 'vacuum' is often used in connection with the measurement of pressures below that of the atmosphere. This term can be ambiguous unless carefully defined; it is used in some contexts to denote a negative gauge pressure, and in others a very low absolute pressure. Such very low pressures are frequently measured in *torr*, one torr being the pressure exerted by a column of mercury 1 mm high.

8.3 Methods of measurement

Since pressure is defined as force per unit area, the problem of measuring it is analogous to that of measuring force. Common methods of measuring force are by elastic deformation (e.g., the extension of a spring) and by comparison with a known weight. These methods are also used for pressure measurement, though the mechanisms are somewhat different in the two cases, because of the necessity of first applying the pressure to a surface of suitable area to produce a force. For pressure measurement, the weights of liquid columns are generally more convenient for comparison purposes than solid or 'dead' weights. (A column of given height produces a certain *pressure* at its base, irrespective of cross-section—see section 8.4.1.) Elastic-deformation and liquid-column methods are well suited to the static measurements required in process instrumentation. They are less suited to dynamic measurements, principally because of mechanical inertia, which cannot be completely eliminated from instruments based on these principles. This is particularly true of liquid-column methods, in which the movement of substantial masses of liquid may be involved. The field of dynamic pressure-measurement is covered principally by piezo-electric and strain-gauge systems (section 8.6).

8.4 Liquid columns

An instrument employing the liquid-column principle for measuring pressures is called a *manometer*. Besides being used for routine measurements, manometers are frequently used as laboratory standards against which other pressure-measuring instruments may be calibrated.

8.4.1 Principle of the method. The action of a manometer depends on the relationship between the pressure p_0 at the surface of a liquid, and the pressure p_1 at some depth h below the surface. By considering the equilibrium of a column of liquid of height h (Fig. 8.1a), this relationship may be seen to be

$$p_1 = p_0 + \rho g h, \tag{8.1}$$

where ρ = density of the liquid, and g = local value of the gravitational acceleration. Thus the pressure at depth h exceeds the pressure at the surface by ρgh. Often the pressure acting on the surface of a liquid is the pressure of the atmosphere. Then if gauge pressures are being used, $p_0 = 0$, and the pressure at depth h is simply ρgh.

An important corollary of eq. (8.1) is that the pressures at all points at the same distance below the surface are equal. This is true only where a single liquid is under consideration. If there is a liquid interface, the simple principle as stated above no longer applies. Consider the arrangement of Fig. 8.1b, in which two liquids, A and B, are contained in a tank with a partition between them. The principle of constant pressure at constant depth applies to the two points X_1 and X_2, because they are both within the liquid A. It does not apply

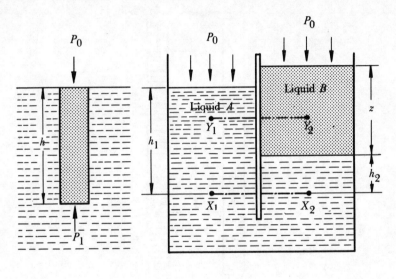

(a)   (b)

Figure 8.1   Relationship between pressure and depth

to Y_1 and Y_2. Note that the pressure at the point X_2 could be calculated from consideration of its depth below either of the liquid surfaces. Working from the surface of liquid A, the pressure at X_2 is given directly by eq. (8.1) as $(p_0 + \rho_A gh_1)$, where ρ_A is the density of liquid A. Applying the same principle to the right-hand section of the tank, the pressure at the liquid interface is $\rho_B gz$ (ρ_B being the density of liquid B), and the pressure at X_2 exceeds this by $\rho_A gh_2$. The pressure at X_2 may therefore be expressed either as $(p_0 + \rho_A gh_1)$, or as $(p_0 + \rho_B gz + \rho_A gh_2)$.

8.4.2 Simple manometers. Although the basic principle of all manometers is the same, they vary in design. The most elementary type is a simple U-tube (Fig. 8.2) containing a suitable liquid. The relationship between the pressures on the two sides may be obtained most easily by applying eq. (8.1) to the points A and B. As these points are at the same level,

$$p_1 = p_0 + \rho_m gh \qquad (8.2)$$

where ρ_m is the density of the liquid. If p_1 is the gauge pressure and p_0 is the pressure of the atmosphere, this reduces to $p_1 = \rho_m gh$.

The important features of the U-tube manometer are: (a) the result is independent of the bore of the tube,† so that accurately sized tube is unnecessary: (b) since the liquid moves up in one limb and down in the other, reference must be made to the levels of both sides when a reading is taken. This is

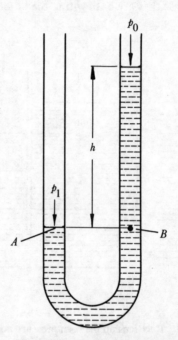

Figure 8.2   U-tube manometer

an inconvenience if frequent readings are required. If the bore is known to be uniform, the drop in level on one side will equal the rise in level on the other; it is then possible to observe one side only, and measure $h/2$. If the manometer scale is to be calibrated in true pressure units, e.g., kN/m^2, the fact that only half the true liquid head is being measured can be taken into account in the calibration. It is common, however, for simple manometers to be calibrated in terms of the head of manometer liquid—e.g., so many mmH_2O or mmHg. (Water and mercury are common filling liquids for manometers; paraffin is also used extensively, but paraffin manometers are usually calibrated in

† Very small bores—say less than 5 mm—should not be used, as capillary effects can cause errors.

mmH$_2$O, rather than mm of paraffin.) If this form of calibration is used, the scale used for a uniform-bore U-tube read on one side only will obviously be only half its nominal length; e.g., the length of scale representing 100 mmH$_2$O for a water-filled U-tube will be 50 mm long. This represents a 50 per cent loss of sensitivity, which is undesirable for low-range manometers. The sensitivity may be restored almost to its original value by using tubes of different cross-sectional areas, A_1 and A_2, (Fig. 8.3). The relation between the changes in the level of the liquid in the two sides (y_1 and y_2) may be obtained from the

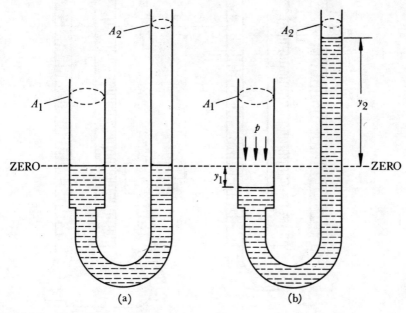

Figure 8.3 Use of tubes of different cross-sectional areas: (a) at zero; (b) measuring

concept of continuity: the volume of liquid y_1A_1 which has left the larger limb has appeared as y_2A_2 in the measuring limb. Hence:

$$y_1A_1 = y_2A_2. \qquad (8.3)$$

If a gauge pressure p is applied to the larger limb, then equating pressures at the level XX on the two sides of the manometer gives—

$$p = \rho_m g(y_1 + y_2). \qquad (8.4)$$

Normally a scale is fixed adjacent to the right-hand limb to read the values of p in terms of y_2. To calibrate this scale from theoretical considerations, a relation between p and y_2 is required. This relation may be obtained by eliminating y_1 from eq. (8.3) and (8.4). If the scale is calibrated in mm of the manometer liquid, the divisions of the scale will be somewhat smaller than their nominal values. (They would be equal to their nominal values only if A_1 were made infinite.) Since the areas of the tubes now appear in the relationship

105

between pressure and observed height, these areas must be constant, and accurately known.

8.4.3 Improvements to the simple manometer. Modifications may be made to the basic forms of manometer described above to improve accuracy, sensitivity, or ease of reading.

The accuracy of a simple U-tube manometer is limited principally by the inability of an observer to judge the exact position of the liquid meniscus

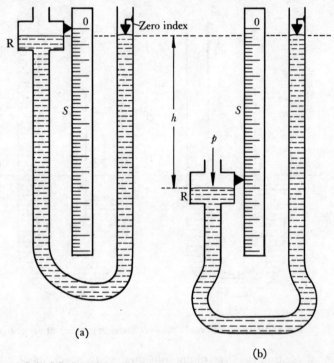

(a)

(b)

Figure 8.4   Moving-reservoir manometer: (a) at zero; (b) measuring

relative to an adjacent scale. Many optical devices, such as anti-parallax devices, have been employed to overcome this difficulty. Another approach to the problem is to use a manometer with a moving reservoir (Fig. 8.4). In use, the reservoir R is lowered until the liquid level in the right-hand side is restored to its original position. The distance moved by the reservoir, measured on the scale S, then equals the head of manometer liquid corresponding to the applied pressure. This type of manometer is unaffected by non-uniformity of the tube bores, provided the volume of the flexible tube remains constant during use.

The simplest way of increasing sensitivity is to incline the measuring limb (Fig. 8.5). The movement of the meniscus for a given pressure increase is thereby increased. Comparing Fig. 8.5 with Fig. 8.3, it can be seen that the head of liquid y_2 is now represented by the length l of the measuring tube, so that the increase in sensitivity is in fact proportional to the sine of the angle of inclination of the tube.

Ease of reading can be improved by combining an unequal-limb mano-meter with a conventional circular-scale display. The indicating or recording mechanism may be operated by a float supported by the manometer liquid, usually in the larger diameter limb. Instruments of this kind are used exten-sively in the process industries, where regular readings are required over long periods.

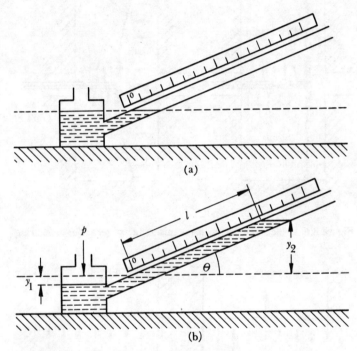

Figures 8.5 Inclined-tube manometer: (a) at zero; (b) measuring

8.5 Elastic-deformation methods

The principle of measuring pressure by elastic deformation requires that (a) a force should be derived from the pressure by applying it to a known area, and (b) this force should be used to deform an elastic member, such as a spring. The area to which the pressure is applied may be distinct from the elastic member, or the two functions may be combined in one element. The resulting displacement (i.e., the deformation) may be used for the direct operation of a mechanical indicator, or it may form the input to a displacement transducer. Instruments based on the principle of elastic deformation are more compact

107

than those using liquid columns, but they are more prone to inaccuracies caused by the effects of ageing and hysteresis in the elastic elements.

A simple illustration of the elastic-deformation principle is provided by the *slack-diaphragm* mechanism (Fig. 8.6). Application of pressure p to the left-hand side of the diaphragm produces a force pA on the diaphragm, where A is the effective diaphragm area. This force is resisted by the spring, which is compressed by the rigid centre plate of the diaphragm. If the spring is of

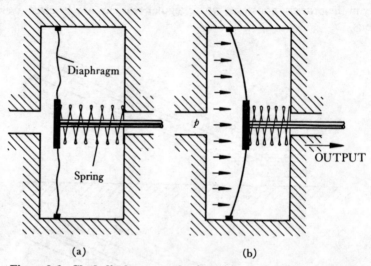

(a)   (b)

Figure 8.6   Slack-diaphragm mechanism: (a) at zero; (b) measuring

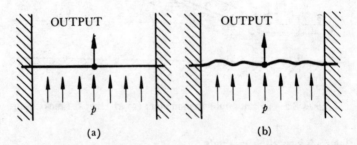

(a)   (b)

Figure 8.7   Metallic diaphragms: (a) plain; (b) corrugated

stiffness k, the movement of the plate due to the pressure p will be pA/k. Practical design considerations limit the magnitude of this movement, and substantial magnification is required if a mechanical indicator is to be operated directly from it.

In the slack-diaphragm gauge, the 'deformation' and 'area' functions referred to above are performed by separate members (the spring and the diaphragm respectively). At the expense of further restriction of the output movement, the two functions may be combined, using a metallic diaphragm (Fig. 8.7). Metals with good elastic properties, such as beryllium copper, are used for these diaphragms, which may be either plain or corrugated. Plain diaphragms have a very restricted range of output movement, and are normally used only in conjunction with sensitive electrical displacement

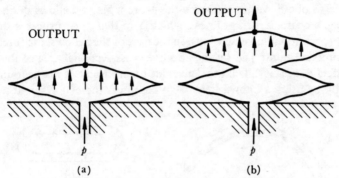

Figure 8.8   (a) single capsule; (b) capsule stack

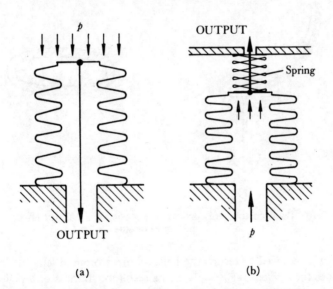

Figure 8.9   Bellows: (a) used alone; (b) combined with spring

transducers. Corrugated diaphragms have a somewhat greater range of output movement, and if combined with a high-magnification linkage, may be used for the direct operation of mechanical indicators. Increased sensitivity may be obtained by combining a number of corrugated diaphragms to form a *capsule* or *capsule stack* (Fig. 8.8).

An alternative to the capsule stack is the *bellows* (Fig. 8.9). Bellows are produced from one piece of material by a series of pressing operations and,

109

if made in sufficient numbers, are cheaper to produce than capsule stacks. They may be used alone, as in Fig. 8.9a, or in conjunction with a spring, as in Fig. 8.9b. When they are used alone, the pressure is applied to the outside of the bellows, as bellows perform satisfactorily only when used at or below their natural lengths. The use of a spring in conjunction with the bellows makes it possible to obtain various sensitivities from a single bellows design. A bellows has a characteristic stiffness, which, like that of a spring, is defined as (force)/(corresponding extension). In the case of the bellows, the force applied is the pressure multiplied by the effective cross-sectional area of the bellows. (The effective area is difficult to determine theoretically. It can be found experimentally by using a known load W to compress the bellows, and noting the

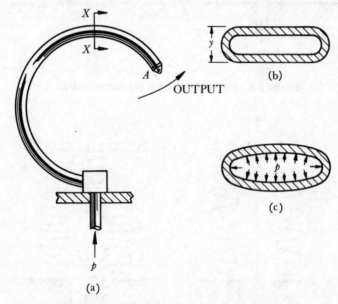

Figure 8.10   Bourdon tube: (a) profile; (b) section on XX; (c) effect of increasing internal pressure

pressure p required to return the bellows to its original length. The effective area A is then given by $pA = W$.) The resultant stiffness of a bellows–spring combination is the sum of the separate stiffnesses of the bellows and the spring.

The elastic-deformation devices so far described, with the exception of the plain diaphragm, which has a very restricted output movement, depend for their action on substantial flexure of relatively thin membranes. Their usage is consequently limited to the lower end of the range over which industrial pressures have to be measured. The upper part of the range is covered by the *bourdon tube*, an elastic-deformation device rather more complex in principle than those described so far. Bourdon-tube elements are commonly used for pressure ranges from 100 kN/m^2 to the highest pressures in normal industrial use (about 300 MN/m^2). Bellows, capsules, etc., are seldom used for differential pressures above 200 kN/m^2 (i.e., the pressure difference across these elements seldom exceeds this figure; the absolute values of the pressures on the two sides of the element may be substantially higher).

Figure 8.10a shows the profile of the commonest form of bourdon tube; Fig. 8.10b shows, to an enlarged scale, the cross-section of the tube, and Fig. 8.10c the change in this cross-section caused by increasing the pressure inside the tube. The principal effect of the increased pressure is to increase the length of the minor axis y of the cross-section. The result of this increase is to cause the output point A to move in the direction indicated on the diagram. In the traditional bourdon gauge, this motion is converted to rotary motion of an indicating pointer by a quadrant and pinion gear.

The sensitivities of bourdon tubes may be altered by changes in their dimensions, the principal controlling factors being the length of the minor axis y, the thickness of the tube walls, and the total length of the tube. The total length may be increased merely by increasing the radius of the circular arc, or by making it in the form of a helix. Though bourdon tubes have been made for pressure ranges as low as 0–10 kN/m^2, they are not normally employed for ranges below 0–100 kN/m^2. The inherently more sensitive devices discussed earlier in this section are preferred for the lower ranges.

8.6 'Dynamic' pressure transducers

The pressure-measuring devices so far described produce a *displacement* output, which may either be used to operate a mechanical indicator, or converted to an electrical signal by means of a displacement transducer, such as a differential transformer. Devices of this kind are unsuitable for measuring rapid fluctuations of pressure. The limitations on their use in this respect depend principally on the magnitudes of the displacement and of the mass being displaced—e.g., a metallic diaphragm is capable of more rapid response than is a mercury manometer. In this context, the mass being displaced is not only that of the moving parts of the transducer, but also that of any fluid which is displaced because of changes in the fluid capacity of the input side of the transducer. For liquids, this fluid mass may be large if the transducer is connected to the pressure vessel by a length of pipe. The masses concerned in gas-pressure measurements are much smaller; the use of connecting pipework is, however, still undesirable, because the compressibility of the gas in the pipe causes attenuation of rapidly fluctuating pressure signals. Pressure transducers for dynamic measurements are therefore mounted directly in the walls of the pressure vessel whenever possible. In many applications this requirement means that the transducer must withstand high temperatures, and may have to be water-cooled.

Several types of electrical pressure transducer, in which the mass displacement is small, have been developed specifically for dynamic applications. For optimum dynamic performance, the most outstanding are those based on the piezo-electric crystals (section 4.4). Piezo-electric transducers have no moving parts. However, the crystal or crystal-stack must compress slightly under load; some effects of mechanical inertia will therefore be apparent if the rate of change of load is sufficiently high. The dynamic performance of piezo transducers is discussed in chapter 14. Their chief limitations are that they are relatively insensitive (the minimum range is about 100 kN/m^2) and cannot be used for the measurement of static pressures.

Strain-gauges in conjunction with elastic elements may be used as an alternative to piezo transducers for dynamic pressure measurements. Any of the types of gauge described in section 4.2 may be used—i.e., they may be bonded or unbonded, or 'integrated' with the element. Suitable elastic elements are plain diaphragms, and cylindrical tubes with sealed ends.

Whatever the type of strain gauge employed, it is usual for a complete bridge of four active gauges to be incorporated in the transducer. The techniques for obtaining an output from the bridge, and for temperature compensation, are as for other strain-gauge applications. If maximum speed of response is not essential, strain-gauge pressure transducers have many advantages over the piezo-electric type. They are more sensitive (ranges down to 30 kN/m^2 are feasible), and are capable of both static and dynamic measurements.

The sensitivity of strain-gauge pressure transducers is limited basically by the need to develop an adequate force to strain the gauge itself. This sensitivity limit determines the minimum useful pressure range. Dynamic pressure transducers for lower pressure ranges may be based on the principle of varying capacitance, employing a plain diaphragm as one plate of a parallel-plate capacitor. Increasing the pressure on one side of the diaphragm decreases the mean separation of the capacitor plates, thus increasing the capacitance. The changes in capacitance may be measured by means of an a.c. bridge (section 3.4.3). Transducers of this type with ranges as low as 1 kN/m^2 have been produced. Low pressure ranges, however, necessitate relatively large diaphragms, and have correspondingly lower speeds of response. Capacitive transducers may also be used for higher pressures, though their dynamic performance is not so good as piezo-electric or strain-gauge types.

8.7 Differential pressures

It is sometimes required to measure the difference of two pressures, neither of which is equal to the prevailing atmospheric pressure. This requirement arises in flow-measuring applications, where rate of flow is deduced from the differential pressure across an orifice or venturi tube (section 9.4); in this application, the magnitude of the differential seldom exceeds 100 kN/m^2.

In principle, any of the pressure-sensitive devices so far described could be adapted to measure differential pressures. Measurement of gauge pressure is, in fact, measurement of the difference between an absolute pressure and the prevailing atmospheric pressure. Any other differential pressure within the range of a particular device may be measured, provided the physical arrangement of the equipment allows a second pressure to be applied to it. This may be difficult; when used for the measurement of gauge pressure, one side of the sensitive element is left open to the atmosphere. Usually the output of the device (e.g., a mechanical displacement) is brought out from this 'open' side, since no problems of sealing then arise. If, however, the device is to be adapted to measure differential pressures, both sides must be completely sealed. This may lead to design complications and increased cost, particularly where the output takes the form of a substantial mechanical displacement. Most differential-pressure instruments for static measurements are based on diaphragms, bellows, or manometers; these elements may be adapted fairly easily to accept the two input pressures.

8.8 Absolute pressure measurement

The problem of measuring absolute pressure may be regarded as that of measuring a difference of two pressures, one of the pressures being zero.

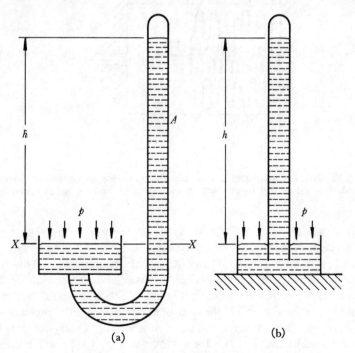

Figure 8.11 (a) Manometer for absolute pressure; (b) usual form of barometer

Again the same basic transducers may be employed as for gauge-pressure measurements, provided that it is possible to subject one 'side' of the sensitive element to zero pressure. This means that a chamber on one side of the element (liquid column, diaphragm, etc.) should be completely evacuated. Complete evacuation is not possible in practice, but a sufficiently good approximation to it may be obtained to enable conventional transducers to be used for absolute pressure measurements down to a few mmHg.

Figure 8.11a shows a single-limb manometer in a form suitable for absolute

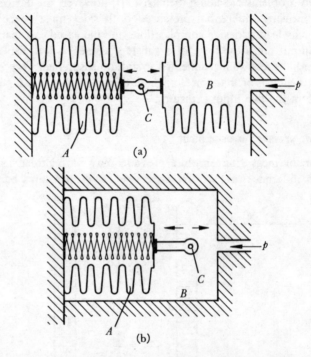

Figure 8.12 Bellows arrangements for absolute pressure measurement; space *A* is evacuated, *B* is connected to pressure to be measured, and output is taken from *C*

pressure measurement, the space above the mercury in limb *A* being evacuated. Equating the pressures in the two sides at the level *XX* gives $p = 0 + \rho_m g h$, since zero pressure is exerted on the surface of the liquid in *A*. This type of manometer is invariably mercury-filled. (Mercury has the advantage that it does not readily vaporize; vaporization of the liquid would destroy the vacuum in the closed limb.) If the measured pressure *p* is the pressure of the atmosphere, the manometer is called a *barometer*. Mercury-column barometers are usually made in the form shown in Fig. 8.11b, which does not differ in principle from the conventional manometer shown in Fig. 8.11a.

Absolute pressures may also be measured by elastic elements. Two possible arrangements employing bellows are shown schematically in Fig. 8.12. The double-bellows arrangement may be more convenient if a mechanical output is required, as no sealing-glands are necessary.

8.8.1 High absolute pressures. Absolute pressures of the order of 1000 kN/m² and above are normally measured by merely offsetting the zero of a gauge-pressure instrument by an amount equal to the mean prevailing atmospheric pressure. This is incorrect in principle, since it takes no account of the variations in atmospheric pressure, but at high pressures these variations would not be discernible with normal industrial measuring equipment.

8.8.2 Very low pressures. Absolute pressures below about 0·5 kN/m² cannot be measured satisfactorily by the 'force-operated' methods so far described,

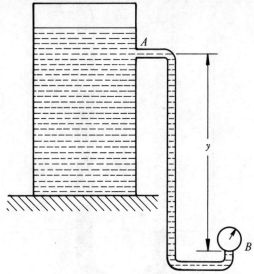

Figure 8.13   Static-head error

partly because of the lack of sensitivity of the devices themselves, but also because it is difficult to obtain a sufficiently good vacuum with which to compare the measured pressures. Radically different techniques are therefore required. One such technique involves measuring the rate of heat conduction from a heated filament in the evacuated space. This depends on the number of collisions between the gas molecules and the filament, which in turn depends on the pressure of the gas. A description of this method, and of other methods applicable to very low pressures, may be found in refs. 1 and 3.

8.9   Head corrections

Where the pressure to be measured is that of a liquid, errors may be introduced due to the columns of the liquid in the connecting lines between the measuring point and the display. Consider the arrangement shown in Fig. 8.13, where the pressure at point A in a liquid of density ρ_l is measured by a gauge at B, a point at distance y below the level of A. The pressure at B will always exceed that at A by a constant amount $\rho_l g y$. This error will appear on the gauge unless allowance is made for it in calibration. In fixed installations this is of little importance, as the zero of the instrument may be offset by the required amount at the time of installation.

For instruments based on the liquid-column principle, the correction required is not constant. Figure 8.14 shows a simple U-tube, containing liquid

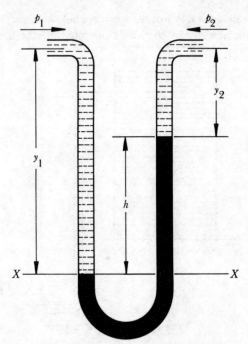

Figure 8.14   Effect of second liquid in manometer

of density ρ_m, used to measure a pressure differential in a liquid of density ρ_l. Equating the pressures in the two sides at the level XX gives:

$$p_1 + \rho_l g y_1 = p_2 + \rho_l g y_2 + \rho_m g h,$$

that is,

$$(p_1 - p_2) = \rho_l g (y_2 - y_1) + \rho_m g h = (\rho_m - \rho_l) g h \qquad (8.5)$$

Comparison with eq. (8.2) shows that the sensitivity has in fact been increased in the ratio $\rho_m / (\rho_m - \rho_1)$.† Again, if the instrument is intended for a specific

† Strictly, in deriving eq. (8.2), the pressure due to the column of gas of length h in the left-hand limb should have been taken into account. In most practical cases the error caused by ignoring this is negligible, unless the gas is at very high pressure.

application, and the value of ρ_l is known, the scale can be calibrated appropriately. General purpose manometers, however, are normally calibrated for use with air, and if used for liquid-pressure measurements, the necessary correction must be applied by the user.

8.10   Calibration of pressure-measuring equipment

Laboratory standards for checking pressure instruments are normally provided by:

(a) Manometers, for pressures up to about 200 kN/m².
(b) Dead-weight testers, for higher pressures.

Not all manometers are suitable for use as standards. In general, designs incorporating float mechanisms are unsuitable (because of the likelihood of

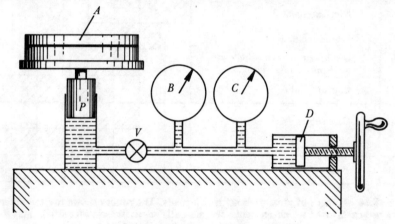

Figure 8.15   Dead-weight tester

friction errors), as are types for which the accuracy of the reading is dependent on the bores of the tubes. Simple U-tubes fitted with anti-parallax devices, and moving-reservoir manometers with vernier scales, are commonly used. A relatively wide range of pressures may be accommodated by the use of different filling liquids. For accurate work, corrections to the manometer readings may be necessary. Equations (8.2) and (8.5) show that the reading of the manometer is dependent not only on the difference in the pressures applied to the two sides, but also on the density of the manometer liquid ρ_m and the value of the gravitational acceleration g (and on the density ρ_l of the fluid exerting the pressure, where this is not negligible). Since g varies with location, and ρ_m and ρ_l depend on temperature, corrections should be made for any differences in the values of these quantities from their respective values when the manometer was calibrated. When manometers are used for calibration purposes, a source of variable pressure is required. This can be provided by a compressed-air supply and sensitive pressure regulator, or by adjustable liquid heads.

The *dead-weight tester* (Fig. 8.15) is a hydraulic device for producing accurately known pressures. Pressures are developed by placing the masses A on a piston P of known area, the pressure being transmitted through the liquid to B, the device under test. Most dead-weight testers also incorporate a hand-operated plunger D. If the valve V is closed, the apparatus may then be used for the comparison of two pressure-measuring devices, B and C, without the use of masses. This method of use is more rapid if a number of instruments have to be checked; if the accuracy of C is known (by first checking it against pressures developed by the loaded piston) a series of

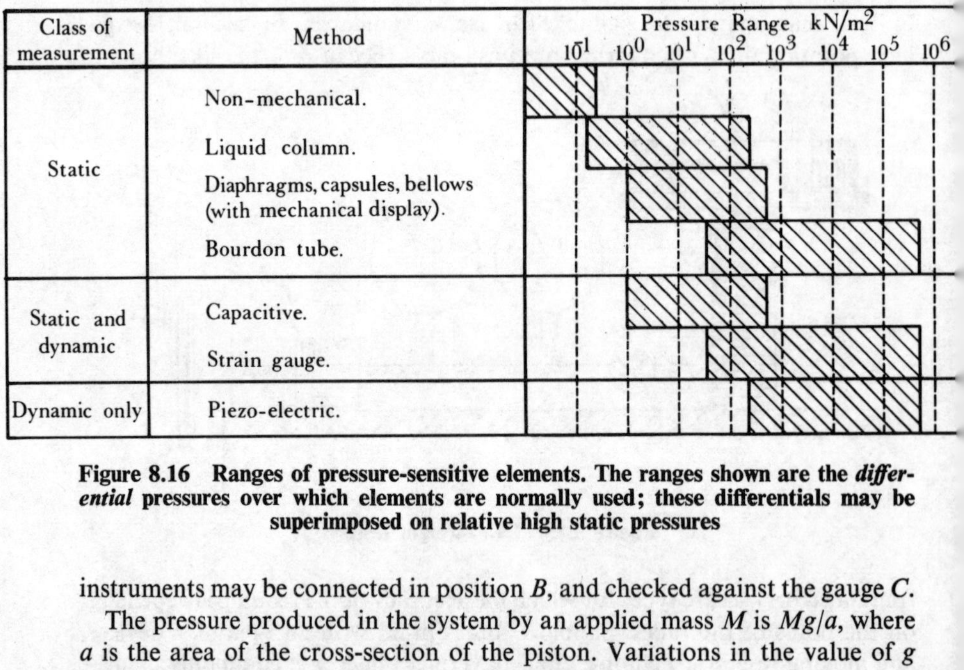

Class of measurement	Method	Pressure Range kN/m^2 10^{-1} 10^0 10^1 10^2 10^3 10^4 10^5 10^6							
Static	Non-mechanical.								
	Liquid column.								
	Diaphragms, capsules, bellows (with mechanical display).								
	Bourdon tube.								
Static and dynamic	Capacitive.								
	Strain gauge.								
Dynamic only	Piezo-electric.								

Figure 8.16 Ranges of pressure-sensitive elements. The ranges shown are the *differential* pressures over which elements are normally used; these differentials may be superimposed on relative high static pressures

instruments may be connected in position B, and checked against the gauge C.

The pressure produced in the system by an applied mass M is Mg/a, where a is the area of the cross-section of the piston. Variations in the value of g must therefore be taken into account if accurate results are required.

Manometers and dead-weight testers are suitable for static calibrations only. For dynamic calibrations, the problems of producing and measuring the test pressures are less straightforward. Some approaches to dynamic pressure calibration are discussed in ref. 4.

Summary

Pressure is normally measured in kN/m^2, relative to the prevailing atmospheric pressure. Low pressures may be measured in terms of the height of the column of a particular liquid which they will support—e.g., in mmHg or mmH_2O.

The principal methods for making static measurements of pressure depend either on the deformation of elastic elements, or on the pressure exerted by a liquid column. Elastic elements are more compact than liquid columns, and have more rapid responses.

Dynamic measurements of pressure may be made with capacitive, strain-gauge, or piezo-electric transducers. Capacitive and strain-gauge transducers are in fact based on elastic elements, but the masses and mechanical displacements involved are normally less than those of similar elastic elements with mechanical outputs; their dynamic responses are therefore better. Very thin diaphragms may be used for capacitive transducers, which are consequently more suitable for the lower pressure ranges. Strain-gauge and capacitive transducers measure both static and dynamic pressures. Piezo transducers are suitable only for dynamic measurements.

The ranges over which the different classes of pressure-measuring element are normally used are indicated in Fig. 8.16.

Examples

1. A mercury manometer of the type shown in Fig. 8.3 is to have a float in the left-hand chamber carrying the core of a differential transformer, to give an electrical output. The manometer is to measure a differential air pressure over the range 0 to 100 kN/m², which is required to cause a displacement of the transformer core of 15 mm. If the internal diameter of the float chamber is 50 mm, find the correct diameter for the right-hand chamber. (Density of mercury = 13·6 Mg/m³; g = 9·81 m/s².)

(Ans.: 7·14 mm.)

2. A differential bellows arrangement for measuring absolute pressure (Fig. 8.12a) uses two bellows, each of natural length 50 mm, effective area 1500 mm², and stiffness 0·5 N/mm. Bellows A is evacuated, and contains a spring of stiffness 3 N/mm. Find the required natural length of the spring, if the bellows are to be equally compressed to a length of 40 mm when a pressure of 100 kN/m² absolute is applied to B. Also find the displacement of the output point C for a change of 10 kN/m² in the applied pressure.

(Ans.: 90 mm, 3·75 mm.)

3. A paraffin manometer of the type shown in Fig. 8.3 has a flexible connection between the two limbs, permitting it to be converted to an inclined-tube manometer (Fig. 8.5) for greater sensitivity. A scale, linearly calibrated from 0 to 500, is attached to the right-hand limb. The same scale is to be used in the two positions of the tube, representing an applied pressure of 0 to 500 mmH₂O in the vertical position, and 0 to 50 mmH₂O in the inclined position. Given that the surface area of the liquid in the left-hand side is 1200 mm²,

and the bore of the tube is 8 mm, find (a) the length of the scale between the 0 and 500 graduation marks; (b) the inclination of the tube to the horizontal in the inclined position. (Relative density of paraffin = 0·80.)

(Ans.: 600 mm, 3°35′.)

4. Figure 8.17 shows schematically the construction of an unbonded strain-gauge pressure transducer. Two rigid links, *AB* and *BC*, are freely supported at *A* and *C*, and hinged together at *B*. Four pre-stressed strain gauges are mounted on rigid pillars attached to the links, as shown in the diagram. Each gauge has a net cross-sectional area 0·2 mm^2 and a gauge factor of 2·0, and the modulus of elasticity of the gauge material is 150 GN/m^2. Pressure is applied to the diaphragm *D* which has an effective area of 1000 mm^2, and negligible stiffness. If the gauges are connected in the form of a four active-arm bridge, fed from a 3 V d.c. supply, estimate the bridge output into an 'infinite impedance' detector when the applied pressure is 200 kN/m^2.

(Ans.: 13·3 mV.)

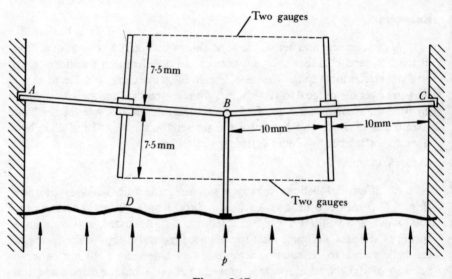

Figure 8.17

5. A piezo-electric pressure transducer gives an output of 1 mV per 100 kN/m^2 input. It feeds into an amplifier which may be considered as having infinite input impedance, negligible output impedance, and a voltage gain of 25. The amplifier output is taken to an oscilloscope having calibrated vertical sensitivities of 1, 5, 20, 100, and 500 mV/mm, the viewing area on the oscilloscope screen being 100 mm × 100 mm. The transducer is used to measure a pressure fluctuating at a frequency of approximately 50 Hz between upper and lower levels of about 700 kN/m^2 and 100 kN/m^2 respectively. Assuming

that the trace seen on the screen is steady and that its peak-to-peak amplitude can be estimated correctly to within ± 1 mm, what is (a) the optimum setting of the vertical sensitivity, and (b) the likely maximum reading error in a measurement of the peak-to-peak amplitude of the wave, in kN/m^2?

(Ans.: 5 mV/mm, ± 20 kN/m^2.)

References

1 J. T. Miller, *Revised Course in Industrial Instrument Technology*, United Trade Press, 1964.
2 E. B. Jones, *Instrument Technology*, Butterworth's Scientific Publications, 1965.
3 Ernest O. Doebelin, *Measurement Systems: Application and Design*, McGraw-Hill, 1966.
4 T. G. Beckwith and N. Lewis Buck, *Mechanical Measurements*, Addison–Wesley, 1961.

9. Flow and viscosity

The term *flow measurement* normally refers to measurement of *rate* of flow, expressed either in mass units or volume units per unit time. It may also refer to the measurement of the total quantity which has passed the metering device in a particular time, i.e., the integral (with respect to time) of the rate of flow. In continuous processes, it is usually the rate of flow which is of primary interest. The *integrated* or *totalized* flow is required in filling operations (e.g., in aircraft refuelling), or where the fluid is being sold.

A flow-measuring device may be required to indicate or record rate of flow, total flow, or both of these quantities. Though most forms of flowmeter may be adapted to perform either function, a particular type of measuring device is often better suited to one function than to the other. Similarly, a measuring device may respond either to mass flow or to volume flow. The majority of flow-measuring systems respond basically to volume flow. If the fluid is a liquid, the distinction may be unimportant, as the variations in density will be negligible in many applications. An instrument which in fact responds to volumetric liquid flow may therefore be calibrated in mass units without introducing significant error. The same does not apply to gas flowmeters. Minor changes in either the temperature or pressure of a gas cause substantial changes in its density; the conversion of a volumetric reading to a mass reading therefore requires knowledge of both pressure and temperature. Though automatic compensation for density changes is possible, this inevitably involves complication of the equipment.

The units normally employed for rate-of-flow measurement are m^3/s and kg/s for volumetric and mass flows respectively. Submultiples of these units of quantity, and/or multiples of the time units, may be more appropriate for small rates of flow.

9.1 Selection of flow-measuring equipment

In chapter 8, it was seen that the choice of equipment for pressure measurement was dictated largely by the range of pressures to be measured, and by the required rate of response. Range and dynamic response are of less importance when deciding the type of flow measuring equipment best suited to a particular application. Most flow transducers respond to fluid velocity,

122

which, for a given flow-rate, is determined by the cross-sectional area of the pipe or duct in which the flow takes place. Usually, this area is such that it will produce adequate velocity to operate any chosen class of transducer. Further, the need for good dynamic response arises less often in flow measurement than in pressure measurement.

The selection of flow-measuring equipment depends primarily on the nature of the metered fluid and on the demands of the associated plant. An aircraft fuel meter requires to be compact and must not be affected by changes in orientation, but it has to handle only clean and non-corrosive fluid. Many industrial flowmeters, on the other hand, have to work with fluids which are corrosive or contain foreign matter, but the equipment is fixed in position and may be relatively large.

The more common methods of measuring flow in closed channels are described in sections 9.2 to 9.6 inclusive. A brief note on flow measurement in open channels (i.e., where the metered fluid has a free surface) is given in section 9.7.

9.2 Positive displacement

The term *positive-displacement meter* is applied to a flow-measuring device so designed that the metered fluid repeatedly fills, and is exhausted from, a space of known volume. The total flow passed is then equal to the known volume multiplied by the number of 'occupations' of the space. The chief advantages of this class of meter are that it can measure down to very low flow rates, and that there is, ideally, no leakage past the metering device. Positive-displacement meters may conveniently be regarded as positive-displacement pumps working in reverse—i.e., instead of power being supplied to the mechanism to produce movement of the fluid, power is taken from the fluid to operate the mechanism.

Like pumps, positive meters may be either reciprocating or rotary. The principle of a reciprocating meter may be seen from Fig. 9.1. In the position shown, valve X is open to the cylinder A, and the valve Y is open to cylinder B. The pressure of the incoming fluid pushes the dual piston assembly to the left, expelling fluid from B. (This fluid will have entered B on the previous stroke.) At the end of the stroke, the positions of valves X and Y are reversed by a mechanism (not shown) operated by the piston assembly, and the assembly is forced back to the right. The total volumetric flow may be deduced by counting the number of reversals of the piston, if the swept volume is known.

Two drawbacks inherent in the mechanism as described are that it is virtually impossible to produce an effective seal between pistons and cylinders without introducing excessive friction, and that failure of the mechanism blocks the flow line. High frictional forces between piston and cylinder are likely to be unacceptable because of the resulting high power losses. (Power could be applied from an external source, making the device a *metering pump*,

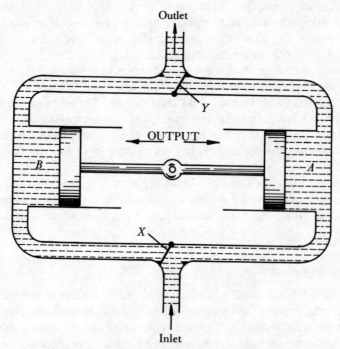

Figure 9.1 Positive-displacement principle (reciprocating)

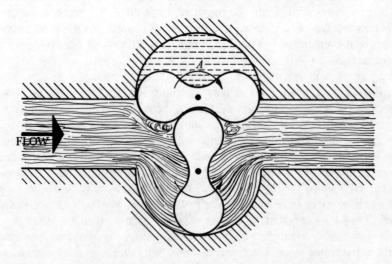

Figure 9.2 Positive-displacement principle (rotary)

rather than a meter.) Pistons and cylinders are, in fact, seldom used in practice for meters of this type. In one alternative arrangement, used for low-pressure gas meters, the piston and cylinder units are replaced by flexible bellows.

A reciprocating system is not well suited to rate-of-flow measurement, because of the non-uniform angular velocity of any output shaft driven by the mechanism. Meters of this type are therefore used mainly for totalizing applications. If a positive rate-of-flow meter is required, the rotary type (Fig. 9.2) is more convenient. Essentially this consists of two interlocking rotors mounted in a cylinder in such a way that, for every revolution of each rotor, a volume of fluid corresponding to twice the area *A* is passed through the meter. Since the rotation is continuous, a rate-of-flow display may be obtained by measuring the speed of rotation of one of the rotor shafts. For accurate results, the clearances between the rotors and the cylinder must be very fine. The need for close tolerances, and the complex contour of the rotors, make this type of meter relatively expensive to manufacture. The close tolerances also restrict the meter to clean-fluid applications.

9.2.1 Semi-positive meters. There are a few established types of flowmeter which are designated *semi-positive*, since, although they are displacement meters, the 'known volume' is not so clearly defined as it is in the types described above. Semi-positive meters are generally cheaper to produce than true positive meters, and rather less accurate. They are extensively used for applications where inexpensive meters are required in quantity (e.g., for domestic metering, in countries where water consumption is charged according to consumption). Meters of this class are described in refs. 1, 2, and 5.

9.3 Turbine meters

The term *turbine* is used here to encompass all flow-measuring devices incorporating some form of multi-vane rotor which is driven by the metered fluid. The most usual arrangement consists of a single row of blades rotating about an axis parallel to the direction of flow, as shown in Fig. 9.3. Provided that friction torques are sufficiently small, the speed of rotation of the rotor is proportional to the volumetric rate of flow over a wide range of flow rates.

Excessive friction torque, and consequent errors, may be caused by wear or corrosion of the bearings. Bearing design is complicated by the necessity for a thrust face at *A*, since the forces exerted on the rotor by the fluid must have an axial component. As the resultant lateral force on the rotor is zero (if its weight is ignored), the diameters of the shaft journals may be small, thus producing small friction torques. The thrust face, on the other hand, must either be of relatively large diameter, or be subject to relatively rapid wear. In either case, excessive friction torque will eventually be experienced. One simple method of relieving the thrust load is to mount the rotor with its axis vertical, with the fluid impinging on the lower end; the thrust is then reduced by the weight of the rotor. More sophisticated arrangements are available, in which the thrust is relieved by hydrodynamic forces derived from the metered fluid (ref. 2).

Figure 9.3 shows only the rotor of the metering device, with no indication of how a display may be obtained from it. Over a specified flow range, the rotor will revolve a given number of times per volumetric unit of flow passed.

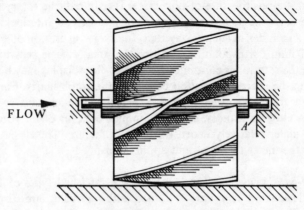

Figure 9.3   Turbine meter

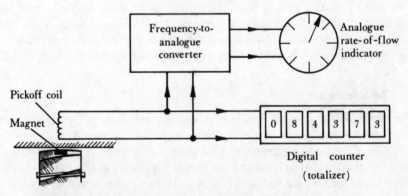

Figure 9.4   Turbine flowmeter installation with electrical output

A count of the number of revolutions therefore indicates the total flow, and the speed of rotation represents the rate of flow. Many turbine meters are purely totalizers. A totalized output is somewhat simpler to obtain in practice than the rate-of-flow output. This is particularly true if the rotor is mechanically connected to the display, which is common practice for the less expensive meters of this type. If a mechanical connection is employed, the display usually takes the form of a cyclometer-type counter driven through a reduction gearbox; the problem of taking the drive through the rotor casing may be solved by means of a magnetic coupling.

Current practice favours the use of an inductive pickoff (section 4.7) to obtain an output from the rotor, rather than the mechanical arrangement referred to above. The output then takes the form of voltage pulses, which may be counted by an electronic digital counter (section 5.5) to give the total flow. Alternatively, the display may be a digital or analogue frequency meter, giving the rate of flow. (Electronic conversion of pulse rate to an analogue voltage is comparatively simple.) Equipment of this kind often incorporates a digital display of total flow, combined with an analogue display of rate of

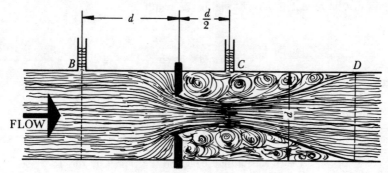

Figure 9.5   Orifice plate

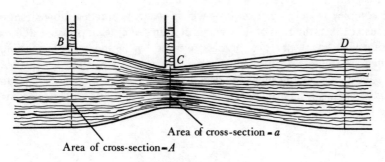

Figure 9.6   Venturi tube

flow. A complete totalizing and rate-of-flow installation may therefore comprise the parts indicated in Fig. 9.4. Although the use of electronic output equipment usually means an increase in cost (principally because of the cost of the display units), it has the advantages of reducing the mechanical load on the rotor, and of making a remote display possible.

9.4   Differential-pressure methods

The methods of flow measurement so far discussed incorporate some form of mechanism which is driven continuously by the metered fluid. Differential-pressure methods, by contrast, depend on the measurement of a change in pressure caused by a constriction in the pipe-line. The forms of constriction most commonly used for this purpose are the circular orifice plate (Fig. 9.5) and the venturi tube (Fig. 9.6).

Referring to Fig. 9.6, the basic theoretical relationship between the volumetric rate of flow and the measured pressure difference may be found by the application of Bernoulli's theorem, combined with the concept of volume continuity, to the cross-sections of the tube at B and C respectively. This relation is derived in most elementary books on mechanics and fluid dynamics, and will not be repeated here. It yields the result:

$$Q = \frac{a}{\sqrt{1-(a/A)^2}} \sqrt{\frac{2\Delta p}{\rho}}, \tag{9.1}$$

where

Q = rate of flow, in volumetric units
a = area of cross-section of tube at C
A = area of cross-section of tube at B
ρ = density of the fluid
Δp = pressure difference between the points B and C.

Bernoulli's theorem, from which eq. (9.1) is derived, is basically a one-dimensional energy relationship, which takes no account of the energy losses and complex velocity distributions which occur in practical flow situations. Because of this, the rate of flow corresponding to a given pressure difference is somewhat less in practice than is predicted by the theoretical equation. In elementary treatments of the problem, it is customary to allow for this by the introduction of an empirical coefficient C_d in the equation, which is assumed to be constant for a particular constriction and a given fluid. The relationship then becomes

$$Q = \frac{C_d a}{\sqrt{1-(a/A)^2}} \sqrt{\frac{2\Delta p}{\rho}}. \tag{9.2}$$

In the case of the venturi, the values of C_d do not differ very greatly from unity; 0·97 would be a typical value.

Referring now to Fig. 9.5, the theory used to derive eq. (9.1) is still applicable if applied to the cross-sections at B and C, C being the minimum cross-section of the flow stream (the *vena contracta*). However, the area of this minimum cross-section is generally not known. The area of the orifice itself is therefore used for the area a in eq. (9.2), the necessary compensation for the error so caused being made by adjusting the value of C_d. Since the area of the orifice is substantially greater than that of the vena contracta, this means that the values of C_d for orifices are smaller than they would be if the area of the vena contracta were used in the formula. Values of C_d for orifices, as a result, are usually in the range 0·62 to 0·65.

It will be apparent from comparison of Figs. 9.5 and 9.6 that a venturi tube occupies more space than an orifice plate; it is also much more expensive. The main advantages of a venturi tube are: (a) lower overall pressure loss; (b) less tendency to trap any suspended material in the metered fluid. The question of overall pressure loss is likely to be significant at high rates of flow, or where the available pressure head producing the flow is limited, as is often the case in the water-supply industry. In addition to the two described here, other forms of constriction—notably the Dall tube and the venturi nozzle—are used to generate differential pressures. Details of these forms of constriction (usually referred to as *primary elements*) may be found in ref. 3.

The assumption that the value of C_d is constant for a particular fluid and primary element is not strictly correct, though in many instances the value may be taken as constant without introducing significant errors. The procedure for finding the C_d value for a particular application is also given in ref. 3.

Equation (9.2) is the basic equation for incompressible (i.e., liquid) flow. The corresponding equation for compressible flow is more complex. In practice, the theoretical complications of the 'compressible' flow equation may be evaded by the use of the 'incompressible' equation, with the addition of only one further coefficient, provided that the velocity of the fluid is subsonic (ref. 3).

9.4.1 Measuring the differential pressure.

9.4.1 *Measuring the differential pressure.* Methods of pressure measurement were described in chapter 8, most of the methods described being applicable to differential pressures if required. Although differential-pressure instruments used industrially in conjunction with orifices and venturi tubes are frequently referred to as flowmeters, they do not differ in principle from similar instruments used in other pressure-measuring applications.

The differential pressures to be measured in flow-metering installations are quite low—usually less than 100 kN/m² and 5 kN/m² for liquids and gases respectively. (Equation (9.2) shows that for given values of Q, a, and A the differential pressure is approximately proportional to ρ, the density of the fluid. Consequently, for the same volumetric flow rate, the pressure differentials obtained from gas flows are very much less than those obtained from liquids.) Figure 8.16 shows that these pressure ranges are conveniently covered by manometers, or by the more sensitive of the elastic elements. There is thus a wide range of devices which may be used for measuring the differential pressure produced by the primary element. Practical considerations, however, may exclude some of these in particular cases—e.g., the metered fluid may be incompatible with the materials of the device. If incompatibility is unavoidable, some form of seal (usually another liquid) must be used to avoid contact between the incompatible materials.

Where manometers are used for measuring liquid differential pressures, the pressures due to the columns of the metered fluid in the manometer tubes must

Engineering Measurements

be taken into account, and appropriate corrections made (section 8.9). Although these corrections are also theoretically necessary in gas-flow measurement, they are usually negligibly small, because of the low density of the gas in comparison with the manometer liquid.

9.4.2 Installation of the differential-pressure device. Certain precautions are necessary in the installation of the connecting pipe-work between the primary element and the measuring device. These precautions are concerned mainly with preventing spurious fluids from collecting in the pipes—e.g., with the prevention of gas pockets in pipes which should contain liquid, and of liquids

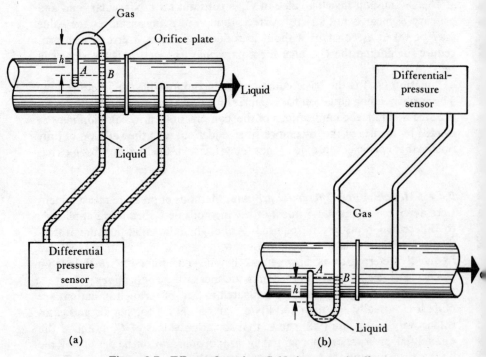

Figure 9.7 Effects of spurious fluids in connecting lines

in pipes which should contain gas. The effect of such spurious fluids is that the differential pressure at the connections to the measuring device is not equal to that developed by the primary element, so that an error in the measured value must result.

Figure 9.7 indicates how these errors may be produced. The particular arrangements illustrated may appear somewhat fanciful, but similar configurations are encountered in practice where there are obstructions in the preferred path of the connecting lines. In each of the cases illustrated, the pressure at the point B in the connecting line differs from that at the point A by an amount ρgh, where ρ is the density of the liquid concerned in each case.

130

If the line had been completely filled with the metered fluid, the two pressures at *A* and *B* would have been equal; this is the condition for which the measuring device would have been calibrated. There must, therefore, be an error in the measured differential pressure, which may be serious in the case of a low-range instrument, even though *h* may be only a few mm.

Connecting pipe-work must therefore be arranged so that unwanted liquids will drain away, either into the main, or into suitably arranged traps, and unwanted gases will rise, again either to the main, or to venting points. The likelihood of unwanted fluids appearing in the connecting lines is reduced by the correct choice of the point of connection into the main. For gas-flow measurement, these points should be near the top of the main; for liquid-flow measurement, they should be near the bottom, though not at the lowest point, as any solid matter in the main will then tend to collect in the connecting pipes and cause blockages. More detail of the correct installation of flow-measuring equipment based on the differential-pressure principle is given in ref. 3.

9.4.3 *The pitot-static tube.* The pitot-static tube, usually called simply the pitot tube, and perhaps better known as an air-speed indicator for aircraft,

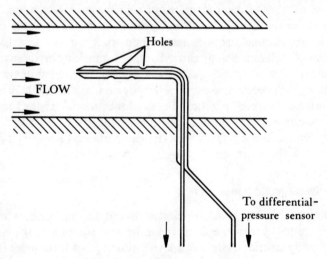

Figure 9.8   Pitot-static tube

is sometimes used for flow measurement. Although it generates a differential pressure, from which the rate of flow is deduced, the pitot tube works on a principle different from the constrictive devices described above, in that it measures the velocity at a particular point in the cross-section of the fluid stream. Since the velocity varies across the stream, it is generally necessary to take measurements at a number of different points in order to compute the flow. (If the manner in which the velocity varies across the section of the pipe or duct is known precisely, rate-of-flow may be deduced from a single determination of velocity.)

Figure 9.8 shows schematically a pitot tube installed in a pipeline. The 'tube', in fact, comprises two concentric tubes, the inner tube having its open end facing the oncoming fluid. The outer tube has a closed end, but has a number of holes in its walls, both tubes containing the same fluid as is flowing in the main pipeline. With the arrangement of holes shown in Fig. 9.8, the pressure in the outer tube is the 'static' pressure in the line. The total pressure in the inner tube, however, is greater than this, being made up of the static pressure plus a pressure due to the impact of the fluid stream on the stationary fluid in the tube. Application of Bernoulli's theorem (ref. 4) shows that velocity v at this point in the cross-section is given by

$$v = \sqrt{\frac{2\,(p-p_0)}{\rho}}, \qquad (9.3)$$

where p_0 is the static pressure in the line, p is the pressure at the entrance to the inner tube, and ρ is the density of the fluid.

Thus, the velocity at a particular point in the fluid may be determined from the pressure differential generated by the pitot tube. If the rate of flow is required, a number of determinations of velocity must be made at different points in the cross-section. It will be apparent from this that the method is unsuitable for routine measurements. Industrially, it is often used when special tests of a plant are being carried out, or for making preliminary tests of flow rate in order to specify permanent flow-measuring equipment for an existing line. The process of measuring flow by means of a pitot tube is referred to as 'making a traverse'; practical details of the process may be found in ref. 4. Flow measurement by pitot is used mainly for gas lines. The differential pressures produced are usually low (typically about 10 mmH$_2$O), and are measured with the more sensitive forms of manometer.

9.5 Electromagnetic flowmeters

Rate of flow may be measured, for electrically conducting fluids, by measuring the e.m.f. induced across the fluid stream when it passes through a magnetic field. A flow-measuring system employing this type of transducer is conventionally referred to as an *electromagnetic flowmeter*.

The principle employed in this form of flowmeter is directly analogous to the principle of electromagnetic induction for solid conductors, namely that a conductor moving through a magnetic field in such a way that it cuts the lines of force will have an e.m.f. induced in it. For a given conductor and direction of motion, the magnitude of the induced e.m.f. depends on the strength of the field and the speed at which the conductor is moving. If a liquid flowing in a pipe is regarded as being made up of a large number of thin conducting discs (Fig. 9.9), it will be appreciated that an e.m.f. will be induced in each disc, just as in any other conductor, if it moves through a magnetic field in the direction indicated. (This is an over-simplified analogy, since the velocity distribution across the pipe is non-uniform). A continuous measurement of this e.m.f. may be made, at a given point in the pipeline, the magnitude of the e.m.f. being proportional to the mean velocity of the fluid.

The e.m.f. is measured by means of two insulated electrodes built into a non-magnetic length of pipe; these electrodes are completely flush with the inner surface of the pipe, so that no obstruction of flow is caused. Unfortunately, the e.m.f.s produced by the method are very small—typically less than 1 mV—and the resistance of the fluid is often very high. The electromagnetic flowmeter is thus an example of a transducer with a small e.m.f. output and

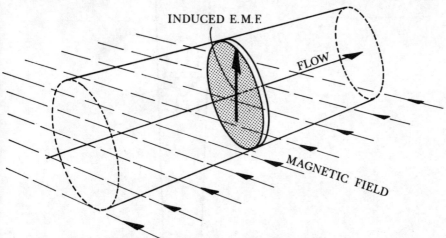

Figure 9.9 **Electromagnetic flowmeter principle**

large internal impedance. Sophisticated 'transmission' equipment is consequently required between the transducer and the display, with a buffer amplifier (section 6.2) as a first stage.

In this brief discussion of the electromagnetic flowmeter, it has been assumed that the magnetic field is unidirectional, and the output is consequently a unidirectional e.m.f. Practical equipment usually employs an alternating magnetic field. The main reason for this is that it prevents *polarization* of the electrodes (i.e. the collection of bubbles on the electrodes due to electrolytic action). Consequently the output e.m.f., and the initial stages of the transmitted signal, are also alternating in form.

The primary advantage of the magnetic flowmeter is the complete absence of obstruction in the flow line. This makes it particularly suitable for fluids containing solid matter. Although the presence of solids may alter the conductivity of the fluid, this will have little effect on the measurement if the output is fed to an amplifier of sufficiently high input impedance. The main disadvantage of the method is that it can be used only for fluids of a certain minimum conductivity; this limitation precludes its use for measurement of gas flow.

9.6 Variable-area methods

The possibility of using a variable-area aperture for measuring rate of flow can be appreciated by supposing an orifice plate to be available, for which the orifice diameter may be varied at will. Suppose now that the area is varied with flow-rate, in such a way that the pressure difference across the orifice

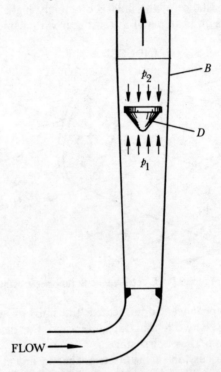

Figure 9.10   Variable-area, fixed-differential meter

remains constant. Equation (9.2) shows that the rate of flow through the orifice under these circumstances is proportional to $a/\sqrt{1-(a/A)^2}$.

In practical flow-measuring situations, the value of $\sqrt{1-(a/A)^2}$ is never much below unity. (In a typical case the ratio of orifice diameter to pipe diameter might be 0·6; $(a/A)^2$ is then 0·13, and $\sqrt{1-(a/A)^2}$ is 0·93.) It can therefore be said, as a first approximation, that the flow rate under the conditions specified above is proportional to the area of the aperture. If these conditions can be met, measurement of the area provides a means of measuring flow.

The conventional orifice is obviously unsuitable for making measurements in this way. What is required is a mechanism which will automatically change the area of the aperture in such a way that the pressure across it remains constant; the area must then, according to the simplified theory, be proportional to the rate of flow. An arrangement which meets this requirement is shown in Fig. 9.10, the orifice being replaced by the annular space around the displacer D, which is free to move vertically in the tapered tube B. The displacer is heavier than the fluid it displaces, and is held in equilibrium by the forces due to the pressure difference across it.

The equilibrium position of the displacer under steady flow conditions must be such that the upward force due to this pressure difference is equal to the 'apparent' weight of the displacer. Since this is constant, the pressure difference must be constant. (This statement neglects viscous forces, which can be substantial.) But it has been shown above that, if the pressure drop remains constant, the area of the aperture must be proportional to the

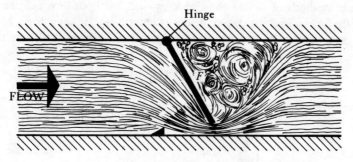

Figure 9.11   Gate meter

rate of flow. An automatic means of adjusting the area of the aperture has thus been established, since the displacer must take up the position corresponding to constant pressure difference. Any desired relationship between area and the movement of the displacer may be produced by giving the tube the necessary profile. Usual practice is to employ a transparent tube, with an engraved scale on it or adjacent to it, and to provide only rate-of-flow readings. Though other read-out arrangements are possible, they lack the essential simplicity of the direct-reading type. The method is equally suitable for both gases and liquids; it is particularly useful for measuring very low flow rates.

Other forms of variable-area meter are available, such as the gate meter (Fig. 9.11). The 'gate' is the hinged flap F, which is opened by the pressure difference across it. Increasing the angular deflection of the flap corresponds to increasing the pressure drop. The device thus works on a combination of the variable-area and variable-differential principles. The main merit of the gate meter is the very wide range of flow rates which can be measured with a given meter.

9.7 Measurement in open channels

The principles of flow measurement described in sections 9.2 to 9.6 inclusive are those most commonly encountered in the field of mechanical engineering. In certain specialized fields—e.g., waterworks and effluent-treatment plants—flow rates in open channels have to be determined. This is normally done by measuring the changes in the level of the liquid surface resulting from some form of constriction in the flow channel. The constriction commonly takes the form of a weir over which the liquid flows, rate of flow being a function of the weir dimensions, and of the level of the liquid at some point upstream of the weir. Rates of flow may therefore be measured continuously by instruments operated by floats which respond to the liquid level. A treatment of this aspect of flow measurement may be found in ref. 5.

9.8 Calibration of flowmeters

Absolute methods of calibration-checking—i.e., methods in which the quantity of fluid passing the metering device is determined by some form of measuring tank—are to be preferred where possible. Such methods are usually

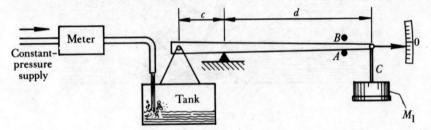

Figure 9.12   Calibration by weighing tank

quite feasible where the fluid is a liquid, and are applicable to both totalizing meters and rate-of-flow meters. For checking rate-of-flow readings it is necessary to maintain a constant flow rate during the test, and to record the time taken for a known quantity of fluid to pass.

In tests of this kind, the 'end errors' which normally occur when the flow is started and stopped must be avoided; in other words, the start and finish of the test should occur during a longer period of steady flow. One of the most convenient ways of arranging an absolute calibration check of a liquid flowmeter is to use a weighing tank, as shown schematically in Fig. 9.12. Flow is started with a mass M_1 on the hanger C, the moment of the weight of M_1 about the pivot being greater than that of the empty tank, so that the balance arm is resting against stop A. After a time the increasing weight of the contents of the tank causes the beam to swing through the horizontal position. This instant is taken as the start of the test. A second mass M_2 is then placed on the hanger, bringing the beam back into contact with the stop A, and the test is continued until it again swings through the horizontal position. By the principle of moments, the mass of liquid passed during the test is then equal to $M_2 d/c$. For a totalizer check, it is merely necessary to read the display at the beginning and end of the test. For a rate-of-flow test, the duration of the test must be recorded, and a check must be made at regular intervals throughout the test (preferably by means of an independent flow indicator) to ensure that the flow rate has remained constant.

The approach outlined above is less easily adapted to gas-flow measurements. 'Gasometer'-type receiving vessels provide a possible means of making an absolute determination of volumetric flow, but the associated calculations are complicated by the necessity of taking pressure, temperature and humidity into account. A comparative approach is more practicable, using an orifice and some simple form of manometer as the standard. The magnitudes of the errors which may be experienced in measurements with orifice plates are discussed in ref. 3.

Any flow-measuring system which is physically divided into different functional parts may be checked in parts rather than as a whole. Although this may not be considered as satisfactory in principle as a check of the whole system, it may be more practicable, and can give useful information if one part of the equipment is inherently more liable to error than other parts. This practice is frequently followed in the case of differential-pressure instruments working in conjunction with orifice plates or venturi tubes, particularly where the instrument concerned is relatively complex. The primary element in an installation of this kind is unlikely to develop errors, provided that it is kept clean and free from mechanical damage. The remainder of the equipment may be checked periodically by applying the differential pressures to it which correspond to specified rates of flow.

9.8.1 Density corrections. Since eq. (9.2) contains ρ, the density of the metered fluid, it follows that flowmeters operating on the differential-pressure principle are subject to errors due to density changes. Where the metered fluid is a liquid, errors from this cause are unlikely to be large; gases, on the other hand, experience substantial density changes for relatively small changes in temperature and pressure.

For a given metering installation and fluid, eq. (9.2) can be reduced to

$$Q = k \sqrt{\frac{\Delta p}{\rho}}, \qquad (9.4)$$

where k is a constant for the installation. If, then, the display is calibrated in terms of the true volumetric flow for a density ρ_c, the indicated flow rate Q_i for a particular pressure differential Δp is given by

$$Q_i = k \sqrt{\frac{\Delta p}{\rho_c}}. \qquad (9.5)$$

137

If, in subsequent use, the actual density of the fluid is ρ_a, the same pressure differential Δp will represent a true rate of flow Q_a given by

$$Q_a = k \sqrt{\frac{\Delta p}{\rho_a}}, \tag{9.6}$$

whence

$$Q_a = \sqrt{\frac{\rho_c}{\rho_a}} Q_i. \tag{9.7}$$

For a differential-pressure operated meter measuring volumetric flow, it is therefore necessary to apply a correction factor of $\sqrt{\rho_c/\rho_a}$ to the indicated readings. A similar argument shows that, for a meter of this type calibrated in mass units, or in volume units reduced to some standard conditions (e.g., standard cubic metres), the required correction factor is $\sqrt{\rho_a/\rho_c}$.

9.9   Viscosity

The rate of flow of a fluid through any part of a plant depends on the viscosity of the fluid, as well as on the applied pressures and the geometry of the plant. In the foregoing discussion of flow measurement, no direct reference was made to the effects of viscosity. Most industrial flow-measuring installations are, in fact, concerned with low-viscosity fluids, usually under circumstances in which the viscosity variations (which occur with changes in temperature) are not sufficient to affect the measuring system significantly. Theoretical computations of flow rate do, however, take the viscosity of the fluid into account—e.g., in orifice calculations the effect of viscosity on the discharge coefficient C_d is allowed for.

In some engineering processes, quantitative knowledge of viscosity may be essential, not only because of its effect on rate of flow, but also because of its influence on other aspects of the physical behaviour of the fluid. This applies particularly to processes—such as fuel injection and paint spraying— where successful atomization of the fluid depends on maintaining its viscosity within certain limits.

9.9.1   Definition of viscosity. The meaning of the term viscosity is best seen in mathematical terms. Imagine a plane of area A in a fluid (Fig. 9.13), which is moving at a velocity δv relative to a parallel plane in the fluid at distance δx from the first plane. To produce this relative motion, a force P must be applied by some means to the first plane, to overcome the internal friction in the fluid between the two planes. For pure fluids, the relationship between P, A, v and x is such that P/A is proportional to $\delta v/\delta x$, or as $\delta x \rightarrow 0$,

$$P/A = \eta(dv/dx) \tag{9.8}$$

where η is called the *dynamic viscosity*, or simply the viscosity, and is constant for a given liquid at a specified temperature. (The term *kinematic viscosity* is also used in some contexts. It is defined as η/ρ, where ρ is the density of the fluid.) Many solutions, as well as pure liquids, follow this law, but there are some solutions and mixtures which do not. The concept of viscosity may still be useful for this latter class of liquids—i.e., a value may be attributed to η, but this value depends not only on temperature, but also on the value of the velocity gradient dv/dx. Liquids for which η is independent of the velocity gradient are referred to as *Newtonian*, and those for which its value varies with the velocity gradient are called *non-Newtonian*.

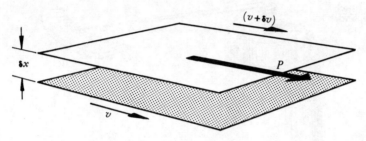

Figure 9.13

9.9.2   Units of viscosity. From eq. (9.8) it can be seen that $\eta = (P/A)\,(dx/dV)$. The SI unit of viscosity is therefore $(N/m^2)(ms/m)$, or Nsm^{-2}. (This may also be expressed as $Kgm^{-1}s^{-1}$.) Before the introduction of SI units, the most commonly used unit of viscosity was the *poise*, or dyne s cm^{-2}. By making the appropriate substitutions, it can be seen that 1 SI unit of viscosity is equal to 10 poise. A number of other so-called 'units' of viscosity are in common use, based on the readings of particular commercial instruments. If such units are employed, comparisons of viscosities determined by different instruments have to be made by reference to the appropriate conversion tables or graphs.

9.9.3   Methods of measurement. The majority of viscosity measurements are made on laboratory samples. The process is therefore a discontinuous one, and most viscometers are designed for this type of usage. Although there is a wide variety of designs available, they fall into two general classes. In the first class, a viscous force or torque is measured; very frequently, the measurement is of the torque transmitted through the fluid from a rotating member to a restrained member. In the second class, the time is measured for some specified relative motion to take place between the fluid and some solid body or surface with which it is in contact. The designs in either case must be such that the measured quantity is dependent on viscous forces, and as far as possible independent of other variables. In view of the dependence of viscosity on temperature, it is essential in any measurement of viscosity that the temperature of the fluid sample should be accurately known.

Figure 9.14 shows schematically the type of mechanism which may be employed to measure the torque transmitted through a liquid. The outer cylinder, which contains the liquid under test, is rotated at constant speed. Viscous drag due to the liquid between the cylinders produces a torque on the inner cylinder, which would therefore rotate continuously if it were not restrained by an equal and opposite torque developed by the spring C. As the

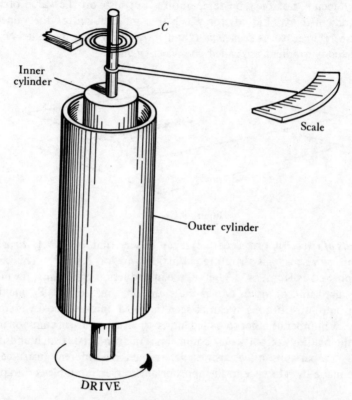

Figure 9.14   Viscous-drag viscometer

spring torque is proportional to the angle turned through, this angle may be used as a measure of the viscosity.

In designs based on this general principle, the liquid may be contained in one of the cylinders, as in Fig. 9.14, or it may be in a separate container, and both cylinders immersed in it. Whatever the detail of the design, it is virtually impossible to avoid 'end effects' of some kind, and this makes purely theoretical calibration of this type of viscometer difficult. Usually calibration is empirical, using liquids of known viscosity.

Many 'relative-motion' types of viscometer rely on timing the motion of a liquid sample passing through a capillary tube under constant pressure. The resistance to flow through a capillary tube is proportional to the viscosity of the liquid and to its velocity. If the pressure applied to the liquid to force it through the tube is kept constant, then the resistance to flow must be constant (ignoring any question of acceleration, which would be very slight). It

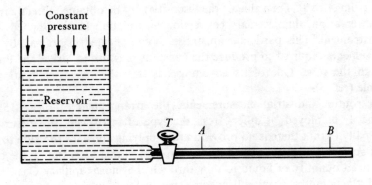

(a)

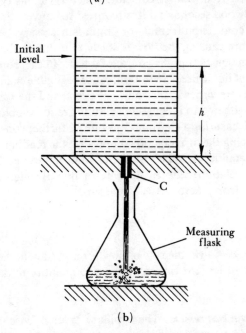

(b)

Figure 9.15 Capillary viscometers: (a) constant-pressure type; (b) Redwood type. In a practical apparatus of either type, the reservoir and capillary would be surrounded by a constant-temperature bath

follows that under these circumstances the viscosity is a function of the velocity only, and it may therefore be determined by measuring the velocity.

The essentials of two types of capillary viscometer are shown in Fig. 9.15. In the first type (Fig. 9.15a) a reservoir of liquid is maintained at constant pressure. To make a measurement, the tap T is opened and the liquid allowed to pass along the capillary tube, the time being taken for the liquid 'front' to move from A to B. The value of the viscosity may be obtained directly from this observation, the necessary conversion information being supplied with the instrument. This particular apparatus is complicated in practice by the arrangements required to produce the constant pressure to 'drive' the liquid through the tube. One of its advantages is that theoretical calibration is possible (ref. 6).

For routine industrial measurements, the arrangement of Fig. 9.15b is commonly employed; it differs from the type of instrument just described principally in that there is no provision for applying constant pressure to the liquid surface, which is open to the atmosphere in this case. In use, the time for a fixed quantity of liquid to flow through the short capillary C is determined, the liquid being initially at some specified level in the upper container. The measured time is taken as a direct measurement of viscosity—e.g., for the commonly used Redwood viscometer, which is of this type, viscosity is measured in 'Redwood seconds'; if it is required to convert this figure to true viscosity units, a conversion formula or graph is necessary.

Since the pressure causing the flow is solely that due to the liquid head h, it does not remain constant in the course of a test. (In the 'constant-pressure' type, the quantity of liquid used in a test will cause negligible change in the head.) Rate of flow therefore varies in the course of a test, and the specified quantity of liquid must be adhered to if consistent results are to be obtained—i.e., it is not a question of measuring a constant flow rate. A further consequence of this method of producing the 'driving' pressure is that the readings obtained are a measure of the kinematic viscosity (η/ρ), rather than of the viscosity η. Reference 6 shows that the relation between the rate of flow through a capillary, Q, and the pressure drop p across it is of the form

$$Q \propto \frac{p}{\eta} \tag{9.9}$$

Since, in this case, $p = \rho gh$, the rate of flow for a particular value of h will be proportional to ρ/η; i.e., the time for a specific quantity to pass will be proportional to η/ρ.

9.9.4 Continuous measurement. The capillary types of viscometer outlined above are unsuited to continuous measurement, which is required in some industrial processes. Continuous readings may be obtained from rotating-cylinder instruments, if suitable arrangements are made for a continuous sample of the liquid to flow through the apparatus. In some applications it may be possible to overcome the sampling difficulty by inserting the viscometer directly in the main liquid line. As in laboratory measurements, temperature must either be closely controlled, or corrections made for temperature variations.

Another form of viscometer which has been used for continuous measurement is basically similar to the displacer-type variable-area flow meter described in section 9.6. The essential difference between the viscometer and the flowmeter lies in the design of the displacer. In the flowmeter, the displacer is designed to be unaffected by viscosity, whereas in the viscometer, it is designed to be sensitive to viscosity. It is not feasible to make the displacer insensitive to flow; the rate of flow through the viscometer must therefore be maintained constant, by either manual or automatic regulation.

Summary

Flow-measuring equipment may be designed to measure rate of flow, total flow, or both, and may display the measurement in either mass or volume units.

The principles of measurement most commonly used may be classified as positive-displacement, turbine, differential-pressure, electromagnetic, and variable-area respectively. The positive method relies on the repeated filling of a space of known volume. Turbine meters employ a rotor driven by the metered fluid, the speed or total number of revolutions of the rotor giving rate of flow or total flow respectively; the method is suitable only for clean fluids.

A differential-pressure flow-measuring installation comprises a differential producing device (the primary element) connected to a pressure-measuring instrument. There is a square-law relationship between the pressure differential and the rate of flow. Except in the case of the pitot tube, the differential-producing element is a constriction in the flow line, usually a circular orifice or venturi tube. When installing differential-pressure equipment for flow measurement, care must be taken to ensure that the lines connecting the pressure instrument to the flow line are arranged so that no 'unwanted' fluid can become trapped in them.

The electromagnetic flowmeter is unique in that it presents no restriction in the flow line. Variable-area flowmeters have the advantages of being relatively simple, and capable of measuring small rates of flow.

Liquid flowmeters may be calibrated by positive methods—i.e., by retaining the liquid passed through the meter and determining its mass or volume. Calibration procedures for meters measuring gas flows are more complex.

Viscosity is usually measured either by determination of the torque transmitted by the fluid from a rotating to a restrained member, or by timing some relative motion between the fluid and a solid surface with which it is in contact. In all measurements of viscosity, the temperature of the fluid must be taken into account.

Examples

1. A simple U-tube mercury manometer is used to measure the pressure differential across a venturi tube in a pipeline containing light oil. The connecting lines to the manometer are completely filled with the same oil. If the manometer scale was originally calibrated in kN/m^2 to measure air pressures, what will be the percentage error in the readings of the pressure differential across the orifice?

Data: density of oil = 8000 kg/m^2; density of mercury = 13 600 kg/m^3; density of air under calibration conditions may be neglected.
(Refer to section 8.9. Ans.: indicated readings 5·9 per cent high.)

2. The differential pressure across an orifice in an air line is measured by a simple water manometer. The manometer registers a differential head of 100 mmH_2O when the rate of flow in the line is 10 000 m^3/h of air at a density of 2 kg/m^3 (on the upstream side of the orifice). A proposal is made to use the same measuring installation to measure the rate of flow of water in the line, using mercury in place of water in the manometer. Estimate the difference in the levels of mercury in the two sides of the manometer which would be obtained for a rate of flow of 2000 m^3/h of water. (Assume that the discharge coefficient remains constant, and neglect effects of compressibility of the air.)

(Refer to section 8.9. Ans.: 159 mm.)

3. An electromagnetic flowmeter is calibrated for measuring the rate of flow of an effluent of conductivity such that the impedance of the liquid between the electrodes is 500 kΩ. The output from the electrodes is taken to an amplifier of input impedance 5 MΩ. After installation of the meter, the effluent is subjected to a purifying process which decreases its conductivity by 25 per cent before it passes through the meter. What error would this change be expected to cause in the indicated rate of flow, if the meter is not recalibrated to suit the new conditions?

(Refer to section 6.2. Ans.: all indications 2·3 per cent low.)

4. A flow-measuring device operated by the differential pressure from an orifice plate is calibrated to measure the volumetric flow of a gas at 30°C and 200 kN/m^2 absolute. What correction factor would have to be applied to the readings if the actual conditions of the gas are 20°C, 150 kN/m^2 gauge, and the atmospheric pressure is 100 kN/m^2? Assume that the gas follows the law $P/(\rho\,T)$ = constant, where P and T are the absolute pressure and temperature respectively, and ρ is the density of the gas.
(Relative density of mercury = 13·6. Ans.: 0·88.)

References

1 E. B. Jones, *Instrument Technology*, Vol. 1, Butterworths, 1965.

2   J. T. Miller, *Revised Course in Industrial Instrument Technology*, United Trade Press, 1964.
3   BS 1042: 1964, Part 1, *Flow Measurement*.
4   BS 1042: 1943, *Flow Measurement*.†
5   A. Linford, *Flow Measurement and Meters*, Spon, 1961.
6   A. Dinsdale and F. Moore, *Viscosity and its Measurement*, Chapman & Hall, 1962. (Institute of Physics and Physical Society monograph.)

† Most of this British Standard has been revised, and is included in ref. 3; at the time of writing the data relating to pitot tubes is still under revision.

10. Temperature

Although the unit of temperature, the kelvin, is a basic unit, it cannot be represented by a single primary standard, either of the 'fixed' or 'reproducible' class. The nature of temperature necessitates that the unit should be defined in terms of the *difference* between two standard temperatures.

The two temperatures chosen for this purpose are that of melting ice and that of condensing steam respectively, at a pressure of one standard atmosphere (101·3 kN/m^2). A kelvin is defined as one hundredth of this interval; it is the same as the degree Celsius (°C, formerly called the degree Centigrade). The Celsius and kelvin scales differ only in that the zero on the Celsius scale is the temperature of melting ice, whereas the zero of the kelvin scale is the *absolute zero*, corresponding to −273·15°C.

Two standard temperatures would suffice to define a temperature scale, if suitable means for extrapolation beyond these temperatures were available. In practice, there is no satisfactory means of doing this, so more than two standard temperatures have to be defined. The scale resulting from these standard temperatures is known as the *International Practical Temperature Scale of 1968* (generally referred to as *IPTS–1968*). The standard temperatures on which it is based are called *primary fixed points*, these points being identified in practice by changes of state—i.e., boiling points and freezing points— of a number of pure substances. (More strictly, these points should be referred to as *temperatures of equilibrium* between liquid and vapour, or between solid and liquid.) The lowest and highest temperatures defined in this way are −259·34°C and +1064·43°C, these being respectively the *triple point* of hydrogen (the temperature at which solid, liquid, and vapour exist together in equilibrium), and the freezing point of gold. Clearly, if a fixed point is identified as a boiling point, the pressure must be specified.

In order to establish the scale completely, a means of interpolation between the fixed points is required. Resistance thermometers are used for this purpose for temperatures below 630°C, and thermocouples between 630°C and 1064°C; above 1064°C, radiation methods are used to extrapolate the scale. These methods of measurement are described in the course of this chapter. Further information on IPTS–1968 may be obtained from ref. 1.

10.1 Methods of measurement

Changes in the temperature of a body may be apparent from the resulting changes in the body itself; these changes include expansion, change of state, and change in the nature and intensity of the radiation from it. These effects of temperature, and also some important electrical phenomena, are used as bases for temperature measurement. The methods most commonly employed in practice may be classified as follows.

(a) *Expansion* of solid, liquid, or gaseous materials.
(b) *Change in electrical resistance* of metals and semiconductors.
(c) *Thermo-electric e.m.f.s* which are generated at the junctions of unlike metals.
(d) *Intensity of radiation* from a particular area of the hot material.

The principles of these four classes of measurement are discussed in sections 10.3 to 10.6 inclusive.

10.2 Sources of error

There are certain problems in temperature measurement which are sufficiently general to merit mention before the individual methods of measurement are described. Possibly the most important of these is the problem of ambient temperature errors. Most temperature-measuring systems consist of a sensing part, or transducer, plus transmission and display elements. The transducer (except in radiation pyrometry) has to be at the temperature being measured, whereas the transmission and display elements are at the temperature of the surroundings; these elements are therefore likely to be subjected to fluctuations in ambient temperature, which may cause errors in the measurement unless compensating techniques are employed.

Another general cause of error is *thermal lag*. When a change in temperature occurs, the transducer must reach the new temperature before it can send the appropriate signal to the display. The time required for it to reach the new temperature depends on its thermal capacity, and on the rate of heat conduction through any protective sheathing with which it may be surrounded. In the design of temperature transducers, due attention must be given to maximizing the rate at which heat is conducted to the transducer, and to minimizing its thermal capacity.

Thermal lag causes only dynamic errors. There are other possible reasons for temperature differences between the transducer and the substance in which the measurement is being made. These include radiation to and from the transducer, and conduction of heat away from the hot substance through the transducer to the environment. (If there is a flow of heat, there must be a temperature gradient, and hence a measuring error.) Radiation and conduction cause both static and dynamic errors, which can be serious in measurements of gas temperatures (ref. 2).

147

10.3 Expansion

Most materials, whether solid, liquid, or gaseous, expand with increase in temperature. The expansion of solids and liquids is small, and some means of magnification of the expansion is necessary if it is to be exploited as a means of temperature measurement. Although small in magnitude, the expansion of solids and liquids produces adequate *power*† for the direct operation of mechanical indicating devices. Expansion coefficients of gases are substantially higher than those of liquids and solids, but, owing to their compressibility, they are less suitable for operating mechanical indicators.

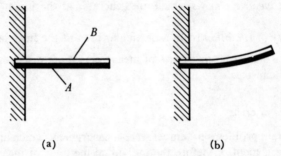

Figure 10.1   Bimetal strip

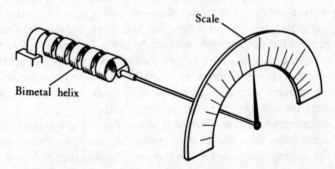

Figure 10.2   Bimetal thermometer

Thermometers using the principle of solid expansion almost always employ a *bimetal strip* (Fig. 10.1). This comprises strips of two metals, having different coefficients of thermal expansion, welded or riveted together so that relative motion between them is prevented. An increase in temperature causes movement of the free end of the strip as in Fig. 10.1b, assuming that metal *A*

---

† The term *power* has a special meaning in the field of instrument design. It is used in connection with mechanisms producing a displacement output from some other form of mechanical input. If, for a certain defined input, the output of such a mechanism were restrained, a force *P* would be required to restrain it; if left free, a certain displacement *x* would take place. The product *Px* gives an indication of *power* in this context; it is a useful concept for comparing alternative methods of measurement.

has the higher coefficient of expansion. The form of bimetal element shown is widely used in thermostatic switches, and as a temperature-compensating device in other instruments. As a measuring device, it is somewhat insensitive, but sensitivity may be improved by using a longer strip in helical form, as shown in Fig. 10.2. This arrangement gives an output in the form of rotation of a spindle, which can conveniently be connected directly to an indicating pointer as shown. The length of this spindle may be up to about 0·6 m, allowing the bimetal element (enclosed in a protective sheath) to be submerged in a hot substance without the indicator itself being subjected to excessive temperatures.

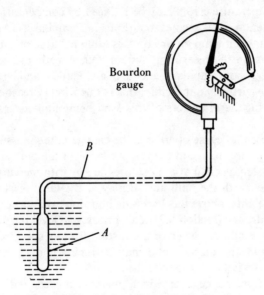

Figure 10.3   Mercury-in-steel thermometer

10.3.1   Fluid-filled systems. The commonest form of liquid-expansion device is the familiar *mercury-in-glass* thermometer. Though it has certain laboratory applications, it is not much used industrially because of its fragility, and because of the inevitable proximity of the display to the measuring point. A type of thermometer employing a similar principle, but of more industrial importance, is the mercury-in-steel indicator (Fig. 10.3). A bulb *A*, the whole of which should be at the measured temperature, is connected by the capillary tube *B* to a bourdon gauge (section 8.5). The system is completely filled with mercury under pressure. Expansion of the mercury due to an increase in the temperature of the bulb produces an increase in the pressure in the system, to which the bourdon tube responds. The gauge can therefore be calibrated in terms of temperature, and will have a near-linear scale. Sufficient power is available to operate a recording pen if required. As the total expansion of the mercury is dependent not only on the bulb temperature, but also on the temperatures of the capillary and bourdon tube, the system is subject to ambient temperature errors. The magnitude of these errors depends on the ratio of the volume of mercury which is at the measured temperature to the volume of mercury at ambient temperature. A reduction in the error may therefore be obtained by increasing the volume of the bulb. This inevitably increases its thermal capacity, and hence the thermal lag. The bulb size is therefore a matter of compromise. The volumes of the capillary and bourdon tube are made as small as the transmission distance and required size of display will allow.

Ambient temperature errors may be reduced by compensation techniques. One arrangement uses a second bourdon and capillary, so arranged that the effects of ambient temperature on this 'dummy' system cancel the corresponding effects on the measuring system. Other methods are available for compensation of both capillary and display. Perfect ambient temperature compensation is virtually impossible; this is the primary reason for transmission distances for thermometers of this kind being limited to a maximum of about 70 m.

A further potential cause of error is the change in the pressure head which is introduced by any change in the relative levels of the bulb and the display. Suppose the system is filled at a mean pressure p_0 with mercury of density ρ, and is calibrated with the bulb and display at the same level. If the bulb is now raised a height h above this level, the bourdon experiences an increase in pressure equal to ρgh (section 8.9). This increase in level introduces an error in the indicator reading. The error is constant for any specified relative positions of the bulb and display, and may be removed by means of the zero adjustment of the indicating mechanism.

The temperature range over which mercury-in-steel indicators may be used is limited by the freezing and boiling points of mercury. (Mercury freezes at $-39°C$. The boiling point depends on the pressure at which the system is filled; it is usually in the range $500°C$–$600°C$.)

Two other types of temperature indicator which are externally similar to the liquid-filled system described above are the *constant-volume gas thermometer* and the *vapour-pressure thermometer*. Neither of these is in fact an expansion device, but their component parts are identical to those of the mercury-in-steel thermometer; only the filling materials and principles of operation differ. The constant-volume gas thermometer uses an inert gas (usually nitrogen) in place of the mercury, and depends for its action on the increase in pressure of the gas at constant volume. (This is an approximation; the volume of the system, and in particular that of the bourdon tube, must increase slightly as the pressure increases.) Its disadvantages, compared with the liquid-filled arrangement, are that the pressure developed for a given temperature change is smaller, and ambient-temperature compensation is more difficult (ref. 2).

Vapour pressure thermometers employ change of state as a measuring principle. The system is filled partly with liquid, and partly with the vapour of the same liquid—i.e., there is a vapour–liquid interface in the bulb. An increase in temperature causes evaporation of some of the liquid, and a consequent increase in the pressure of the vapour. Evaporation continues until the S.V.P.† corresponding to the new temperature is reached, the change in pressure being registered by the bourdon gauge. An inherent advantage of vapour-pressure thermometers is that they are virtually unaffected by changes in ambient temperature, since the pressure depends only on the temperature at the liquid–vapour interface. (A head error may be introduced if the ambient temperature falls within the measuring range of the instrument. When this occurs, there will be a change of state of the fluid in the capillary tube when the measured temperature passes through the ambient value; e.g., when the measured temperature is increasing, the fluid in the capillary tube will liquefy at the moment when the measured temperature reaches the temperature of the tube. This causes a sudden change in the static head on the bourdon, if bourdon and bulb are at different levels.) The general usefulness of vapour-pressure thermometers is restricted by the limited number of liquids having suitable S.V.P. ranges. Because of the nature of the temperature–S.V.P. relationship, the scales of vapour-pressure thermometers are noticeably non-linear.

10.4 Electrical resistance

The resistance of metallic conductors increases with temperature—i.e., they have positive temperature coefficients of resistance; this effect has already been noted in connection with strain gauges (section 4.2), where it represents a potential cause of error in the measurement of strain. Semiconductor materials also experience changes in resistance with temperature; in most cases they have negative temperature coefficients, i.e., resistance *decreases* with increasing temperature. Semiconductor devices with negative temperature coefficients are called *thermistors*. Any type of resistor used for temperature measurement, whether metallic or semiconductor, may be called a *resistance thermometer element*.

The most used material for metallic resistance elements is platinum. The resistance–temperature characteristics of pure platinum are very well defined, and for this reason platinum resistance thermometer elements are used over a wide range to establish the international temperature scale. Reference 3 gives

---

† Saturation vapour pressure: the pressure at which a liquid exists in equilibrium with its own vapour in an enclosed space. There is a fixed relationship between S.V.P. and temperature for a particular liquid.

the relationship between R_t, the resistance of a platinum resistance element at temperature t, and R_0, its resistance at 0°C, as

$$t = \frac{1}{\alpha}\left(\frac{R_t}{R_0} - 1\right) + \delta\left(\frac{t}{100} - 1\right)\frac{t}{100} \qquad (10.1)$$

for the range 0°C to 630°C, α and δ being constants. The relative values of

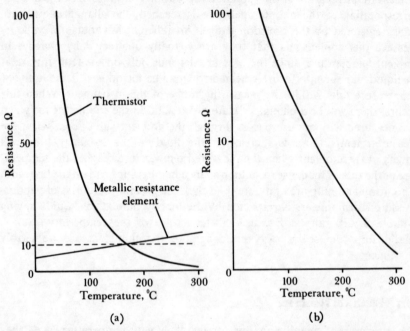

Figure 10.4 (a) **Metallic resistance element and thermistor characteristics compared;** (b) **same thermistor characteristic plotted to logarithmic resistance scale**

α and δ are such that, at the lower end of the range, a platinum resistance element has a nearly linear characteristic represented by

$$R_t = R_0(1 + \alpha t) \qquad (10.2)$$

Other metallic resistance elements follow similar laws, the value of the constant α depending on the material. For platinum, its value is 0·00391 per degC. This gives an indication of the sensitivity of the material. A more useful figure for a particular element is its *fundamental interval*, which is defined as the change in resistance corresponding to a change in temperature from 0°C to 100°C.

Thermistors are more sensitive than wire-wound elements and have non-linear characteristics. The characteristics of a typical thermistor and a platinum resistance thermometer are compared in Fig. 10.4a. These graphs emphasize the difference between the two types of resistance element. In

152

practice, thermistor characteristics are normally plotted to a logarithmic resistance scale, as in Fig. 10.4b. The physical shapes and dimensions of thermistors vary widely; they are commonly in the form of small discs or cylinders of a few millimetres diameter.

The standard method of using resistance thermometer elements for temperature measurement is to incorporate them in a Wheatstone bridge (section 3.4.2). The bridge may be of the unbalanced, manually balanced, or self-balancing type. Modifications to the standard form of the bridge are necessary if the leads connecting it to the resistance element are long—i.e., if they have resistances which are significant compared with that of the element; such leads will cause errors due to their changes of resistance with changes in ambient

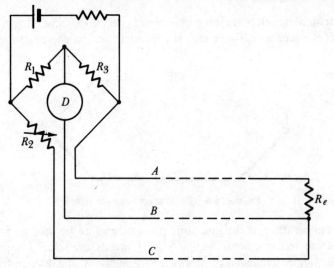

Figure 10.5   Three-wire compensation for resistance element

temperature. The difficulty may be overcome by connecting identical leads into the balancing arm of the bridge. Figure 10.5 shows the most usual arrangement, known as the *three-wire system*, applied to a balanced bridge. The lead A is in the same arm as the resistance element, and the lead C is in the adjustable, or balancing, arm. If the leads A and C are identical, changes in the resistance of A will be balanced by changes in the resistance of C. Bridge balance is unaffected by changes in the resistance of lead B, as this forms part of the detector line. For this method of compensation to be successful, the bridge resistances R_1 and R_3 must be equal (i.e., R_2 must equal R_e at balance; if the bridge is not arranged in this way, the leads C and A must have resistances in the ratio $R_1 : R_3$). Details of other arrangements of compensating leads, and further possible modifications to resistance-thermometer bridge circuits, may be found in ref. 4.

The normal operating range for metallic resistance thermometers is $-220°C$

to $+600°C$, and for thermistors $-100°C$ to $+160°C$ (ref. 3). These limits may be exceeded under certain conditions, using specially designed elements.

The active parts of both thermistors and wire-wound resistance thermometers have small thermal capacities, and are therefore capable of relatively rapid response. However, for most applications they require some form of protective sheath, which adds to the thermal capacity and reduces the rate of heat conduction to the element; in the case of wire-wound elements, the thermal capacity is further increased by the former on which the coil is wound.

10.5   Thermo-electric e.m.f.s

If two dissimilar metals are joined, there is, in general, a very small e.m.f. established at the junction. This e.m.f. is dependent on the choice of metals, and

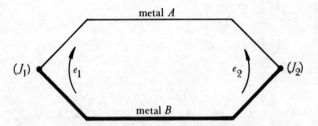

Figure 10.6   Basic thermocouple circuit

on the temperature of the junction; it may therefore be used as a basis for temperature measurement. A junction of metals used for this purpose is called a *thermo-junction*. For most thermo-junctions, the temperature–e.m.f. relationship is very nearly linear. If two thermo-junctions, J_1 and J_2, are joined to form a circuit as in Fig. 10.6, they form a thermocouple.† The e.m.f.s e_1 and e_2 in this circuit will be equal if the temperatures of the junctions are equal. If the junction temperatures are unequal, there will be a resultant e.m.f. equal to $(e_1 - e_2)$ causing current to flow in the circuit.

10.5.1   Law of intermediate metals. In practice, a means of measuring the resultant e.m.f. must be provided; this usually involves the introduction of a third metal into the thermocouple circuit. A basic thermo-electric law, the *law of intermediate metals*, states that the net e.m.f. in the circuit is unaltered if a third metal is introduced, provided that the two junctions between the new metal and the circuit are at the same temperature. The new metal may be introduced anywhere in series with the existing circuit; e.g., it could occupy

† The term *thermocouple* is now conventionally used for a single thermojunction, consisting of two lengths of wire joined at one end. This usage will be followed here, and the combination of two such junctions, as in Fig. 10.6, will be called a *thermocouple circuit*.

either of the positions shown in Fig. 10.7. The net e.m.f. will be unaffected, if the points X and Y are at the same temperature.

This would be expected for the arrangement of Fig. 10.7a, since the two new thermojunctions are in fact identical. It is perhaps less evidently true for the arrangement of Fig. 10.7b, which is the important case in practice. Here the junction J_2 has been 'split', and the third metal, C, introduced *into* the junction. A measuring device, such as a moving-coil meter, may therefore be introduced into the junction. A further important consequence of the law of intermediate metals is that the wires forming the junction can be soldered or brazed together, without altering the performance of the junction.

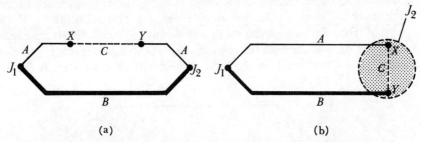

Figure 10.7   Introduction of intermediate metal into thermocouple circuit

10.5.2   Measurement of thermocouple outputs. The output from a thermo-couple circuit may be pre-amplified before being taken to a display instrument, but is commonly taken directly to a moving-coil meter (section 5.1), an amplifying meter (section 5.2), or a potentiometer (sections 3.4.1 and 5.4). Ideally, the display should indicate the true net e.m.f. in the circuit; the corresponding temperature can then be obtained directly from e.m.f. temperature tables† for the particular type of thermocouple used. In principle, only the potentiometer can read the true e.m.f., since it takes no current, but the error in the reading of a high-impedance amplifying meter is often negligibly small. The same is not true for direct-deflection meters. Consider the simple arrangement of Fig. 10.8, which is similar to Fig. 10.7b except that the 'intermediate metal' C has been replaced by a direct-deflection meter M. To ensure sufficient current to deflect the movement, the meter resistance must be small, since thermocouples produce only a few millivolts per 100 degC difference in temperature between the junctions. Industrial moving-coil thermocouple instruments commonly have a resistance of about 50 Ω; the resistance of the thermocouple and its leads may be about 10–20 Ω. There will therefore be a substantial *loading error* (section 5.1.1) if this method of measurement is used. This does not invalidate the method, as the meter can be calibrated

---

† Temperature e.m.f. tables for common types of thermocouple are available from the British Standards Institution (BS 1826–9 inclusive). Most suppliers of thermocouples also publish tables.

directly in terms of temperature, for a given 'external' resistance (i.e., the resistance of the thermocouple and leads). If this resistance is changed, the system must be recalibrated. (The manufacturer will specify the external resistance for which the meter is calibrated. If the thermocouple or lead resistances are changed, the total circuit resistance can usually be returned to its original value by altering the value of a series coil provided for this purpose inside the meter.) Direct-deflection thermocouple meters are thus susceptible to errors caused by changes in the resistance of the thermocouple and its leads. Such changes may be caused by deterioration with age, or merely by the effects of ambient-temperature changes on the various circuit elements, such as the thermocouple leads and the meter coil. The general approach to this problem is to 'swamp' these resistance changes by the inclusion in the circuit of relatively high resistances of a metal having a negligible temperature coefficient. As this increases the total circuit resistance, the extent to which it can be done is restricted by the limited sensitivity of the meter. A further

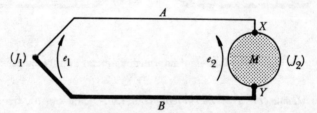

Figure 10.8   Measuring thermocouple output

consequence of this susceptibility to changes in circuit resistance is that resistance has to be taken into account in any check on the calibration of the meter. Circuit resistance problems are virtually absent when amplifying meters or potentiometers are used to measure the output; this is one of the advantages of these two types of display over the direct-deflection meter. Direct-deflection meters, on the other hand, have the advantage that they do not require any auxiliary source of power.

10.5.3   Reference-junction compensation. The methods referred to above for the measurement of the thermocouple output all respond to the *resultant* e.m.f. in the circuit. That is, they necessarily measure $(e_1 - e_2)$, where e_1 is the e.m.f. generated at the junction J_1, and e_2 is the e.m.f. generated at the 'junction' J_2, which has now been split to accommodate the measuring device (Fig. 10.8). Thermocouple tables give e.m.f.s for a range of temperatures of the *hot* or *measuring* junction J_1, at one particular value of the temperature (normally 0°C) of the *reference* junction J_2. An instrument calibrated to the tabulated figures will therefore read correctly only if the reference-junction temperature is 0°C. For any other temperature of the reference junction, the reading requires correction. This may be achieved by automatic or manual adjustment of the measuring system, or by merely applying an arithmetical correction to the readings.

The nature of the required correction may be seen from the basic premise that a specific junction e.m.f. corresponds to a particular junction temperature. Suppose that the measuring device is one which takes no current, so that the true net e.m.f. in the circuit can be measured. If the junctions are at temperatures T_1 and T_2 respectively, the measured e.m.f. will be $(e_1 - e_2)$. Knowledge of this e.m.f. does not allow T_1 to be found directly from the temperature–e.m.f. tables for the thermocouple. If the tabulated e.m.f.s are for a reference-junction temperature of $0°C$, T_1 may be found only if $(e_1 - e_0)$ is known, where e_0 is the e.m.f. of a thermo-junction at $0°C$. The method of finding $(e_1 - e_0)$ is as follows: the measured e.m.f. $(e_1 - e_2)$ could be written as

$$(e_1 - e_0) - (e_2 - e_0).$$

Rearranging this statement gives

$$(e_1 - e_0) = (e_1 - e_2) + (e_2 - e_0), \tag{10.3}$$

or,

tabulated e.m.f. for measured temperature

$$= \text{measured e.m.f.} + \text{tabulated e.m.f. for reference-junction temperature.}$$

The right-hand side of this equation can be evaluated if the reference-junction temperature is known. The e.m.f. corresponding to the measured temperature can then be calculated, and the temperature itself found from the appropriate temperature–e.m.f. table. Equation (10.3) is often referred to as the *law of intermediate temperatures*.

In self-balancing potentiometers working with thermocouples, the necessary correction for reference-junction temperature is usually carried out automatically. A potential difference equal to $(e_2 - e_0)$ is developed across a temperature-sensitive resistor, and added to the measured e.m.f. The potentiometer is therefore always responding to $(e_1 - e_0)$, and no further correction is required. Direct-deflection meters sometimes employ bimetal strips, which automatically offset the zero by the required amount. Manual resetting of the zeros of these meters is also frequently resorted to, though it is not very satisfactory if the reference junction is subject to large fluctuations in temperature. Manually operated bench potentiometers, if they are general-purpose instruments, do not usually incorporate reference-junction compensation. Bench potentiometers are used extensively for checking other thermocouple instruments, and for accurate checks on thermocouple outputs. When making such checks, the necessary reference-junction corrections must be applied arithmetically. Care should be taken to do this correctly: it should be remembered that eq. (10.3) is a relation between e.m.f.s, not a relation between temperatures. Thus, if a thermocouple output is being measured, the correct procedure is to add the e.m.f. corresponding to the reference-junction temperature to the measured e.m.f., then find the tabulated temperature corresponding to this resultant e.m.f. (The common practice of finding the temperature corresponding to the measured e.m.f., and adding this to the reference-junction *temperature*, gives the correct result only if the thermocouple has a truly linear temperature–e.m.f. relationship.)

Reference-junction compensation is not required if the classical solution of holding the junction at 0°C (or at any other reference temperature) is adopted. This is sometimes done where a large number of thermocouples can make use of a common constant-temperature enclosure.

10.5.4 Thermocouple construction. Several combinations of metals are commonly used in the construction of thermocouples. It is conventional to divide these into two classes: *base* and *rare* metals respectively. Base-metal

Table 10.1 Common types of thermocouple

Materials	Approximate sensitivity, mV/degC	Approximate maximum temperature, °C
Copper/constantan	0·05	400
Iron/constantan	0·05	850
Nickel–chromium/nickel–aluminium†	0·04	1100
Platinum/platinum–rhodium	0·01	1600

† Commonly known as 'chromel/alumel'.

thermocouples are used wherever possible, as they are more sensitive, cheaper, and have nearly linear characteristics. Their chief limitation is that they are not as suitable as rare-metal couples for high-temperature operation, because of their low melting points or proneness to oxidation.

A brief comparison of four common types of thermocouple is given in Table 10.1. All those listed, except platinum/platinum–rhodium, are base-metal thermocouples. The details given in the table, namely sensitivity and maximum working temperature, are two of the factors influencing the choice of a thermocouple. A further factor is the nature of the atmosphere in which it is to operate; this, with the working temperature, determines the rate of oxidation, and hence the life of the thermocouple.

Thermocouples are usually made from wires of the two constituent metals, though other configurations are possible—e.g., a wire of one metal inside a tube of the other, with the junction at one end of the tube. This arrangement is known as a *concentric* thermocouple; the tube performs the double function of thermocouple metal and protective sheath. Thermocouple wires may be of any thickness, as this has no bearing on the e.m.f. generated for a given junction temperature. Thicker wires have longer life, but increase the rate at which heat is conducted away from the junction. This may cause the junction to be at a temperature significantly below that which it is intended to measure.

The thermo-electric e.m.f. corresponding to the junction temperature will be generated by any form of junction, provided that electrical contact is made between the two thermocouple metals, whether or not the contact is through an intermediate metal. Junctions are usually made by brazing or welding, though special applications may demand special techniques. Temperatures of cutting tools have been measured by using the cutting tool as one member of the junction, and the work being machined as the other. When thermo-junctions of this kind are employed, the output should be measured by a means which will be insensitive to the inevitable resistance variations of the junction, and care must be taken to avoid other thermo-junctions in the circuit.

For most applications, the thermocouple has to be inserted in a protective sheath, which may be of metal or refractory material. Metal sheaths are to be preferred where possible on account of their better thermal conductivity; refractory sheaths are necessary at very high temperatures, or where vapours given off by metal sheaths would damage the thermocouple. (Platinum/platinum–rhodium thermocouples always require refractory sheaths, or refractory lined metal sheaths, for this reason.) Better heat conduction between the sheath and the couple may be obtained by allowing the junction to make contact with the end of the sheath. There is no objection to this, even when using a metallic sheath, provided that there is no other electrical connection between the sheath and the measuring circuit. For further practical information concerning thermocouples and sheaths, the reader is referred to the appropriate British Standard (ref. 2).

10.5.5 Compensating leads. In the discussion so far on the measurement of thermocouple outputs, it has been assumed that the thermocouple was of sufficient length to reach from the measuring point to the display instrument. This is seldom the case in practice. Industrial thermocouples usually terminate at a connecting head attached to the end of the sheath. The length of the complete assembly may vary from a few centimetres to a metre or so, to suit the application. Almost invariably further leads are required to connect the thermocouple head to the display.

If copper leads are used for this purpose, the circuit reference junction is transferred to the thermocouple head (Fig. 10.9). The whole of this circuit beyond the head corresponds to the intermediate metal, C, in Fig. 10.7b. Automatic compensation for reference-junction temperature will now be ineffective, unless it is based on the temperature of the connecting head, instead of on the instrument temperature. In process-instrumentation schemes, signal converters incorporating reference-junction compensation are sometimes built into the thermocouple head; the output from the converter is then a signal in a standard d.c. range (section 6.4.1) which is already corrected for reference-junction temperature. The more conventional arrangement is for each lead from the thermocouple to the display to be made of the same metal as the thermocouple wire to which it is attached, or of a metal thermo-electrically similar to it. (Substitute metals, which produce no e.m.f. when joined to the corresponding thermocouple metal, are used either to reduce expense, or because the thermocouple metal has high electrical resistance.) The use of the correct cable transfers the reference junction to the display, where the necessary corrections can be made by the methods described in section 10.5.3.

The leads used to extend the thermocouple in this way from the thermocouple head to the display (or to some other point at known temperature)

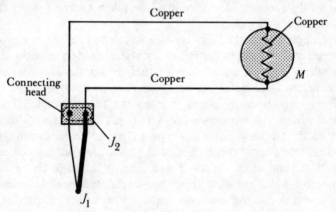

Figure 10.9   Use of copper connecting leads

are called *compensating* leads or cables. The name is somewhat inappropriate, as they do not compensate in any true sense, as do the compensating leads in a resistance-thermometer circuit. The term *thermocouple extension leads* has been suggested as a more suitable alternative, but is not widely used at present. It is important to ensure that the correct cable is used with a particular type of thermocouple. Compensating cable is supplied to any required length by thermocouple manufacturers, and is colour-coded for identification.

10.6   Radiation

Instruments which employ radiation principles fall into two general classes: *total-radiation pyrometers* and *selective-* (or *partial-*) *radiation pyrometers* respectively. The first is sensitive to all the radiation which enters the instrument, and the second only to radiation of particular wavelengths. An important common feature of both types is that they make no contact with the hot material. They are therefore particularly suited to the measurement of high temperatures, in the range where transducers based on 'contact' principles would be destroyed, either by melting or by rapid oxidation. Other applications where radiation methods may be preferred include the measurement of local surface temperatures, and of the temperatures of moving objects. A radiation pyrometer imposes virtually no load on the temperature source—i.e., it does not have to be heated up to the temperature of the source.

10.6.1 **Total radiation.** A total-radiation pyrometer receives virtually all the radiation from a particular area of the hot material, and focuses it on a sensitive temperature transducer. The term *total radiation* includes both the visible (light) and invisible (infra-red) radiations. Infra-red radiation, which is associated with the transfer of heat energy, is similar in physical nature to visible radiation, but has longer wave lengths; it may be focused by similar techniques, provided that the appropriate optical materials are used. Ordinary glass is unsatisfactory in this respect, as it absorbs infra-red radiation.

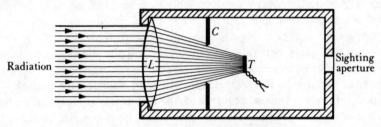

Figure 10.10   Total-radiation pyrometer

Figure 10.10, which is not intended to be optically realistic, shows a total-radiation pyrometer in its simplest form, consisting of a single lens L focusing the radiation through a calibrating aperture C onto a temperature transducer T. Mirrors are sometimes preferred to lenses as a means of focusing, because of the absorption problem referred to above. The transducer can be a thermocouple or resistance thermometer, but is more usually a *thermopile*. A thermopile comprises a number of similar thermocouples connected in series; if there are n measuring junctions in the thermopile, the output at a given temperature is n times that which would be obtained from a single junction. Since it is the rise in temperature of the transducer (resulting from the radiation falling on it) which is used as a measure of the source temperature, the sensitive part of the transducer should have small thermal capacity, in order to produce an acceptably fast response.

The theory underlying the operation of total-radiation pyrometers is that the rate of radiation from a body A (the source) to a body B (the pyrometer) is proportional to $(T_A^4 - T_B^4)$, where T_A and T_B are the respective absolute temperatures of the bodies. At source temperatures above 1000°C it is usually sufficiently accurate to consider the radiation from A to B as being proportional to T_A^4. (Suppose T_A is 1300 K and T_B is 300 K; then T_B^4 is less than 0·5 per cent of T_A^4.) However, at lower temperatures—say below 500°C—the effects

161

of variations in T_B become significant. For low-temperature pyrometers, it may be necessary to control the temperature of the instrument case at some constant value to ensure that the accuracy of calibration is maintained.

Because of the fourth-power law, the characteristic of a total-radiation pyrometer is very non-linear, and sensitivity in the lower temperature ranges is poor; an output of 2 mV for a temperature change from 0°C to 500°C would be typical. In spite of this relatively low sensitivity, it is in this range that total-radiation pyrometers are now normally used, since better results may be obtained in most high-temperature applications with selective-radiation instruments. The main objection to a low output is that stray pickup signals may be comparable in magnitude with the measured-value signal. As with other transducers, this difficulty may often be overcome by incorporating a miniature amplifier in the transducer unit. The transmission lines then carry signals which are large enough to be little affected by pickup. The output from a total-radiation pyrometer, whether amplified or not, is usually taken either to a moving-coil meter, or to a self-balancing potentiometer.

Pyrometers incorporating thermocouples or thermopiles do not require compensating cable between the pyrometer and the display. The sensitive element is required to measure its own temperature change, due to the radiation it receives, relative to the temperature of the immediate surroundings—i.e., the body of the instrument. This is achieved by locating the reference junction or junctions within the body of the instrument, in a position shielded from direct radiation from the source.

10.6.2 Selective radiation. The principle employed in selective-radiation pyrometers is that the intensity of radiation of a particular wavelength (i.e., of a particular colour, in the case of visible radiation) is a function of the temperature of the source (ref. 5). The best-known instrument of this type is the *disappearing-filament optical pyrometer*, in which radiation of the selected wavelength is compared with radiation of the same wavelength from a reference source. The lens L (Fig. 10.11) forms an image of the temperature source in the same plane as the lamp filament B. An absorption screen A, which permits only a known proportion of the incident radiation to enter the instrument, may be included for high-temperature work. The lamp filament, superimposed on the image of the source, is viewed through the eyepiece E and the filter F; the purpose of the filter is to select light of a particular wavelength from both the filament and the source. An adjustable resistor R permits the operator to control the current through the filament until the filament and source appear to be of equal brightness—i.e., until the image of the filament 'disappears' into that of the source. The filament current is then read from the meter M; if the current–temperature relation for the filament is known, its temperature may be found; the temperature of the source is then equal to that of the filament. Usually the meter is calibrated to read temperature directly, so that conversion from current to temperature is not required.

Optical pyrometers provide a useful method for measuring temperatures above the ranges covered by contact devices. They are capable of better accuracies than total-radiation instruments, but have two inherent limitations which prevent their wider use: firstly, they are confined to temperatures at which visible radiation is emitted (i.e., temperatures above 700°C); secondly, they require an operator, and are thus not capable of providing continuous readout.

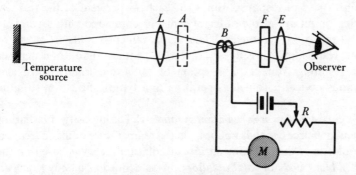

Figure 10.11 Disappearing-filament optical pyrometer

Figure 10.12 Radiation pyrometer (photo-electric type) measuring temperature of steel during rolling. (*Photo by courtesy of Land Pyrometers Ltd.***)**

Continuous readout may be obtained, while retaining the selective-radiation principle, from pyrometers based on light-sensitive cells. Instruments of this type are sometimes called *continuous optical pyrometers*. Various types of photo-electric sensor have been used in this way: those which appear to have been most successful industrially employ photo-voltaic cells. A photo-voltaic cell, or 'solar cell', produces an e.m.f. output which is dependent on the intensity of the incident radiation. The cells commonly used in radiation pyrometers in fact respond to wavelengths in the infra-red region, rather than to visible light, and may be used to measure temperatures down to about 400°C. The optical systems employed are similar to those of total-radiation pyrometers, the photo-voltaic cell replacing the temperature-sensitive element.

An outstanding feature of pyrometers based on photo-voltaic cells is their very high speed of response: times to reach 98 per cent of the full response to a 'step' input are of the order of 1 ms, as compared with several seconds for total-radiation pyrometers. This improvement results from the sensing element responding directly to radiation, rather than to a temperature change resulting from the absorption of radiation. Figure 10.12 shows a continuous optical pyrometer operating in a typical industrial situation.

10.6.3 *Sources of error in radiation pyrometry.* The intensity of radiation from a particular source depends not only on the temperature of the source, but also on the nature of the radiating surface. Radiation theory is based on the concept of a *black body* or *total radiator*; this is defined as a body which absorbs and re-radiates all the radiation falling on it (i.e., it does not transmit or reflect any radiation). Practical temperature sources are not perfect black bodies in this sense.

The ratio of the radiation from a surface at a given temperature to that from a black body at the same temperature is called the *emissivity* of the surface. Emissivity must be taken into account in the calibration of any radiation pyrometer. If the nature of the radiating surface is changed, *emissivity errors* are likely to be experienced. This can cause practical difficulties—e.g., the emissivity of hot steel changes if a scale is formed on it. Selective-radiation pyrometers are less affected by emissivity errors than are total-radiation pyrometers (ref. 7).

Radiation may be absorbed by the atmosphere between the temperature source and the pyrometer. The magnitude of the errors caused by atmospheric absorption depends largely on the nature of the impurities—such as smoke and water vapour—which are present. Each type of impurity absorbs radiation within a certain defined band of wavelengths. In the case of 'selective' instruments, the importance of intervening impurities therefore depends on whether or not this waveband coincides with that to which the instrument responds. Compensation may be made during calibration for absorption, provided that the absorption remains constant under working conditions; in industrial situations this is generally not the case.

Most radiation pyrometers intended for continuous use have *fixed focus* optical systems. This means that the radiation from the 'target area' of the source is correctly focused on the detector only if detector and source are at some specified distance apart. The effect of changing the distance between the 'target' and the pyrometer is illustrated in Fig. 10.13. For simplicity, the calibrating aperture has been omitted from the diagrams, and a target of the same diameter as the lens has been assumed. Figure 10.13a shows the ideal arrangement, in which the image of the target S coincides with the detector T. All radiation from the point A on the target which is included in the angle θ_a enters the instrument, and is focused on T. Other radiation from the point A, such as the rays p and q, does not fall on the lens. Radiation from other sources (e.g., the ray r) may enter the lens, but does not fall on the detector.

Figure 10.13b shows the effect of reducing the target distance. The amount of radiation from the target entering the lens is in fact increased $(\theta_b > \theta_a)$, but radiation from the point A does not now fall on the detector; the image of the target is in fact at $A'B'$. However, radiation from the central portion of S does fall on T, and the 'external' radiation r does not. As all the radiation falling on the detector still emanates from the target area, the new conditions can usually be allowed for in calibration.

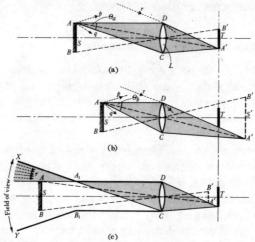

Figure 10.13 Effect of changing distance between pyrometer and target

If the target distance is increased (Fig. 10.13c) the situation is more serious. Although all the radiation received by the pyrometer from the target now falls on the detector, some 'external' radiation, r, also does so. This cannot be allowed for in calibration. Increasing the distance is therefore unsatisfactory, unless the target area can be enlarged; for satisfactory performance, it is essential that the target should completely fill the field of view bounded by the lines XA_1D and YB_1C. Pyrometer manufacturers invariably specify the requirements of a particular instrument with respect to target area and target distance.

10.7 Dynamic temperature measurements

Photo-electric radiation pyrometers are well suited to dynamic temperature measurements in those applications where it is physically possible to apply them—i.e., where a surface temperature is required, and where the pyrometer can be positioned to receive the radiation from that surface. If rapid response is required from a 'contact' type of temperature sensor, bare thermocouples or resistance elements are frequently used. These elements can be made from very fine wire; the element itself therefore has a small thermal capacity. If a sheath has to be used, the response will be very much slower, because of its thermal resistance and capacity. There are various methods by which the rate of heat conduction to sheathed thermocouples can be improved. Concentric construction, and contact between the couple and the sheath, have already been mentioned; another method is to introduce a small quantity of conducting material into the end of the sheath, so that the thermo-junction is immersed in it. Low melting-point metals have been used for this purpose. Some more specialized methods of making dynamic temperature measurements are described in ref. 8.

10.8   Calibration of temperature instruments

Two approaches to temperature calibration are possible: 'spot' checks at fixed points, or comparison with another measuring device of known accuracy. In addition to the primary fixed points referred to at the beginning of this chapter in connection with the definition of IPTS–1968, a number of *secondary fixed points*, covering the range $-259°C$ to $+3387°C$, have been defined for calibration purposes (ref. 9). However, the use of fixed points may not be satisfactory if the temperatures which are of particular interest are remote from the available fixed points. The comparison method must then be used; this requires a reference standard, such as a thermocouple or platinum resistance thermometer which has previously been calibrated by some competent authority. A further requirement of the comparison method is a means of ensuring that the standard and the device under test are at the same temperature. Specially designed baths containing water, oil, or suitable salts are used for this purpose (ref. 9).

The 'fixed-point' method is commonly used industrially, particularly for thermocouple checking. The usual procedure is to immerse the transducer in a molten metal of known freezing point, and plot a cooling curve. The freezing point is identified on the curve by the 'flat' portion representing a reduced rate of cooling due to latent heat of solidification.

In systems where the transducer is separable from the display, an independent check of the display is possible. This is common practice for instruments operating with resistance thermometers or thermocouples. Electrical quantities (resistances or e.m.f.s respectively) corresponding to particular temperatures are substituted for the transducer outputs, and the responses of the display observed. When this is done for thermocouple instruments, care must be taken to make any necessary correction for reference-junction temperature: e.g., for a self-balancing potentiometer with automatic reference-junction compensation, the input required for a particular temperature is the tabulated e.m.f. for that temperature *less* the e.m.f. corresponding to the reference-junction temperature, since the compensation system will automatically add the reference-junction e.m.f. to the input.

High-temperature calibration of radiation pyrometers presents special problems (ref. 2). Optical pyrometers may be calibrated by comparison with a tungsten-filament lamp of known temperature–current relationship (i.e., with an N.P.L.-certified calibration). Total-radiation and photo-electric pyrometers can be checked at fixed points identified by changes of state of certain refractory materials (ref. 2), or by comparison with thermocouples over the lower parts of their ranges. Except where the calibration is done by comparison, using the temperature source with which the pyrometer is normally associated, the source emissivity must be taken into account. In many industrial applications, the emissivity of the source is not accurately known.

Summary

The chief methods of temperature measurement may be classified under the following headings: (a) expansion, (b) electrical resistance, (c) thermo-electric, (d) radiation. The respective normal working ranges of these methods are shown in Table 10.2.

Table 10.2   Working ranges for methods of temperature measurement

Method	Temperature, °C	
	Min.	Max.
Expansion	0	600
Electrical resistance	−220	600
Thermo-electric	−200	1600
Radiation	0	3000

Liquid and gas expansion systems consist of a bulb containing the operating fluid, connected by a capillary tube to a bourdon-tube display. The presence of the fluid in the transmission and display elements makes the arrangement susceptible to ambient-temperature errors. Though compensating techniques are possible, the useful transmission range is limited.

Electrical-resistance thermometry is based on the change of resistance with temperature of a sensitive element, usually a metallic coil or a thermistor. The characteristics of wire-wound resistance thermometers are nearly linear; thermistors are more sensitive than metallic elements, but their characteristics are non-linear. Resistance elements are invariably connected into bridge circuits. If the leads to the element are long, compensating leads are required in the balancing arm of the bridge.

Thermo-electric e.m.f.s are developed at the junctions of dissimilar metals, the magnitude of the e.m.f. being temperature dependent. A thermocouple circuit consists of two thermojunctions: the measuring junction and the reference junction. Usually the reference junction is not apparent as a junction, because it is 'split' to accept the display instrument. Provided that the two instrument terminals are at the same temperature, its presence in the junction does not affect the net circuit e.m.f. To relate this e.m.f. to the temperature of the measuring junction, reference-junction temperature must be taken into account. Thermocouple outputs may be measured with direct-deflection meters, amplifying meters, or d.c. potentiometers. If a direct-deflection meter is used, the meter indication is dependent on the total circuit resistance. Compensating cable of the appropriate type is required between the thermocouple head and the reference junction.

Radiation pyrometers may be divided into two main classes—total-radiation and selective-radiation respectively. Total-radiation pyrometers can cover the lower temperature-ranges, but are liable to greater errors than the selective types. Optical pyrometers compare visible radiation with that from a calibrated lamp, and are manually operated; they are confined to temperature ranges above 700°C. Photo-electric pyrometers have very rapid responses, and can be used down to 400°C.

Examples

1. A resistance thermometer with a fundamental interval of 10 Ω is connected by two copper wires into a Wheatstone bridge, with no compensating lead. Each of the connecting wires has a resistance of 4 Ω at the ambient temperature at the time of calibration. If the range of the bridge indicator is 0–250°C, find the approximate error, as a percentage of f.s.d., which will be caused by a 10 degC change in the temperature of the leads. (Take the temperature coefficient of resistance of copper as 0·0044 per degC, and assume the temperature–resistance characteristic of the resistance thermometer to be linear over the working range.)

(Ans.: 1·4 per cent.)

2. A mercury-in-steel indicator comprises bulb, capillary, and bourdon tube, all three parts being of stainless steel. The volumes of mercury in the bulb, capillary, and bourdon, are 20 000, 2000, 3000 mm^3 respectively, and no provision for ambient temperature compensation is made. What error, in degC, would be expected in the indications for a change in ambient temperature of 15 degC?

(Ans.: 3·8 degC.)

3. The simple potentiometer circuit of Fig. 10.14 is to work from a platinum/platinum–rhodium 10 per cent thermocouple and have a measuring range

of 900°C–1200°C; the scale-readings are to be correct for a reference-junction temperature of 20°C. The slidewire resistance is 2·5 Ω, and the circuit is standardized to give 1·08 V between *A* and *B*. Find the values of the resistances *X* and *Y*.

(Data from thermocouple tables for platinum/platinum–rhodium 10 per cent with 0°C reference junction:

e.m.f. for   20°C = 0·112 mV
e.m.f. for   900°C = 8·446 mV
e.m.f. for 1200°C = 11·946 mV.

Refer to section 3.4.1. Ans.: 5·95 Ω, 763 Ω.)

4. An iron/constantan thermocouple of resistance 2 Ω is connected by compensating leads of total resistance 13 Ω to a moving-coil meter of resistance 45 Ω. The meter is calibrated in mA, full-scale deflection being 0·5 mA.

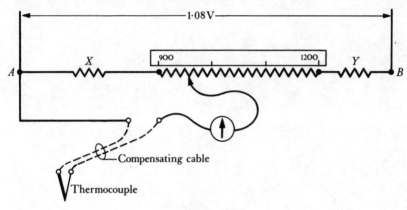

Figure 10.14

What will be the meter reading when the measuring junction is at 480°C and the meter terminals are at 25°C?

(Data from thermocouple tables for iron/constantan thermocouples with 0°C reference junction;

e.m.f. for   25°C = 1·28 mV
e.m.f. for 480°C = 26·27 mV.

Ans.: 0·42 mA.)

References

1 National Physical Laboratory, *The International Practical Temperature Scale of 1968*, HMSO, 1969.
2 BS Code 1041:1943, *Temperature Measurement*.
3 BS 1904:1964, *Specification for Industrial Platinum Resistance Thermometer Elements*.
4 BS 1041: Part 3:1969, *Code for Temperature Measurement: Industrial Resistance Thermometry*.

5 BS 2082:1954, *Code for Disappearing-Filament Optical Pyrometers.*
6 T. Land and G. Torr, *Continuous Optical Pyrometers based on the Silicon Photovoltaic Cell*, paper presented at the National Physical Laboratory, New Delhi, 1967. (Reprinted by Land Pyrometers Ltd.)
7 R. Barber and T. Land, 'The Place of Photovoltaic Detectors in Industrial Pyrometry', paper included in ref. 8.
8 A. I. Dahl (ed.), *Temperature—its Measurement and Control in Science and Industry*, Vol. 3, part 2; Reinhold, 1962.
9 C. R. Barber, *The Calibration of Thermometers*, HMSO, 1970.

11. Time, motion, and vibration

Methods of measuring time, linear and angular velocity, acceleration, and vibration amplitude are considered in this chapter. The measurement of vibration amplitude is, in fact, a measurement of displacement, which has already been discussed in other contexts. However, vibration amplitude is a particular case of displacement which presents special problems, and is most conveniently considered in connection with other vibration measurements.

11.1 Time measurement

The unit of time, the second, is a basic SI unit. It is defined in terms of a characteristic vibration of the caesium atom, which is believed to have constant period. Working standards for time measurement are provided by a number of physical systems which possess the ability to repeat some particular action at regular intervals. This action, which is always some form of oscillation, may be mechanical, electrical, or atomic in nature.

In discussing time, reference will often be made to frequency. In practice, time standards and frequency standards are virtually identical. If an event is known to occur at 10 kHz to a certain degree of accuracy, it can be used either as a time standard (by counting a certain number of cycles) or as a frequency standard.

11.1.1 Mechanical methods. Purely mechanical systems commonly used for timing are: (a) a swinging pendulum, and (b) a spring and wheel combination (a *balance wheel*) making torsional oscillations. Both devices are familiar as the basis of clock mechanisms. Reference to books on elementary mechanics will show that, subject to the physical 'constants' of these mechanisms remaining truly constant, they will oscillate with constant period.

No physical system of this kind can be completely free from energy losses, caused by air resistance, friction, and, in the case of spring-controlled mechanisms, losses in the spring itself due to imperfect elastic properties. If these losses did not occur, the system would oscillate continuously without an energy supply; in practice, a small energy input is required to maintain the action, and to provide power for any output taken from the system. In conventional clock mechanisms, this energy is provided by the main spring, or by a falling weight. The injection of energy into the oscillating system takes the form of small repetitive forces, applied at the correct instant during the cycle to maintain the oscillation. This is achieved by arranging that the application of the force is triggered by the oscillating mechanism itself.

Mechanical systems are simple and reliable, but have limited accuracy and resolution. Accuracy is affected by ambient conditions—e.g., changes in temperature, which cause changes in physical dimensions, and thus change the period of the oscillation. Resolution cannot be better than the time required for one cycle, which is typically 0·5 s. Although it would be possible to produce oscillating mechanisms with much shorter periods, mechanical triggering of the maintaining force becomes impracticable at high frequencies.

In a carefully controlled environment, stabilities of better than 0·1 s per day have been obtained with highly refined mechanical clocks, but this order of performance cannot be expected of industrial mechanical timing devices. Many engineering applications call for the measurement of very short time-periods; errors caused by the limited resolution of mechanical timers may therefore be serious. Further errors may result from the starting and stopping operations of the timer, particularly where these are performed manually. Most mechanical timers—e.g., stopwatches—are, in fact, manually operated. It is seldom possible to arrange for automatic start and stop signals to be initiated by the event being timed, as can be done with electrical timing devices.

11.1.2 *Electrical methods.* Many electrical timing devices are operated from the electrical mains supply, and rely on the frequency of this supply as their time standard. An example is the domestic mains-operated clock. The frequency of the public electrical supply in the UK is 50 Hz, and there is a statutory requirement that this should be maintained within ±1 per cent. Although errors approaching this magnitude are rare, variations up to about 0·5 per cent may occur for short periods. A timing-device based on mains frequency as its standard cannot therefore be relied upon for better accuracy than this if used to measure short time-intervals. However, the same does not apply to timing over long periods, since corrections are applied to the mains frequency so that the mean long-term error is very small.

The accuracy and resolution obtainable from the mains is adequate for a large number of industrial applications. Where better performance is required, oscillators of higher frequency and better stability must be used. Some such oscillators are in fact electro-mechanical, rather than purely electrical—i.e., they are based on a mechanical vibration. The vibration is that of a single member, rather than of a mechanism (thus making higher frequencies possible), and the energy supply maintaining the vibration is electrical. Tuning forks may be used as a basis for electro-mechanical oscillators of this kind. Vibrations of the fork are sensed by an inductive pickoff coil, the inductance of the coil being varied by the change in air gap between the coil and the fork. This change in inductance is developed electronically into a power output of the same frequency, and of the correct phase, to maintain the vibration of the fork by means of an electro-magnet.

Electro-mechanical oscillators are relatively rare in practice; most precision timing devices used in engineering are based on oscillators incorporating a stabilized electrical resonant circuit to determine the oscillator frequency. A resonant circuit consists of a combination of inductance and capacitance. (The relevant theory may be found in elementary electrical text books.) These circuits behave in a manner which is analogous to that of the mechanical oscillatory systems used in mechanical and electro-mechanical timers. A pendulum, if deflected from its equilibrium position and released, oscillates at its characteristic frequency: a resonant circuit, if subjected to a steady voltage which is then removed, produces a sinusoidal voltage at its characteristic frequency. Like the mechanical oscillations of the pendulum, the electrical oscillations will die away if energy is not supplied to maintain them. To obtain the correct phasing of the input energy in the electrical case, the resonant circuit has to be combined with a valve or transistor circuit.

The characteristic frequencies of electronic circuits of this type are affected by external factors, particularly temperature. In their basic form, they are therefore unsuitable for precise time measurement. To be useful as a time or frequency standard, an electronic oscillator requires to be *stabilized*. This is normally achieved by incorporating a quartz crystal in the circuit. The crystal is maintained in a state of continuous mechanical oscillation, at its own natural frequency of vibration for a particular mode of restraint. Piezo-electric charges (section 4.4) are developed, due to the cyclic strains in the crystal. These charges may be exploited to 'lock' the frequency of the oscillator to the mechanical frequency of the crystal. The arrangement produces a very stable oscillator of known frequency. Stabilities of the order of 0·001 per cent are claimed; frequencies are typically in the range 10 kHz to 1 MHz.

Whatever the method of obtaining the stabilized frequency, timing is achieved by counting the number of cycles between two events marking the start and finish of the timed period. This number must be large enough to avoid serious resolution errors (since any count can produce an error of up to the duration of one cycle). Hence for the precise measurement of short time intervals, a high-frequency oscillator is required.

The general-purpose counter–timer–frequency meter (section 5.5) uses the principle described above, and is the type of instrument most commonly used for precision timing in experimental work. Frequency-based methods may also be employed for controlling times in routine industrial processes, such as automatic welding. However, the order of accuracy required in such applications seldom justifies the cost of equipment based on stabilized oscillators. Timers using mains-driven synchronous motors, combined with a gearbox and cam-operated switches, are often employed for this purpose. An alternative, for relatively short periods (up to about 2 minutes) is to use a resistance–capacitance time-delay circuit.

Figure 11.1 shows the essentials of a simple time-delay circuit of this kind. If the switch S has been in the position 1 for an 'infinite' period, the voltage v across the capacitor will equal the supply voltage V. If now S is switched to the position 2 at the start of the process to be timed, the capacitor starts to discharge through the resistor at a rate determined by the values of the capacitance and resistance respectively. After a certain period, v will have fallen to a point where a control device will operate. One can imagine, for instance, that v is applied to the coil of a relay which will release at some particular voltage; this voltage will be reached at some definite interval after S has been operated. Practical circuits are more complex than that shown, because the presence of the relay coil in the circuit of Fig. 11.1 would interfere with the timing action.

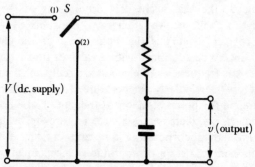

Figure 11.1   Time-delay circuit

11.1.3   Atomic methods. As the primary time standard is defined in terms of an atomic vibration, it would be expected that attempts would be made to develop atomic working standards. Atomic clocks have, in fact, been developed, for which accuracies of one part in 10^{11} are claimed (ref. 1).

The inclusion of the atomic stage represents a further stabilization process in the type of crystal-controlled oscillator referred to in section 11.1.2. Although the performance of a crystal-stabilized electronic timer is adequate for most industrial applications, the crystal frequency is slightly affected by temperature and age. Atomic frequencies appear to be completely unaffected by these variables, with the consequence that timing devices based on atomic vibrations have exceptional long-term stability; they are, therefore, particularly well suited to precision timing over long periods. At the time of writing, atomic 'clocks' have been used in connection with space research, but have not come into general industrial use.

11.2   Linear velocity

Velocity is the first time derivative of displacement. In principle, it can be determined by measuring very small corresponding increments of displacement and time. A typical technique would be to detect the arrival of the moving object at two successive points in its course by photo-electric pickoffs (section 4.7), using the signals from the pickoffs to start and stop an electronic timer. The distance/time approach is extensively used for measuring uniform velocity; in this case the increments do not have to be small, and high orders of accuracy can be achieved.

The choice of method for measuring linear velocity depends on the distance over which the measurement is to be made. If this is relatively short, use can be made of fixed reference points; this is not possible for large distances, such as are involved when measuring the speeds of vehicles under normal running conditions. Ships and aircraft present particular problems in this respect, and it is practicable in these cases only to measure speed relative to the supporting medium—water or air respectively. Linear velocities in

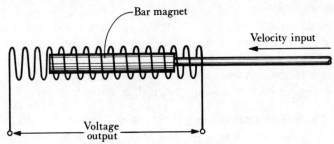

Figure 11.2 Velocity transducer

some industrial processes may be inferred from measurement of a related angular velocity; e.g., in the production of continuous sheet materials, the speed of the product may be deduced from that of a roller over which it passes. A similar technique is used for motor vehicles, where speed is determined by measuring the angular velocity of the wheels.

Velocities relative to fluids are determined by methods which have already been described in connection with flow measurement (chapter 9). Most rate-of-flow instruments in fact measure the average velocity of the fluid relative to the measuring device; rate of flow is then inferred from the cross-sectional area of the flow stream and the measured velocity. For aircraft, the pitot tube (section 9.4.3) is universally employed. It offers little resistance to motion through the air, and at aircraft speeds produces sufficient pressure differential to operate the more sensitive pressure transducers. The speeds of ships are generally measured by devices similar in principle to turbine flowmeters (section 9.3).

Different approaches are required to the problems of velocity measurement where the associated displacements are small. The essential difference in such applications is that the velocities are almost always changing rapidly. An electromagnetic velocity transducer (Fig. 11.2) may provide a satisfactory solution. In principle, this consists simply of a coil surrounding a bar magnet, the magnet being free to move through the coil. One of the members, usually the coil, is attached to a fixed reference, and the other is attached to the moving object. Relative movement between the two components induces an e.m.f. in the coil. This induced e.m.f. is proportional to the rate at which the magnetic flux cuts the turns of the coil—i.e., it is proportional to the velocity of the magnet relative to the coil. The relationship is truly linear only over the centre portion of the travel, because of flux passing out of the ends of the coil in the extreme positions. The voltage output can be fed to an oscilloscope directly, if the sensitivity of the system is sufficiently high, or to a u.v. recorder or oscilloscope via a suitable amplifier. An alternative to this form of transducer is to differentiate the output from a displacement transducer. (Electronic differentiation of electrical signals is an established technique.)

11.3 Angular velocity

'Static' measurements of angular velocity are easier to make than similar measurements of linear velocity. Linear velocity is, therefore, often inferred from a related angular velocity, as in the motor-vehicle case already quoted. Instruments for measuring the speeds of rotating shafts are called tachometers; they may depend on mechanical, electrical, electronic, or optical principles.

11.3.1 Mechanical tachometers. The long-established fly-ball mechanism (Fig. 11.3) is still used in tachometers. Shaft *A* is driven at the speed to be measured. The masses *B* and *C*, attached to pivoted arms which rotate with *A*, tend to move outwards with increasing speed as a result of centrifugal action. This movement is resisted by the weight of the collar *D*. The equilibrium position of *D* is dependent on the speed of the shaft, and may therefore be used to measure this speed. As illustrated, the mechanism would be suitable for rotation about a vertical axis only; this restriction may be removed if the resisting force is derived from a spring, rather than from gravity.

Of the other types of purely mechanical tachometer, possibly the most important is the *chronometric* type. This works on an intermittent principle, whereby the indicating pointer is driven upscale, at a speed proportional to the input speed, during a mechanically-determined time interval. The pointer then holds its final reading until reset; since the time interval is constant, this final reading must be proportional to the input speed. The mechanism of the chronometric tachometer is somewhat complex, particularly if it is adapted for continuous readout, rather than for spot checks with manual resetting. Its accuracy, however, is generally superior to that of other mechanical tachometers.

Mechanical tachometers impose a load on the shafts to which they are connected. They therefore absorb power, and, where the available power is low, may cause a significant reduction in the shaft speed being measured. In general, electrical methods are to be preferred, except where the tachometer is hand held, or is permanently attached to relatively heavy machinery.

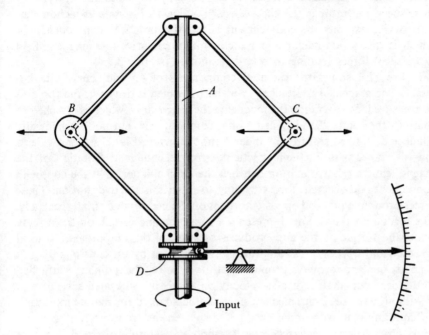

Figure 11.3   Fly-ball mechanism

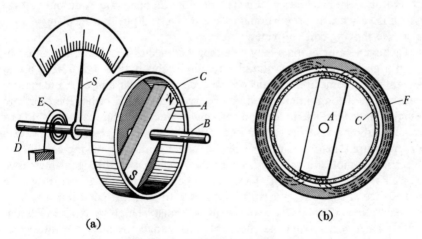

Figure 11.4   Eddy-current tachometer

11.3.2 Electro-mechanical tachometers. Possibly the commonest type of shaft-speed indicator is the *eddy-current* (*or magnetic*) *drag-cup* tachometer. This device exploits the eddy-current effect, the practical consequence of which is that a non-magnetic conductor moving relative to a magnetic field experiences forces tending to retard its motion (section 3.3.4).

Figure 11.4 shows the essential components of an eddy-current tachometer. The magnet *A* is attached to a shaft *B* which is driven at the speed to be measured. Surrounding the magnet is the *drag cup C*, which is attached to shaft *D*, the shafts *B* and *D* being on a common axis, but not mechanically connected. A fixed soft-iron cylinder *F* (not shown in Fig. 11.4a), provides a low-reluctance path for the magnetic flux from the magnet. Rotation of the magnet causes relative motion between the magnetic field and the cup, with consequent eddy-current forces tending to resist this relative motion. These forces produce equal and opposite torques on the magnet and cup respectively. The torque on the magnet represents a small loading torque on the driving shaft; the torque on the cup produces rotation of the output shaft *D* until an equal and opposite resisting torque is developed by the control spring *E*. As eddy-current torque is proportional to velocity, the pointer *S* attached to the drag-cup shaft indicates velocity on a linearly calibrated scale.

Although the drag-cup mechanism could be adapted for remote indication by combining it with some form of displacement transducer, it is more satisfactory to use a *tachogenerator* if remote indication is required. A tachogenerator is a small electrical generator intended solely for the indication of shaft speed; any constant-field electrical generator could be used as a tachogenerator, since machines of this type produce an open-circuit output voltage which is very nearly proportional to speed. This output may be displayed on a simple moving-coil voltmeter.

Tachogenerator outputs may be either a.c. or d.c. To obtain a d.c. output from a generator, a commutator is required; this may be considered a disadvantage in some applications on the grounds of wear and/or maintenance, particularly if long running periods are envisaged. A.C. tachogenerators are usually made with fixed coils and rotating-magnet armature, and thus do not require rubbing contacts of any sort. They do, however, require rectification of the output before it can be fed to a conventional moving-coil meter. Electrical complications arise because the *frequency* of the signal increases, as well as its amplitude, with increase of speed. One result of this is that the impedance of the generator coils increases with speed. If good linearity is to be maintained, the impedance of the display must be high compared with that of the generator, so that the effects of this change are effectively swamped. (The varying impedance in fact produces a variable loading error.)

11.3.3 Digital methods. The electro-mechanical methods described above are satisfactory at speeds up to a few thousands of rev/min—up to 10 000 rev/min in the case of the a.c. tachogenerator—and accuracies may be as good as 1 per cent. Higher speeds and better accuracies are possible using 'pulse' pickoffs in conjunction with digital frequency meters. The pickoff is usually either inductive or photo-electric (section 4.7).

A major advantage of digital methods is that no direct contact with the shaft is required, so that no load is imposed on the shaft by the measuring device. (Inductive pickoffs exert a small retarding torque, but this is negligible

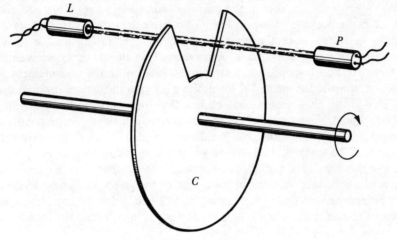

Figure 11.5   Chopper disc

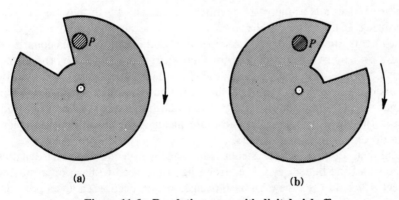

Figure 11.6   Resolution error with digital pickoff

in most applications.) It is, however, usually necessary to fit an attachment to the shaft to generate the voltage pulses. Occasionally it may be possible to use an existing fitting for this purpose—e.g., pulses may be generated by gear teeth, as indicated in Fig. 4.12.

Figure 11.5 shows a simple photo-electric arrangement for generating pulses. The *chopper disc* C interrupts the light beam from the source L, so that the photo-transistor P receives one flash per revolution. A voltage pulse may be developed from this light flash as indicated in section 4.7, and fed to a digital frequency meter. The accuracy of this method depends principally on the error represented by one pulse. It will be recalled that digital meters (section 5.5) measure frequency by counting the number of input pulses which occur in a short period of time, known as the *gating period*. If this period is too short, serious errors can be caused. Suppose that the gating period starts with the disc in the position indicated in Fig. 11.6a and ends with it in the position shown in Fig. 11.6b, after the disc has made approximately $1\frac{1}{4}$ turns. Since the pulses result from light falling on the photo-transistor, two pulses will have been received by the counter, representing $1\frac{1}{4}$ turns; this corresponds to an error of 60 per cent in the measurement. If, however, the disc had made 10^5 revolutions between the (a) and (b) positions, the error from this cause would be less than one part in 10^5. The gating period should, therefore, be chosen to give a sufficiently large count: in general the maximum number of the digits provided on the display (typically six) should be utilized. The factors which the user can control in order to achieve this are (i) the gating-period, and (ii) the number of pulses generated per revolution; this depends on the design of the pulse-generating device. It will be appreciated that where gating period and pulses per revolution are open to choice, a calculation is necessary when interpreting the readout.

11.4   The stroboscope

The stroboscope is a manually operated instrument which may be used for measuring shaft speeds. It imposes no load on the shaft, and no special attachments are required. Stroboscopes are used mainly for occasional spot checks on machinery speeds, and for laboratory work. Basically, the instrument is variable-frequency flashing light, the flashing frequency being set by the operator. The circuit used is based on a variable-frequency oscillator, which cannot be stabilized as effectively as a fixed-frequency oscillator; strobo-scopes therefore provide a less accurate means of frequency measurement than do digital frequency meters.

The method of use of the stroboscope depends on the imperfect dynamic response of the human eye. If a strong light is caused to flash on a moving object which, at the time each flash occurs, always occupies a given position, the object will appear to be stationary in that position. Obviously the method is useful only for types of motion, such as oscillation or rotation, in which an object does in fact occupy a particular position at regular intervals.

For shaft-speed measurement, the method of use is to direct the light at some distinctive mark on the shaft, and to adjust the flashing frequency until the mark appears stationary. Provided that the approximate speed is known in advance, and the flashing frequency has not been allowed to depart too far from this figure, the frequency at which the stationary image is obtained gives the shaft speed, within the limits of accuracy of the stroboscope. If these conditions are not met, or if there are several identical marks on the shaft (e.g., if the spokes of a wheel, or jaws of a chuck, are used as marks) there are possibilities of serious error.

Consider first the case where there is only one mark. If the mark is at A (Fig. 11.7a) each time a flash occurs, a stationary image will appear. This is the case where the shaft speed n (rev/s) equals the flashing frequency f; it would also be the case if n were any whole multiple of f—i.e., if $n = 2f, 3f$, etc. Thus the mere fact that a stationary image is obtained does not determine the shaft speed with certainty. Note that the problem does not occur if $n < f$; if

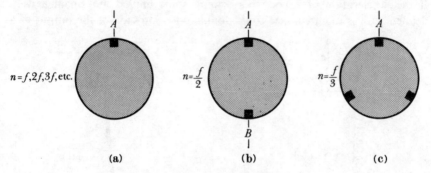

Figure 11.7   Stroboscope patterns (single mark)

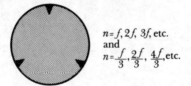

Figure 11.8   Stroboscope patterns (three identical marks)

n is some simple submultiple of f, 'multiple' patterns will be obtained, as indicated in (b) and (c).

The reason for these multiple images may be seen by considering the case where $n = f/2$. Suppose a flash occurs when the mark is at A; with this relationship between speed and frequency, the next flash will occur when the mark is at B (Fig. 11.7b), the next when it is at A, and so on. Thus although the mark will repeatedly be at A when flashes occur, it will also repeatedly be at B at the time of the alternate flashes, and two images of the mark will be seen. An extension of this argument applies for $n = f/3, f/4$, etc. The situation becomes much more complicated if there is more than one mark on the shaft. Consider the case where there are three identical, equi-spaced marks (Fig. 11.8). By considering the positions of the marks as successive flashes occur, it can be seen that not only will the stationary pattern be obtained when $n = f, 2f, 3f$, etc., but also for certain values of n which are smaller than f, namely $n = f/3$, $2f/3$, and also at $n = 4f/3$, $5f/3$, etc. The possibility of error is thus greatly increased.

From the above discussion, it can be seen that it is safest to work with a single mark, and to find the highest flashing frequency at which a 'true' image is seen. As a check that the correct value of n has in fact been found, the frequency may then be doubled; this should produce a double image.

11.5 Acceleration

If the acceleration of a body performing some limited motion in a well, defined path is required, electronic double differentiation of the output of a

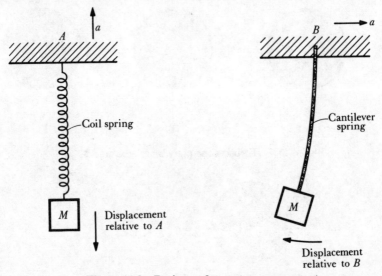

Figure 11.9 Basic accelerometer arrangements

displacement transducer provides a possible means of measurement. A differential transformer (section 4.5.1) may be used in this way, if the core can be attached to the accelerating body, and the coil assembly to a fixed reference. This is not possible in the majority of practical situations where acceleration measurements are required. Typical measuring situations involve moving vehicles, impact, and imprecisely defined vibrations, and do not permit the use of a transducer requiring attachment both to the moving body and to a fixed reference.

An inherently simpler means of measuring acceleration is to use a mass–spring combination of one of the types shown in Fig. 11.9. In both arrangements, one end of a spring member is firmly fixed to the accelerating body, and the other end carries a mass M. If the body is subjected to a steady acceleration a as indicated in the diagram, the spring in each case has to apply the accelerating force Ma to the mass in the appropriate direction.

There will consequently be a displacement of Ma/k of the free end of the spring, where k is the spring stiffness. Since M and k are constants, the deflection is proportional to acceleration in each case. Acceleration may then be measured by any type of displacement transducer of appropriate range. An alternative, for the cantilever arrangement, is to measure the strain on the surface of the cantilever by means of strain gauges. Whatever method is employed to convert the deflection of the spring to an electrical output, the whole of the transducer is mounted on the moving body, so that problems of alignment of its component parts do not arise.

The basic accelerometers described above are members of a class of measuring device known as *seismic transducers*. Seismic transducers are extensively used in the field of vibration measurement, where they are employed for measuring both the displacement and acceleration of the vibrating body. Further consideration will be given to the design and use of this class of transducer when the general problems of vibration measurement have been discussed.

11.6 Vibration

The need to make measurements of vibrations has arisen largely in connection with the growth of the practice of environmental testing. Specifications, particularly in the military field, often require that the equipment should withstand stated levels of vibration; in order to check that the equipment meets the specification in this respect, it is necessary to make quantitative assessments of vibration levels. Vibration measurements are also frequently made in investigations on machinery, where the object is usually either to damp out the vibration, or to trace its cause.

Most vibrations are approximately sinusoidal displacements of the vibrating member about a mean position. A vibration of this kind may be defined by its frequency and amplitude. In the case of a purely sinusoidal vibration, amplitude, velocity, and acceleration are simply related. The displacement x at any time t is given by $x = A \sin \omega t$, where A is the amplitude, and ω is the angular frequency ($\omega = 2\pi f$, f being the frequency of the vibration in Hz). Differentiation of x with respect to t shows that the maximum velocity is ωA, and the maximum acceleration is $-\omega^2 A$. A sinusoidal vibration can therefore be defined by giving its frequency, plus its amplitude, *or* maximum velocity, *or* maximum acceleration.

The choice of the variable to be measured does not restrict the information which can be obtained, even where the vibration is non-sinusoidal. If one of the three variables concerned (amplitude, velocity, or acceleration) is measured, it is possible to determine the other two by carrying out electronic differentiation or integration operations on the original signal. Measurements of vibration may therefore be made with a transducer sensitive to amplitude, velocity, or acceleration. The output of this transducer, after any necessary conditioning of the signal, goes to a display which may indicate or record the original measured variable, or another variable derived from it. Since the transducer output is pulsating, frequency may be measured by feeding it, at some suitable stage in the conditioning process, into a digital frequency meter.

11.6.1   Use of conventional displacement transducers. Capacitive and inductive displacement transducers (sections 4.5 and 4.6 respectively) may be used in some applications for measuring vibration amplitude. All transducers

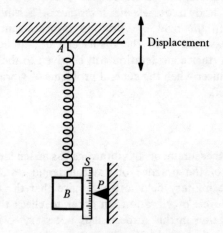

Figure 11.10   Seismic principle

of this kind comprise two members, one of which is capable of displacement relative to the other. For vibration measurements, one of the two members must be attached to the vibrating body, and the other to a fixed reference point. This is practicable only where a truly fixed point is available for the location of the stationary member. If displacement transducers are used in this way, it is important that no relative movement, other than the vibration being investigated, should take place between the vibrating body and the fixed reference. As in the general case of acceleration measurement discussed in section 11.5, it is seldom possible to meet this requirement in practical situations, particularly in 'on-site' investigations. Vibration from a large machine tool, for example, is transmitted, wholly or partly, to the foundations on which it is mounted. It is therefore difficult to find a reference point from which measurements of the machine's vibrations may be made, if conventional displacement transducers are to be used. Most vibration measurements are therefore made with seismic transducers.

11.6.2   Seismic transducers. Transducers working on the seismic principle may be used in two basic ways—the *displacement* and *acceleration* modes

respectively. Although the behaviour of seismic transducers is best explained
by mathematical analysis (sections 14.3.3 and 14.3.4), an appreciation of the
principles involved may be gained from a common-sense approach. Consider
a relatively heavy mass *B* suspended from a point *A* (Fig. 11.10) by means of a
weak spring. For the purposes of a simple demonstration, values of 1 kg and
100 N/m would be appropriate for the mass and spring stiffness respectively.
If the point *A* were subjected to rapid vertical sinusoidal displacements at a
frequency of, say, 100 Hz, experience suggests that the resulting displacements
of *B* would be negligible. In everyday terms, the mass could not 'follow' such
a high-frequency vibration of the support. The effect can be demonstrated
adequately at much lower frequencies, by inducing roughly sinusoidal input
displacements of the point *A* by hand.

If, then, high-frequency vibrations are applied to *A*, then mass *B* will act
as a fixed reference point in space. Thus, if the pointer *P* were also fixed in

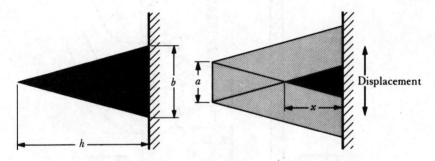

Figure 11.11   Amplitude measurement by direct observation

space it would continue to indicate zero on the scale *S* attached to *B*. If,
however, *P* were rigidly attached to *A*, instead of to a fixed reference, the
motion of *P* relative to *B* would be identical to the motion of *A* in space. At
the high frequencies involved, it would not be possible to take instantaneous
readings from the pointer *P*. However, it is possible to obtain a direct reading
of vibration amplitude with a device of this kind, provided the amplitude is
large enough; although the pointer image is blurred, the ends of its travel will
be discernible. (If direct observation of amplitude is considered feasible, a
more practical method is to use a 'wedge' in the form of an elongated isos-
celes triangle, as shown in Fig. 11.11a, fixed directly to the vibrating body.
Vibration produces an image (Fig. 11.11b) of a well-defined opaque triangle,
surrounded by a blurred region. The amplitude of the vibration may be calculated from measurement of the 'height', *x*, of the opaque triangle. This
method is independent of any seismic mechanism, but is suitable only for
relatively large amplitudes—say above 3 mm.)

The arrangement of Fig. 11.10 does not represent a practical method of measuring vibration amplitude. A modified form, capable of giving an electrical output, is shown schematically in Fig. 11.12. Here the output is obtained from a variable potential divider, and the end A of the spring is attached to the transducer housing, which is rigidly fixed to the vibrating body. A further modification is the addition of the damping device D, consisting of a vane moving in a viscous fluid. The need for this device is not immediately apparent from the discussion so far. It will be seen in section 14.2 that damping is necessary, and that the use of the correct amount of damping increases the range of frequencies over which the transducer may be used.

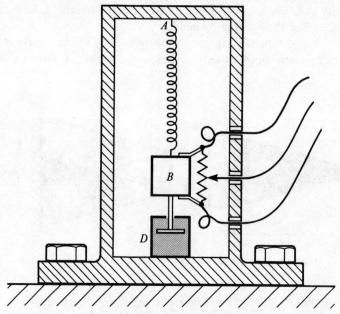

Figure 11.12   Seismic transducer

Because of its limited resolution, and the inevitable wear and friction at the sliding contact, the potential divider is not the ideal means of deriving the output signal. A contactless device, such as a differential transformer (section 4.5.1) is generally preferred. If an output proportional to velocity is required, a velocity transducer similar to that described in section 11.2 may be used. The arrangement shown in Fig. 11.12 is suitable only for measuring vertical displacements. Further modifications are necessary if it is required to work in any other position.

By altering the physical constants of the system represented by Fig. 11.12, it may be used to determine the acceleration of a vibration, rather than its amplitude. The requirements for operation in the acceleration mode are a stiff spring and a relatively small mass. (These requirements are for measuring dynamic accelerations only; static accelerations can be measured by any mass–

spring combination of appropriate sensitivity.) Again a common-sense approach suggests that this result would be expected. A transducer based on a piezo crystal (section 4.4) represents the practical ultimate of high spring stiffness, the stiffness being that of the crystal or crystal stack itself. The associated mass may be as small as is consistent with obtaining a sufficiently large output signal, which depends on the range of accelerations to be measured. (A small mass is preferable; it is often a requirement that the overall mass of an accelerometer should be small, to avoid loading effects—i.e., changes in the nature of the vibration due to the presence of the transducer.) Figure 11.13 shows the essentials of a piezo accelerometer. The mass

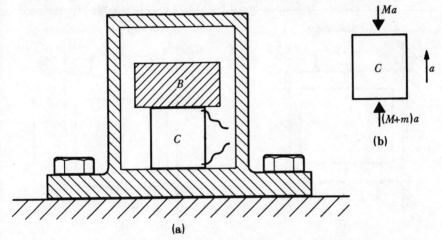

(a)

Figure 11.13   Piezo accelerometer

B is bonded to the crystal (or crystal stack) C, which is in turn bonded to the base of the transducer. The construction of practical accelerometers is often more complex, but the arrangement shown suffices for a discussion of principle.

Consider an upward acceleration of the transducer. The force to accelerate the mass B is provided by the pressure applied to its lower surface by C; this force is equal to Ma, where M is the mass of B, and a is the acceleration. Similarly, there must be an upward accelerating force on the base of the crystal of $(M+m)a$, m being the mass of the crystal. The crystal itself is thus subject to an accelerating force ma, plus equal and opposite compressive forces of Ma on the top and bottom surfaces respectively. The compressive forces produce a strain in the crystal proportional to the acceleration a. A charge proportional to a is therefore developed, which may be converted to a useful output signal as indicated in section 6.1.2.

Piezo accelerometers may be used in this way for vibration measurements at frequencies up to about one fifth of the natural frequency of vibration of the mass–crystal unit. (Since the crystal has stiffness—i.e., it behaves like a spring—the unit has a natural frequency just like any other mass–spring combination.) The reason for this limitation is explained in section 14.3.4. Fortunately, this natural frequency is very high, typically of the order of 100 kHz, so that one fifth of the natural frequency represents a very wide frequency range. Because of the charge-leakage effects associated with all piezo-electric devices, piezo accelerometers can not be used for static acceleration measurements, or for very low frequencies, However, in vibration applications, the lower frequency limit is normally limited by the sensitivity of the transducer (since acceleration is proportional to the square of frequency) rather than by charge leakage.

The basic mass–spring transducer of Fig. 11.12 may be adapted to measure

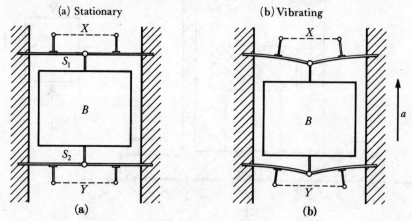

(a) Stationary (b) Vibrating

Figure 11.14   Strain-gauge accelerometer

dynamic accelerations by using a relatively small mass and a stiff spring. This is another way of saying that it should be modified to give it a high natural frequency and low sensitivity. (An increase in natural frequency is inevitably associated with a reduction in sensitivity—see section 14.3.1.) The movement of the mass in this mode is therefore small, so that the output devices which are used for the displacement mode are no longer suitable. Strain-gauge systems are frequently employed, often using unbonded gauges; inductive transducers, similar in form to that shown in Fig. 4.10, may also be used, the seismic mass being the moving armature. Figure 11.14 shows a possible strain-gauge arrangement. The mass B is supported by the spring members S_1 and S_2, to which unbonded strain gauges are attached by pillars. Relative movement of the mass (Fig. 11.14b) reduces the strain in gauge X, and increases the strain in gauge Y. (Only two gauges are shown; in practice four gauges would be used, connected as a four active-arm Wheatstone bridge.)

The natural frequencies of strain-gauge accelerometers are lower than those of piezo accelerometers. Natural frequency remains the factor controlling the usable frequency range of the accelerometer. However, whereas the usable frequency range of a piezo transducer is limited to about 20 per cent of its natural frequency, strain-gauge transducers may often be used satisfactorily up to about 60 per cent of their natural frequencies. This improvement is the result of damping, which may be incorporated in a strain-gauge transducer, but which cannot be applied to a piezo device because of the virtual absence of relative motion between the mass and the housing. The primary advantages of strain-gauge accelerometers over the piezo type are firstly that they are more sensitive, and may therefore be used more successfully for small accelerations, and secondly that they are capable of measuring static accelerations.

11.6.3 Readout from vibration transducers. Most vibration measurements are made in the course of research or of routine testing, and readings are often required only for relatively short periods. Under these circumstances, oscilloscopes or u.v. recorders, following the necessary signal-conditioning equipment, provide suitable displays. These forms of display give an indication of both the amplitude and the frequency of the signal, though frequency may be read with greater accuracy and convenience with a digital frequency meter. Where continuous vibration monitoring is required, it may be sufficient to feed a rectified signal to a simple moving-coil meter, which then indicates vibration amplitude only. This approach is used for aircraft jet engines, where permanent vibration monitoring is now being called for as a safety precaution, since an increase in the level of vibration is an indication of developing fault conditions.

11.6.4 Calibration of vibration equipment. Accelerometers which respond to static inputs may be calibrated by mounting them on a rotating table, so that they are subject to known centripetal accelerations. Although this method is attractive in that it produces accelerations which can be calculated, there are practical problems in making the connections to the transducer. Piezo accelerometers and seismic displacement pickoffs cannot be calibrated by rotary methods. In these cases a sinusoidal vibration of known amplitude and frequency is required. For relatively low frequencies, it is possible to design a mechanism (e.g. the Scotch yoke), which will produce a known vibration from a rotary input of known speed; both amplitude and form of the output motion are then determined by the geometry of the mechanism.

Mechanisms of this kind can operate only at relatively low frequencies; if higher frequencies are required, electro-mechanical vibrators are normally used. These operate on a principle similar to that of a loudspeaker—i.e., attraction and repulsion of a coil carrying an alternating current in a strong unidirectional magnetic field. A variable-frequency, variable-amplitude power source is required to drive the vibrator. For small vibrators, an ordinary laboratory electronic oscillator makes a suitable source, provided that its power rating is sufficiently high.

Electro-mechanical vibrators are readily commercially available. Unlike the purely mechanical vibrators mentioned above, the output of an electro-mechanical vibrator is not accurately determined by its input. If, therefore, it is to be used for calibration purposes, the frequency and one other characteristic of the output (amplitude, velocity, or acceleration) must be measured. Frequency presents no serious difficulty. The output frequency is necessarily equal to the input frequency; this is determined with reasonable accuracy by the calibration of the oscillator, and may be measured with greater accuracy with a digital frequency meter. Amplitude and acceleration measurements present greater problems. For the average user, the most convenient solution is probably a high-grade master accelerometer attached to a vibrator table. Commercial vibrators are available which are designed to accommodate test and calibration transducers in this way. As with other types of standard, the calibration accelerometer can be sent to a specialist laboratory for periodic checking by more sophisticated methods.

There are several *single-point* calibration methods by which accelerometers may be checked in relation to the gravitational acceleration g. Such checks are useful to confirm that the accelerometer is functioning correctly. One method is to hold the accelerometer with its axis vertical, then invert it. The mass in the accelerometer experiences a change in the gravitational force acting on it equivalent to a change in acceleration of $2g$. Further details of calibration methods for accelerometers may be found in ref. 2.

Summary

Time is measured by a variety of physical systems which possess the property of continuously repeating a cyclic operation of constant duration. These systems require an energy input to maintain the cycling process. Most precision time measurements are made with instruments based on crystal-controlled electronic oscillators. Clocks based on atomic phenomena provide the most accurate timing devices, but are not yet in general use.

Methods of velocity measurement depend on the nature of the application. Velocities relative to fluids are measured by techniques which are identical in principle to those used for flow measurement. Timing over known distances may be used for constant velocities, and is useful for calibration checking. For small displacements, velocity transducers based on inductive principles may be employed.

Measurements of angular velocities are required mainly for relatively steady shaft speeds. Instruments used for this purpose are known as tachometers. The eddy-current *drag-cup* type is numerically the most common. It is best suited to display near the measuring point. Remote indication, and better accuracy, can be achieved by tachogenerators. Digital methods of measuring shaft speeds are capable of better accuracies and higher frequencies than other methods, and do not load the shaft; a digital measuring system comprises an inductive or photo-electric pickoff feeding a frequency meter.

Stroboscopes provide a convenient manually operated method of checking shaft speeds without loading the shaft. Serious errors may be incurred if the correct procedures are not followed.

A sinusoidal vibration may be specified by giving its frequency, plus either its amplitude, maximum velocity, or maximum acceleration. Whether or not the vibration is sinusoidal, amplitude, velocity, and acceleration may be derived from one another by electronic differentiating or integrating techniques.

Almost all vibration measurements are made with seismic transducers. A seismic transducer consists of a mass–spring combination enclosed in a housing which is rigidly fixed to the vibrating body. Provision is made for obtaining an electrical output, derived from the relative motion between the mass and the housing. The special feature of seismic transducers is that they operate without a fixed spatial reference. To obtain amplitude measurements, the mass–spring assembly must have a natural frequency substantially below the frequency of the vibration under investigation. The mass then remains virtually stationary in space, and the vibration amplitude is equal to the amplitude of the relative motion between the mass and the housing; this may be measured by means of a conventional displacement transducer. To obtain an acceleration output from a seismic transducer, the natural frequency of the transducer must be substantially above that of the vibration; accelerometers are therefore designed to have high natural frequencies. This may be achieved by the use of a very stiff spring element. In piezo accelerometers, the crystal itself acts as the spring, giving a high natural frequency because of its very high stiffness. The piezo crystal responds to the strain resulting from an accelerating force. Strain-gauge accelerometers have lower natural frequencies than those based on piezo crystals, but can have higher sensitivities, and respond to steady accelerations.

Examples

1. A digital timer with eight-digit readout is stated to have an accuracy of 0·005 per cent of the reading, ±1 in the final digit. Readout is in s, ms, or μs. Assuming that the instrument meets its specification, what are the maximum likely errors when the reading is (a) 05 000 000 μs; (b) 00 000 500 s? What is the maximum nominal accuracy, in time units, with which reading (b) could be made with this instrument?
(Refer to section 5.5. Ans.: 251 μs; 1·025 s; ±26 ms.)

2. A stroboscope is directed at a rotating disc having five equi-spaced radial lines on it. The highest flashing frequency at which a 'true' pattern is observed is 2000 flashes/min.

Give two other flashing frequencies which would produce (a) a five-line pattern; (b) a ten-line pattern.

(Ans.: 1000, 667, 500, etc.; 4000, 1333, 800, etc.)

3. An inductive pickoff operating from a 120-tooth wheel is used with a digital frequency meter to measure the speed of rotation of the shaft on which the wheel is mounted. The gating-period is set to 10^4 μs, and a reading of 0030 is obtained on the four-digit display. What shaft speed does this represent, in rev/s? If the available gating periods are 10^2, 10^3, 10^4, 10^5, 10^6, 10^7 μs, respectively, what would be the optimum setting of the gating period for

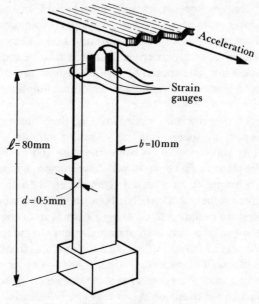

Figure 11.15

making this measurement? (Assume that the shaft speed is known to be constant.)

(Refer to section 5.5. Ans.: 25 rev/s; 10^6 μs.)

4. Show that, for the 'vibrating wedge' method of measuring vibration amplitude (Fig. 11.11), the amplitude of the vibration is given by $b(1-x/h)$.

5. An accelerometer (Fig. 11.15) consists of a mass weighing 0·5 N attached to a spring cantilever. The spring is made from material of modulus of elasticity 200 GN/m² and is of uniform rectangular cross-section. The output is obtained from a strain-gauge bridge comprising four active gauges of factor 2·0 (two each side of the cantilever) supplied from a 3 V d.c. source. Find the bridge output, with the output terminals open-circuited, for a steady hori-

zontal acceleration of 4*g*. (The surface stress on a cantilever at distance *l* from the free end may be taken as $6Pl/bd^2$, where *P* is the load applied to the free end.)

(Refer to section 4.3. Ans.: 11·5 mV.)

References

1   H. Brandenberger, 'Oscillatom, Frequency Standards, and Atomic Clocks', *La Suisse Horlogère*, No. 4, 1966.
2   T. G. Beckwith and N. Lewis Buck, *Mechanical Measurements*, Addison–Wesley, 1961.

12. Force, torque, and power

The SI unit of force is that which produces unit acceleration when applied to unit mass. In terms of basic units, the unit of force is therefore the kg m/s^2—better known as the newton.

Torque is turning moment; it has the dimensions of (force × distance), and is measured in Nm. It will be apparent that the Nm is dimensionally the same as the joule, but the joule is used exclusively as the unit of energy, and the Nm as the unit of torque or *moment of force*. The unit of power, the watt, is equal to a rate of working of 1 J/s.

12.1 Force

Methods of measuring force are in many ways analogous to the methods used for pressure, described in chapter 8. Of the five main techniques used for pressure measurement—elastic deformation, liquid column, dead weight, strain gauge, and piezo-electric—all except the liquid-column technique are commonly used for force measurement. Dead weights, or dead loads (meaning the gravitational pull on a known mass M) provide the most commonly used form of working standard for force. Since by definition the magnitude of this force is Mg, the local value of g must be known if a mass is to be used as a force standard. Many lower-grade standards of this kind are specified in terms of the gravitational force on them, rather than by giving their masses—i.e., a particular value of g is assumed.

The comparison of an unknown force with a dead-weight standard may be made directly by means of a mechanical balance. These are commonly used for weighing (where the real interest is in mass rather than weight), but the balance principle can also be employed to measure force in other contexts, such as in materials-testing machines.

Mechanical balances provide an accurate means of comparison between an unknown force and the gravitational pull on a mass standard. They are not, however, as convenient to use as devices based on elastic-deformation principles.

12.1.1 Mechanical balances. Designs of mechanical balances vary in complexity from the single equal-armed lever to those using multiple levers and

194

sliding masses. The purpose of using more than one lever is to increase magnification, so that conveniently small masses may be used to produce relatively large forces at the measuring point. Sliding masses, on calibrated arms, are used to speed the comparison procedure, and to avoid the necessity for large numbers of accurately known masses.

Figure 12.1 shows the essential features of a simple mechanical balance. The unknown force, in this case the weight W of the mass A, is determined by adjusting the position of the mass B until balance is obtained. If balance was originally obtained with B in the position B_0, then by the principle of moments, $Wa = wx$, w being the weight of B. Since weight is equal to the product of mass and the gravitational acceleration, this relation can also be written as $Ma = mx$, or $M = (m/a)x$, M and m being the masses of A and B respectively. It follows that M is proportional to x. The scale S can therefore be

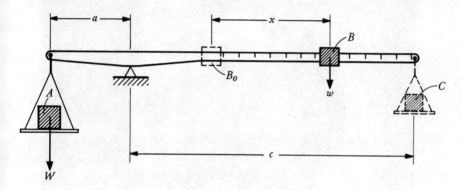

Figure 12.1 Mechanical balance

calibrated directly in terms of M, or in terms of the force W, if a certain value of g is assumed.

The range may be extended by adding a further mass C at the end of the beam. If m' is the mass of C, balance is then obtained when

$$Ma = mx + m'c, \qquad \text{or} \qquad M = (m/a)x + m'c/a.$$

Since $(m'c/a)$ is constant, the calibration marks on the scale can be used for the higher range, provided that the constant quantity $(m'c/a)$ is added to every reading. By choosing suitable values for m', the range can be extended indefinitely in this way, within the limits imposed by the strength of the mechanism.

To measure large forces, it is convenient to increase the magnification of the mechanism by using a system of interconnected levers. The relation between the measured and measuring forces may be determined in such cases by the successive application of the principle of moments. For very high-precision work, however, machines without levers are employed (ref. 1).

12.1.2 Elastic deformation. Elastic bodies, under the action of an applied force, suffer a deformation or deflection which is directly proportional to the force. Measurement of this deformation or deflection therefore provides a method of measuring force.

Figure 12.2   Proving ring mounted in materials-testing machine to verify the machine. (*Photo by courtesy of the National Physical Laboratory.*)

The elastic devices most commonly used for the direct mechanical measurement of force are coil springs in tension, and steel rings in tension or compression. In addition, a wide variety of elastic members is used for indirect measurement, in conjunction with strain gauges or electrical displacement transducers.

Coil springs giving a direct indication of deflection are commonly known as 'spring balances', though they are not balances in the strict sense of the term. A spring balance consists of a spring located at one end, with some arrangement for applying the load to be measured to the free end; the resulting displacement of the free end is shown by a pointer moving over a scale calibrated in force units. (In commercial types, the scale may be calibrated in mass units, assuming a certain value of g.) Direct-reading spring balances are incapable of high accuracies, because of the relatively small displacements obtained. Reading accuracy may be improved by the use of a mechanical magnifying system, such as a rack-and-pinion gear, giving a circular display; modifications of this kind introduce the possibility of increased friction errors (section 13.2.1).

Steel rings, or *proving rings*, are employed as force standards, particularly in connection with the calibration of materials-testing machines, where dead-weight standards would be impracticable because of their physical bulk. A proving ring is a circular ring of rectangular cross-section (Fig. 12.2), which may be subjected to tensile or compressive loads across a diameter. As the deflection is small, the usefulness of the proving ring as a calibration device depends on this deflection being measured accurately. This may be done with a precision micrometer, or by means of a displacement transducer with electrical output. The measuring arrangement in Fig. 12.2 comprises a micrometer screw and fiducial indicator (a spring-loaded mechanical magnifying device, which ensures that all micrometer readings are taken at constant contact load).

Proving rings are normally used within the range 2 kN to 2 MN. The maximum deflection is typically 1 per cent of the outside diameter of the ring; although the deflection may be predicted theoretically, calibration by dead-weight methods is preferable. The NPL has facilities for the calibration of proving rings and other load-measuring devices up to 5 MN by methods based on deadload principles (ref. 1).

12.1.3 Strain-gauge systems.

Strain gauges (section 4.2) may be attached to any elastic member on which there exists a suitable plane area to accommodate them; the arrangement may then be used to measure loads applied to deform or deflect the member, provided the resulting strain in the gauges is large enough for satisfactory measurement. When used for weighing, transducers of this kind are usually referred to as *load cells*; in common with other force transducers, they are sometimes called 'dynamometers' in other applications. This usage of the term 'dynamometer' can be misleading, in view of its long-established association with machines for measuring power.

Factors to be considered in the design of strain-gauge force transducers are (a) stiffness of the elastic member, (b) optimum positioning of the gauges on the member, and (c) provision for temperature compensation. The stiffness of the member must be appropriate to the range of the transducer—i.e., the gauges must be subjected to strains of sufficient magnitude to give a measurable output from the bridge. Sensitivity is also affected by the positions and orientation of the gauges. To obtain maximum sensitivity and full temperature compensation, a four-active-arm bridge is invariably employed.

Strain-gauge transducers can cover a very wide force range. There is virtually no upper limit, as the elastic member can be made as robust as necessary to withstand the load. The lower limit is determined by the sensitivity of the gauges used. Figure 12.3 indicates two possible transducer arrangements: a cylinder, with gauges mounted vertically and circumferentially, and

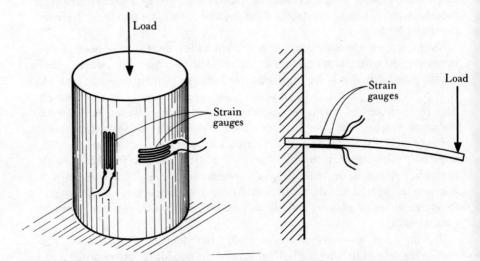

Figure 12.3   Elastic elements for strain-gauge force transducers

a cantilever with the gauges mounted on its upper and lower surfaces near the fixed end. Strain gauges may also be attached to proving rings.

In the cantilever arrangement, gauges in corresponding positions on the upper and lower surfaces of the beam experience equal and opposite strains; two gauges are therefore attached to each surface, and connected as a four-active-arm bridge. In the case of the cylinder, an axial compressive load causes a negative strain in the vertical gauges, and a positive strain in the circumferential gauges. The two strains are not equal in this case. Since the value of the strain is of no interest—the object is to produce a force transducer, to be calibrated empirically—the fact that the strains are unequal does not matter. Provided that the gauges are all similar, temperature compensation will be achieved, and all the gauges will contribute to unbalancing the bridge. The cylinder may be either solid or hollow, depending on the sensitivity required.

Unbonded strain-gauge transducers are also extensively used for force measurement, particularly if high sensitivity is required. Highest sensitivity is achieved when the gauge itself performs the function of the elastic member— i.e., all the input force is used to strain the gauge.

Strain-gauge systems are suitable for both static and dynamic measurements. Dynamic force measurements may also be made by means of piezo transducers. Their primary advantage is their excellent dynamic response; as they do not respond to static loads, their usefulness in the field of force measurement is restricted. If the piezo-electric principle is to be used for force measurement, it is often more convenient to measure the force in terms of pressure, as described below.

12.1.4   *Use of pressure transducers.* As a wide range of pressure transducers is commercially available, it is sometimes convenient to measure force by developing a corresponding hydraulic pressure from it. If only moderate dy-

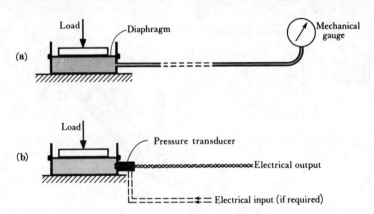

Figure 12.4   Force to pressure conversion: (a) for static measurements; (b) for optimum dynamic response

namic performance is required, transmission to some point remote from the measuring point is possible without the need for a power supply. Where better dynamic response is called for, piezo or strain-gauge transducers are used (section 8.6). These should be mounted close to the measuring point, in the interests of obtaining optimum response. The use of a transducer which requires only very small movements of the liquid simplifies the problem of force-to-pressure conversion. There is no need for sliding pistons, with the inevitable leakage problems: relatively stiff metallic diaphragms may be used.

Figure 12.4 illustrates the essential differences between a mechanical 'static' measuring system and an electrical 'dynamic' system. Force-to-pressure conversion by means of a diaphragm has been indicated in both diagrams; this is feasible in the mechanical system only if the gauge is of a type—such as a bourdon tube—for which the volume changes associated with measurement are small. For the dynamic arrangement, the relative merits of piezo and strain-gauge transducers are as in other applications; while piezo transducers have a better dynamic response, they do not respond to static inputs, and the signal-conditioning equipment is usually more expensive.

12.1.5 Forces in unknown directions. The methods of force measurement

so far described are appropriate only if the line of action of the force to be measured is known. Although this is generally the case, some applications require not only that the magnitude of the force should be determined, but also its direction.

The general approach to this problem is to measure the components of the force in three perpendicular directions; the total force, and its direction, can

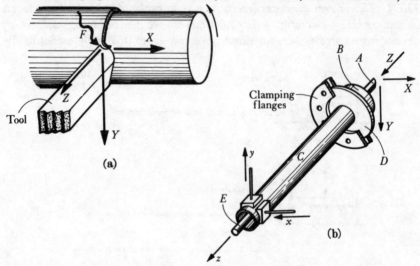

Figure 12.5   Three-dimensional force measurement

then be determined, though often knowledge of the three components is more convenient. Measurements of this kind have to be made in investigations of forces on cutting tools in machining operations. Consider the lathe tool in Fig. 12.5a. There will be a total force F acting on it, which can conveniently be resolved into the components X, Y and Z in axial, vertical and radial directions respectively. To measure these forces, elastic-deformation methods are invariably used. However, as the tool must be rigidly mounted to obtain a satisfactory cut, the deflection of the elastic member or members must be very small.

Solutions to the problem generally involve the fabrication of a special tool-holder incorporating the necessary elastic members. This could be so designed that three flexure members measured the force components independently, each of the three members being strain-gauged to provide individual outputs. An arrangement of this kind is necessarily complex, as three complete strain-gauge bridges are required. Temperature-compensation troubles may be encountered if the flexure members are close to the cutting tool, due to temperature gradients in the assembly.

Flexure combined with sensitive displacement transducers is generally preferred to strain-gauging in this context. One commercial device (Herbert Controls and Instruments Ltd.) uses mechanical magnification in conjunction with inductive displacement transducers. The principle of the method is shown in Fig. 12.5b. The tool A is rigidly mounted in a boss attached to the diaphragm D, which is itself rigidly mounted on the tool carriage. The diaphragm is the flexure member of the assembly; it is, however, sufficiently stiff to allow only very small movement of the tool under load. Movements due to the X and Y components of the total force are magnified by the tube C, which is also rigidly attached to the diaphragm, and which is relatively long compared with the tool. (The tool and tube effectively form a single beam, pivoted at the diaphragm.) Movement due to the Z-component of the force is transmitted to a third displacement transducer by the rod E; this is attached to the diaphragm by a flexible connection, and is consequently unaffected by flexure of the diaphragm due to the X and Y components. Thus displacements x, y, and z can be measured, representing the three components of the force. To minimize the effects of temperature changes, the rod E is made of invar. A measuring system of this kind is calibrated before each investigation. Calibration involves applying known loads in the direction of each force component individually.

12.2 Torque

Measurements of torque are made mainly in connection with determinations of the power developed or absorbed by rotating machinery; the techniques of measurement in this application are complicated by the motion of the shaft. There are many machines, known as *brakes* or *dynamometers*, which both apply and measure torque; these are used exclusively for power measurements, and are described in section 12.3. Other methods of measuring torque are based on measurements of the strain in the shaft itself, or in an elastic element built into the shaft. The strain may be measured directly, or torque may be inferred from the relative displacement of two cross-sections of the shaft at a known distance apart. Devices for determining torque by these methods are known variously as *torque transducers*, *torsiometers*, and *transmission dynamometers*.

12.2.1 Direct strain method. The strain in the shaft may be measured by means of strain gauges attached to its surface. The gauges should be positioned on the shaft to give maximum sensitivity to the strains produced by torsion. Reference to any text covering the theory of two-dimensional stress systems (e.g., ref. 2) will show that, for a shaft subjected to pure torsion, the gauges will be strained in the directions of their major axes if they are mounted at 45° to the axis of the shaft. The usual technique is to mount a complete strain-gauge bridge on the shaft, as in Fig. 12.6. With the torque in the direction shown, gauges T_1 and T_2 will be in tension, and gauges C_1 and C_2 in compression. The arrangement has the following merits: (a) it is fully temperature compensated, (b) it achieves maximum sensitivity for a given torque, and (c) it provides automatic compensation for bending and axial loads, if these should also be present in the shaft. The main difficulties with the method are associated with connecting the bridge to its power-source and display equipment. *Slip rings* may be used for this purpose. These are conducting rings attached to the shaft, but insulated from it, one ring being electrically

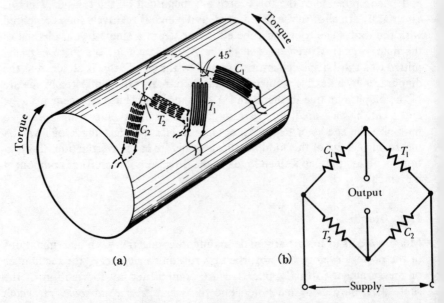

(a) (b)

Figure 12.6 Torque measurement by strain gauges: (a) arrangement of gauges on shaft; (b) electrical connections

connected to each of the four bridge terminals. Rubbing contact is made between the rings and stationary brushes, which are connected to the input and output equipment.

Slip rings are a potential source of trouble in circuits where resistance is critical, because the contact resistance between the ring and brush does not remain constant. The changes of contact resistance are likely to be large compared with the changes in resistance of the gauges. However, this does not rule out their use with the system illustrated; the contact resistances are not in the arms of the bridge, but in the supply and output lines, where relatively large resistance changes can be tolerated without serious errors. In general, slip rings are satisfactory where the contact rubbing velocities are low, and where readings are required only over relatively short periods.

An alternative to slip rings which has been used commercially for connecting supplies to torque transducers is a form of transformer having a stationary primary winding and a rotating secondary winding (Fig. 12.7). The secondary winding is attached to a flange on the shaft, and consequently rotates with it. An alternating e.m.f. is induced in the secondary as in a conventional transformer, and forms the supply to the strain-gauge bridge (or other transducer). Output from the bridge is taken through a similar transformer, differing from the first only in that the primary winding rotates, and the secondary is stationary. This form of supply and output connection is used in conjunction with a carrier frequency system (section 6.1.1).

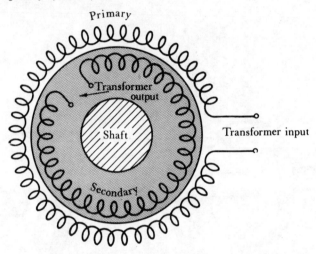

Figure 12.7   Transformer coupling to rotating transducer

The success of the strain-gauge method described above is dependent on the shaft experiencing sufficient strain to generate an adequate measuring signal. This requirement may not be met if the shaft is lightly loaded. In such cases it may be possible to introduce some form of flexible coupling into the shaft, incorporating one or more elastic members to which the gauges may be attached. The elastic members would then be designed to give a sufficiently large deflection under the torque to be measured.

12.2.2   Angular-displacement methods. A more common approach to the determination of torque by means of shaft strain is to determine the relative angular displacement of two attachments set on the shaft at some convenient distance apart. There are various ways in which this relative displacement may be measured; a brief selection of possible methods will be reviewed here.

Possibly the simplest method is that illustrated in Fig. 12.8. Two flanges, *A* and *B*, are mounted on the shaft, carrying a scale and pointer respectively. A torque applied to the shaft causes displacement of the pointer relative to the scale, due to the 'twist' of the length of shaft between the two flanges. For a stationary shaft, this displacement could be read off the scale directly; if the shaft is rotating, direct observation of the reading is possible only if the rate of rotation is extremely slow. However, if a stroboscope (section 11.4) is directed at the scale and adjusted until a stationary image is obtained, a scale reading may be taken. In general the displacement is small, and the reading accuracy is consequently poor. The method is inexpensive, assuming a stroboscope to be available. For power calculations, it has the advantage that the shaft speed is given by the stroboscope flashing frequency.

To overcome the inherently poor sensitivity of the method, the relative

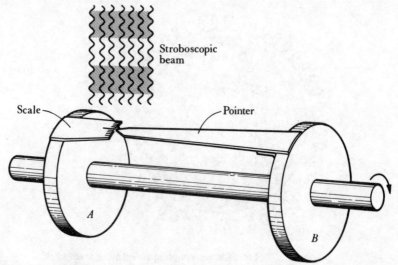

Figure 12.8 Use of stroboscope for torque measurement

angular displacement of the two flanges may be sensed by transducers similar to those used for small linear displacements. A further advantage of this approach is that rapid variations in the torque may be measured. The practical problems of using displacement transducers in this context are associated with the satisfactory mounting of the components of the transducer on the shaft, and with making the necessary electrical connections to it.

Figure 12.9 shows the idea in principle, using an inductive transducer. Flange A carries a coil, and flange B an iron core which moves in and out of the coil according to the relative displacement of the two flanges, thus forming an inductive transducer of the type described in section 4.5.

A more satisfactory arrangement, giving better sensitivity and linearity, is to use four such coil-and-core units, the coils being connected in the form of an a.c. bridge. The cores are arranged so that a torque in a given direction causes an increase in the inductance of two of the coils, and a decrease in the inductance of the other two (Fig. 12.10). Torque transducers based on this principle, and employing the system of contactless transformer coupling described on p. 203 are available commercially (Vibro-meter Ltd.).

Digital timing techniques may also be used to determine the relative displacement of the two flanges. Suppose the flanges are made in the form of single-toothed wheels (Fig. 12.11) the teeth being designed to generate voltage

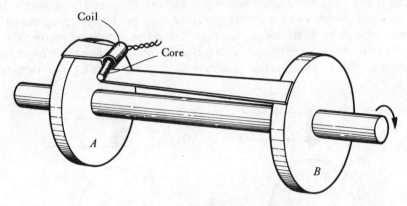

Figure 12.9   Inductive torque transducer

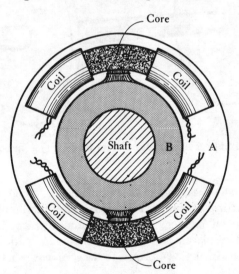

Figure 12.10   Inductive-bridge torque transducer

pulses in the inductive pickoffs C and D respectively. If the two teeth are precisely aligned with each other when the shaft is unstrained, rotation of the shaft at zero torque will produce voltage pulses in C and D simultaneously; if, however, a torque is applied to the shaft producing an angular displacement of A relative to B, there is a time interval between the two pulses which can be measured by an electronic timer. The ratio of this interval to the time for a complete revolution (which could be calculated from the shaft speed) gives the relative displacement as a fraction of a revolution.

There are other ways of obtaining an output signal from digital pickoffs of this kind. If the single-toothed wheels of Fig. 12.11 are replaced by multi-toothed wheels, such as ordinary spur gears, the output from each of the pickoffs will be approximately sinusoidal. The two outputs will be exactly in phase if the two wheels are correctly aligned, and will become progressively more out of phase as the torque increases. The phase difference can therefore be used as a measure of torque. In an experimental installation, it could be measured with an oscilloscope, though methods are available for converting

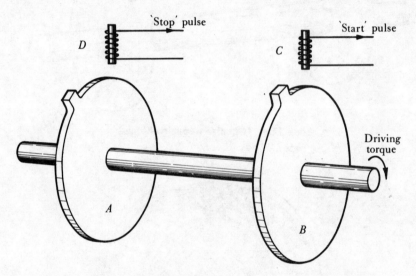

Figure 12.11   Torque deduced from time-interval measurement

phase measurements to analogue or digital signals, which would provide a more convenient form of readout for a permanent installation.

A disadvantage of methods based on inductive pickoffs is that, unlike strain-gauge and displacement-transducer methods, static calibration (i.e., calibration by applying known torques to the stationary shaft) is not possible.

12.2.3 Magneto-strictive transducers. The torque transducers so far described all require fittings of some kind on the shaft, and, in the case of the angular-displacement methods, these fittings may occupy a substantial length of shaft. Magneto-strictive transducers can operate without any attachments or modification to the shaft, and are relatively compact.

The action of magneto-strictive transducers depends on the change which occurs in the permeability of magnetic materials when subjected to strain:

permeability decreases with positive strain, and increases with negative strain. (Magnetic permeability is analogous to electrical conductivity; for a particular flux path, a decrease in permeability increases the reluctance of the path. If, therefore, the material is positively strained in the direction of the flux path, the reluctance of the path is increased.)

In the discussion of the strain-gauge torque transducers in the previous section, it was pointed out that in a shaft subjected to pure torsion, the highest positive and negative strains are experienced in the two directions at 45° to the shaft axis. If flux paths can be established in these two directions, and their changes in reluctance detected, a further method of torque measurement

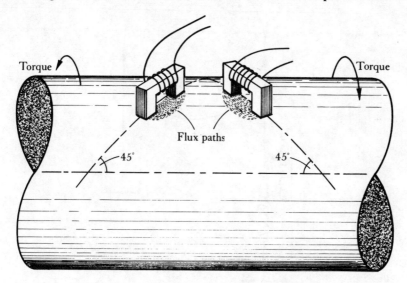

Figure 12.12   Magneto-strictive torque transducer

is available. A possible means of achieving this is indicated in Fig. 12.12. Two a.c.-energized coils, wound on iron cores, are positioned close to the shaft so that their flux paths through the material of the shaft coincide with the directions of maximum strain. If the coils form two arms of an a.c. bridge, the bridge will then be unbalanced by the differential change in the reactance of the coils caused by the changes in the reluctances of their respective flux paths.

The type of pickoff coil shown in Fig. 12.12 is similar in principle to that used in the inductive displacement transducers described in section 4.5. This similarity is, in fact, its weakness in the elementary form shown here, since the bridge balance will be upset by any very small changes in the air gap between the coil cores and the shaft, unless these changes are identical for both coils. More sophisticated coil arrangements may be used to overcome this difficulty, producing a contactless torque transducer in the form of a ring, which occupies only a very short axial length of shaft (ref. 3).

12.3 Power

The conventional methods of determining the power delivered to (or absorbed by) rotating machinery require simultaneous measurements of torque and shaft-speed. (The power corresponding to a torque T Nm in a shaft rotating at ω rad/s is $T\omega$ W, or $2\pi nT$ W, where n rev/s is the shaft speed.) Machines used for torque measurements under test-bed conditions are referred to as *dynamometers*. Besides measuring torque, a dynamometer either absorbs the power

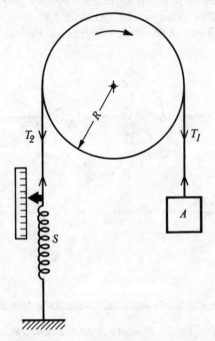

T_2 R T_1

A

S

Figure 12.13   Simple friction brake

output of the machine under test, or provides the power required to drive it, according to the nature of the machine.

12.3.1 Absorption dynamometers. The simplest form of absorption dynamometer is the dry-friction brake (Fig. 12.13). A rope or band is wound round a large wheel coupled to the machine output shaft, the rope or band being attached at one end to the calibrated spring S, and at the other to the mass A. For the purpose of calculating the torque, the rope tensions may be regarded as acting on the wheel. The torque is therefore equal to $(T_2 - T_1)R$. T_2 is measured by the spring S, and T_1 is equal to the weight of A. To calculate power, the shaft speed must be measured separately by means of a tachometer.

In this type of dynamometer, the power output of the driving machine is dissipated as heat developed by friction between the rope and the wheel. The difficulty of dissipating the heat, without reaching temperatures which the materials of the brake cannot withstand, places limits on the power which can be absorbed. A further limitation is that the brake arrangement does not stabilize the speed of the machine under test, since there is no automatic increase in torque with an increase in speed.

Dynamometers for larger power inputs differ from the simple friction brake both in their arrangements for heat dissipation, and in the methods by which the resisting torque is produced. Various machines, such as electrical generators and water brakes, are used as dynamometers. These machines have certain common features. Each incorporates a rotor *A* (Fig. 12.14) which is driven by the machine under test. Rotation of *A* relative to the frame or casing

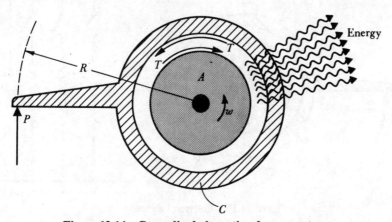

Figure 12.14   Generalized absorption dynamometer

of the machine is resisted by a torque *T*. Since the casing must necessarily experience an equal and opposite torque, *T* may be measured by measuring the torque on the casing, rather than on the rotor. This is done by mounting the casing on bearings on the same axis as the rotor shaft. Then *T* may be found by means of a force transducer mounted at a known radius *R*, measuring the force *P* required to restrain the rotation of the casing. For the machine to be generally useful, a means of controlling the resisting torque at a given input speed is necessary. (For the friction brake of Fig. 12.13, this is achieved by changing the value of the mass *A*.)

In the *water brake*, the casing is partly or completely filled with water. To develop the necessary resisting torque, both rotor and casing must incorporate some form of blades or cavities which create turbulence. Control of the torque is achieved in some designs by adjustment of the water level in the casing, and heat is removed by arranging for a continuous flow of water. The restraining torque applied to the casing is measured by a force transducer at a known radius, as in the general case.

Several types of electrical generator may be adapted for use as dynamo-meters. In any form of generator, resistance to the rotation of the armature is experienced as soon as power is taken from the generator output terminals (section 3.3.3). Electrical generators may therefore be used as absorption dynamometers, the resisting torque being controlled by the field strength, or by adjustment of the current taken from the generator. Energy dissipation is in the form of heat from the electrical load on the generator, which can be adjusted by means of a number of fixed or variable load resistors (Fig. 12.15).

An *eddy-current brake* is also a form of electrical generator, but differs from the more usual forms of generator in that power cannot be obtained from it; it therefore suffers from one of the major drawbacks of the friction

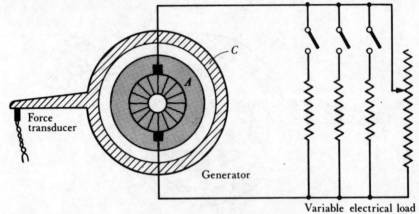

Figure 12.15   Electrical dynamometer

brake—i.e., that the energy has to be dissipated locally as heat. Its advantage over the friction brake is that smoother torque control can be obtained.

The eddy-current brake relies on the resistance to motion experienced by a non-magnetic conductor moving through a magnetic field (section 3.3.4). The field is provided by electro-magnets, and the magnitude of the resisting torque can be varied by adjustment of the current supplied to the magnet coils. The power absorbed appears as heat in the rotor, which may be water-cooled. Torque on the frame of the machine (to which the magnet assembly is attached) is measured in the usual way.

12.3.2   Driving dynamometers. Where the machine under investigation is one which absorbs power (such as a pump or compressor) the driving power must be supplied by the dynamometer. This requirement restricts the choice of the type of machine which can be used. Electric motors are almost uni-versally employed; d.c. machines are preferred, because the speed of a d.c. machine may be controlled over a wide range. The disadvantage of a d.c. driving dynamometer is that the necessary d.c supply is seldom available, so that the cost of generating or rectifying equipment has to be added to that of the dynamometer.

12.3.3 No-load methods. It may be required to measure the power transmitted from one machine to another in the course of normal operation, rather than under 'test-bed' conditions. In such cases the types of dynamometer described in the previous two sections cannot be used, as the measuring device must not impose any significant load on the shaft. The methods of torque measurement described in section 12.2 may be employed, in conjunction with a suitable tachometer.

Some of these methods lend themselves to the direct measurement of power, without making a separate measurement of shaft speed. If the output of the torque transducer used is proportional to its supply voltage, as in the case of a strain-gauge bridge, a direct measurement of power can be obtained from it if the supply voltage can be made proportional to the speed of the shaft. (The bridge output is then proportional to torque × speed.) A voltage proportional to shaft speed may be obtained from a tacho-generator driven by the shaft, either directly or through a gearbox.

12.3.4 Power absorbed in machining. The cutting process in most machine tools involves both angular and linear motion of the tool relative to the work. Power is then absorbed partly by the torque exerted on the rotating member, and partly by the thrust required to produce the linear motion. A complete analysis of power absorption therefore requires measurements of torque, thrust, and both linear and angular velocity.

Where the work rotates, as in a lathe, both thrust and torque can be determined from measurements of the forces on the tool; a method of measuring these forces was described in section 12.1.5. In machines where the tool rotates, such as drilling machines, it is more practicable to measure the forces on the work. To do this, it is necessary to design a special workholder incorporating thrust- and torque-measuring systems. The cutting tool, work, and workholder together then become, in effect, an absorption dynamometer, the tool being the equivalent of the rotor in the generalized dynamometer shown in Figure 12.14. An additional force transducer is incorporated to measure the end thrust on the drill. Apart from this, the design principles are the same as for other absorption dynamometers. Some practical differences arise because the dynamometer, if fitted to a vertical-axis machine, has to be mounted with its own axis vertical, and because the torques to be measured are small in comparison with those encountered in engine testing. The torque is normally determined by means of a force transducer mounted at a known radius, restraining the rotation of the dynamometer body, which is mounted in bearings. (When measuring very small torques, the friction torque of the bearings may be sufficient to cause significant errors; to avoid such errors, some designs support the dynamometer body either wholly or partly by means of the elastic members which also form the basis of the force transducers.) A typical dynamometer for a rotating-tool machine therefore incorporates two force transducers—one for thrust, and the other for torque. Any type of force transducer of appropriate sensitivity may be employed. Force-to-pressure converters with simple mechanical pressure indicators have been used, as have a variety of elastic-deformation systems combined with sensitive displacement transducers.

12.3.5 Electrical power. Another approach which may be useful in investigations on machine tools is to measure the electrical power input to the

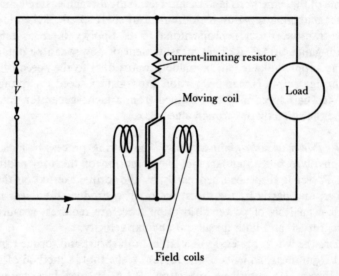

Figure 12.16 Principle of wattmeter

machine. If the power consumed by the machine when running free is subtracted from that consumed during cutting, an estimate of the power used in the machining operation may be obtained. (This method can give only an estimated result, as the power consumed in the motor and transmission increases with load; in practice, the power consumed when running free is often negligibly small.)

Measurements of electrical power may be made with *wattmeters*. Since electrical power is equal to $VI \cos\phi$ (V = supply voltage, I = current, ϕ = phase angle between voltage and current) a wattmeter must be simultaneously sensitive to voltage and current. The simplest form of wattmeter is based on the same principle as the moving-coil meter (section 5.1), except that the field is obtained from the current I, instead of from a permanent magnet. To appreciate the principle of the wattmeter, consider first the d.c. case, where there is no phase angle; $\cos\phi$ is then equal to unity, and the power is simply VI watts. Now suppose the voltage V is applied to the terminals of a moving-coil voltmeter: a current proportional to V flows through the moving coil, causing a deflection which depends on the design of the coil, the stiffness of the control spring, and the strength of the magnetic field. If the other factors remain constant, the deflection is proportional to the current in the coil and the strength of the magnetic field. In the wattmeter, the field is generated by coils carrying the power-circuit current, as indicated in Fig. 12.16; deflection is therefore proportional to the product of the currents in the field coils and moving coil respectively, i.e., to the product VI.

In the case of alternating current, if the current and voltage are exactly in phase, the situation is similar to the d.c. case. The torque at any instant is proportional to the product of the instantaneous values of V and I; it therefore varies from zero to some maximum value, but it does not reverse, since the directions of the two currents reverse simultaneously. An instrument movement with 'ideal' dynamic response would therefore oscillate continuously at twice the supply frequency. However, a movement of normal dimensions is incapable of responding at this speed, and will read an average value. A similar argument applies where the voltage and current are not in phase, since only the component of the voltage which is in phase with the current produces torque on the moving coil.

The electrical power to a d.c. machine, or to a single-phase a.c. machine, may therefore be measured by a wattmeter. Large machines are usually driven by three-phase motors. Measurement of power in three-phase circuits may also be effected by wattmeters. The methods are well established, and may be found in texts dealing with electrical power (e.g. ref. 4).

Summary

Force may be measured by mass-balancing (dead-weight) systems, elastic deformation, or by conversion to a proportional pressure. Mass-balancing methods are based on single- or multiple-lever principles; they are used mainly for weighing, tensile testing, and the calibration of other force-measuring systems.

Many simple elastic-deformation devices are based on coil springs, which give a displacement output of sufficient magnitude for the direct operation of mechanical displays. Various less sensitive elastic elements are also employed, occasionally with mechanical magnification, but more usually in conjunction with strain gauges or with electrical displacement transducers. The forms of elastic member employed include cantilevers, rings, and solid or hollow cylinders, the choice depending principally on the sensitivity required. Strain-gauge transducers of all types employ four-active-arm bridges, thus obtaining maximum bridge sensitivity and full temperature compensation.

The torque in the output shaft of a power-producing machine may be measured by an absorption dynamometer; power may then be calculated, if the shaft speed is also known. The torque and power supplied to a power-consuming machine may similarly be determined by means of a driving dynamometer. A dynamometer may be one of a number of types of machine; its essential features are that it should be capable of absorbing power (or producing power, in the case of a driving dynamometer) and that the frame or casing should be slung in bearings. Rotation is restrained by a force transducer at known radius.

Torque transducers (transmission dynamometers) may be fitted to shafts to measure torque without imposing any appreciable load. They may be based on strain gauges, displacement or magneto-strictive transducers, or non-contacting pickoffs. Except in the strain-gauge and magneto-strictive systems, the general approach is to measure the relative angular displacement of two fixtures at some convenient distance apart on the shaft.

Mechanical power is determined by simultaneous measurements of torque and shaft speed; some more sophisticated systems perform the required computation automatically, and provide a direct indication of power.

Examples

1. Fig. 12.17 shows the essentials of a simple tensile-testing machine. Tensile forces are applied to the specimen *EF* by the mass *M* which may be moved between the points *A* and *B* on the beam *CD*. The mechanism is initially balanced so that the specimen is unstressed when *M* is at *A*; *CD* is kept horizontal during use by an adjustment at the end *F* of the specimen.
   (a) If the range of the machine is 0–20 kN, what is the weight of *M*?
   (b) In order to increase the range, a mass is suspended from the point *C*, such that a tension of 20 kN is applied to the specimen when *M* is at *A*. Wha is the new range of the machine?
   (c) It is proposed to modify the machine by fixing the mass *M* at *A*, straining the specimen by means of the adjustment at F, and obtaining a readout from a strain-gauge force transducer acted on by the end *C* of the beam. What would be the merits and demerits of the new system compared with the old?
(Ans.: 0·4 kN, 20–40 kN.)

2. A transducer intended to measure forces in the range 5 to 40 N consists of four strain gauges mounted on a cantilever (Fig. 12.18). The dimensions *l* and *b* are 50 mm and 10 mm respectively. Find the required depth *d* of the cantilever, if the maximum stress on section *AA* is to be 75 MN/m^2. (The stress, σ, on the surface of a cantilever is given by $\sigma = 6Pl/bd^2$.)

If the gauge factor is 2, the bridge supply voltage is 4 V, and the modulus of elasticity of the material is 200 GN/m^2, find the minimum unbalance voltage of the bridge which will have to be measured for the force range specified. Assume an 'infinite impedance' detector to be used.
(Refer to section 4.3. Ans.: 4 mm, 0·38 mV.)

3. A digital timer is used to determine the torque in a rotating shaft by the method described on p. 205 (Fig. 12.11). Static calibration shows that the length of shaft between the flanges twists one degree for an applied torque of 1000 Nm. In a test with the shaft rotating at 500 rev/min, the torque calculated from the timer readings is 1200 Nm. What is the maximum probable error in the measured torque due to timing error, if the final digit on the timer

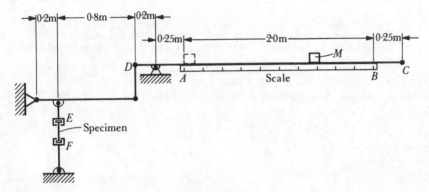

Figure 12.17

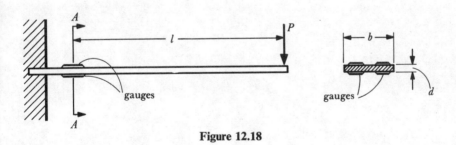

Figure 12.18

display represents units of 10^{-5} s, and the accuracy of the instrument is specified as 0·05 per cent of the reading ± 1 in the final digit?

(Ans.: 2·55 per cent.)

4. A dynamometer fitted to a drilling machine is mounted in bearings which are known to exert a friction torque of approximately $0·004P$ Nm on the dynamometer body, where P is the thrust exerted by the drill.

In a test at a drill speed of 600 rev/min, the mean reading from a force transducer mounted at 120 mm radius (to measure torque) was 80 N, and the mean reading from the transducer measuring thrust was 200 N. The speed of advance of the drill during the test was 0·2 mm/rev. Show that the power used

215

in advancing the drill was negligible compared with that used to produce the torque, and estimate the percentage error due to bearing friction in a power calculation based on the transducer readings.

(Ans.: 7·7 per cent.)

References

1   B. Swindells and R. C. Debnam, *Standards of Force and their Application to Materials Testing Machines*, paper presented at the National Physical Laboratory, 1969.
2   G. D. Redford, J. G. Rimmer, and D. Titherington, *Mechanical Technology*, Macmillan, 1969.
3   O. Dahle, 'Torductor Torque Transducers without Slip Rings for Industrial Measurement and Control', *ASEA Journal*, 1960.
4   C. T. Baldwin, *Fundamentals of Electrical Measurements*, Harrap, London, 1961.

Part 3

Performance

13. Static performance

Reference was made in chapter 1 to the basic concepts of static and dynamic performance, and to the interrelation between the application of the measuring system and the performance required. These basic concepts will be examined in more detail in the remaining two chapters.

In almost all applications, the static accuracy of the measuring system is of importance. There are exceptions to this, a particular case being that of piezo transducers, for which the concept of static accuracy has no real meaning. In contrast, there are other applications of measuring instruments where dynamic performance is of little interest, because the measured quantity itself is incapable of rapid variations. A representative case would be an instrument measuring water level in a large reservoir. Dynamic performance in excess of that required should not be called for in specifying measuring systems, as to do so may involve a great deal of extra sophistication and expense.

13.1 Criteria of static performance

The inexperienced user, if he questions the performance of his measuring equipment at all, is likely to ask 'is it accurate?'; accuracy tends to be regarded as an absolute condition which the measuring system either does or does not enjoy. However, no analogue quantity can be measured with absolute accuracy. Consider a measurement of an unknown length by comparison with a length bar. The length of the bar itself will be known only within certain limits, and the method of comparison will inevitably introduce further uncertainty. It is therefore possible to establish the unknown length only within certain limits, which may be specified, but which cannot be closer than those within which the length of the standard bar is known. All measurement being basically a matter of comparison, a similar argument may be applied to other analogue measurements (and, of course, to any digital measurement of an analogue quantity; the only type of measurement which can be exact is a determination of a number of discrete events).

Accuracy then, is only a relative term, but it is nevertheless important to know *how* accurate measuring devices are. The conventional way of expressing accuracy is by stating the maximum errors to which the system is subject; these may be expressed in terms of the variable being measured, but are more commonly given either as a percentage of the measured value, or as a percentage of the measuring range of the equipment. The latter method is generally preferred. If percentage of measured value is used as the accuracy criterion, the specification of accuracy becomes complex, and may give apparently alarming error figures at the lower end of the scale. Thus an instrument which indicates five units when it should indicate four units has an error of 25 per cent of the true reading; if, however, the range were 100 units, this error would represent only 1 per cent of f.s.d. The actual magnitude of the errors, in terms of units of the measured variable, is likely to be of the same order of magnitude throughout the measuring range of the equipment; errors expressed in terms of percentage of measured value are consequently large in the lower part of the measuring range. This part of the range should not be used if alternative methods of measurement, or alternative ranges, are available.

Any discussion of static accuracy inevitably introduces the concept of *reproducibility*. By reproducibility is meant the ability of the system to display the same reading for a given input, when this input is either presented to it on a series of different occasions, or is held constant over a long period. Other terms may be used to express the same quality, depending on the method of presentation of the input. Thus *repeatability* is used to express the system's ability to display the same output for a series of applications of the same input signal under defined conditions, the intervals between the applications being short; *stability* expresses the same quality for applications of inputs applied at longer intervals of separation; *constancy* is the term used to describe the ability of a system to hold a constant reading in response to a constant input, the conditions of the test (e.g. temperature) being varied in a specified manner. These terms, and others relating to the performance of measuring systems, are defined fully in ref. 1. Like accuracy, these qualities are expressed in terms of the errors which are incurred when tests of the specified types are carried out. Thus a statement such as 'constancy better than ± 1 per cent for 20–40°C' might be encountered in a specification, meaning that the response of the equipment to a sustained input will not vary more than ± 1 per cent of its full range for temperature variations within the limits 20°C to 40°C.

13.2 The nature and causes of static errors

In practice, the existence or non-existence of an error may be of less importance than a knowledge of the magnitude of the error—i.e., accuracy is often less important than reproducibility. A measuring system may have a large constant error, but provided this is known to the user, it may not detract greatly from the usefulness of the system. If, however, errors of a random nature are encountered, so that the user does not know the magnitude of the error at any particular time, the situation is much more serious. One useful classification of errors is therefore to divide them into *constant* and *random* errors respectively.

This classification is not in fact quite so clearly defined as might at first appear. Consider errors caused by temperature changes. Much measuring equipment—particularly electronic equipment—is subject to errors of this kind. If the equipment is used in a constant-temperature environment, the error, if any, will be constant; if, on the other hand, the temperature varies, the error would generally be regarded as random, unless the temperature were continuously measured and due corrections applied.

A further useful classification of errors consists in differentiating between those which are the responsibility of the user (*observer errors*) and those which are inherent in the measuring system. The problem of observer error is confined almost entirely to analogue indicators. Although the ability and attitude of the observer are factors contributing to this class of error, the magnitudes of the errors can be greatly reduced by attention to the design of the display. In particular, errors often result from parallax (i.e., the pointer being a finite distance in front of the scale, and the observer's eye not being on a line perpendicular to the plane of the scale and passing through the pointer), or from inappropriate choice of the number and arrangement of the scale markings. The optimum arrangement of scale markings and numerals depends on the application of the equipment, and on the class of user. A display layout suitable for an industrial panel instrument would not be appropriate for a research instrument designed for the highest possible reading accuracy. In the first instance rapid and frequent readings are required, and a reading error of 1 or 2 per cent may be acceptable; in the second case, only a few readings may be required, and ample time may be available. (If these conditions are not met, some form of automatic recording is normally employed.) The chief differences in the display presentation in the two cases would lie in the number and size of the markings. The panel instrument would have relatively few scale graduation marks, boldly presented to ensure quick and unambiguous reading. References 2 and 3 give extensive recommendations for the design of analogue displays.

13.2.1 *Effects of friction and hysteresis.* Although random errors cannot, by their very nature, be allowed for in taking readings from a display, it is sometimes possible to establish a maximum likely magnitude for such errors. A representative case is that of errors caused by friction in analogue indicators, such as moving-coil meters. Neglecting for the moment the question of friction, the operation of a meter of this kind depends on 'balancing' an input torque T_i, derived from the measured current, against a torque T_r produced by the torsion spring. The movement eventually comes to rest† in the position where $T_i = T_r$. As T_r is directly proportional to the deflection θ, the deflection gives a measure of the input torque, and therefore of the current from which that torque is derived.

† A *damping torque* is in fact required to bring it to rest (section 14.2). This torque operates only when the coil is in motion, and can be neglected here.

Now consider the effect of introducing a friction torque T_f in the bearings of the movement (Fig. 13.1). To determine the effect of this torque, it will be necessary to make some assumptions about the manner in which T_i is applied, to avoid becoming involved with dynamic problems.

Suppose T_i is applied by very slowly increasing the current input to the meter. In the absence of the friction torque, the pointer would move slowly upscale to some position OP, corresponding to the final value of the current. The friction torque, however, will cause it to stop short at a position OP_1, i.e., at an angular deflection $(\theta - \delta\theta)$ instead of the correct deflection θ. If the

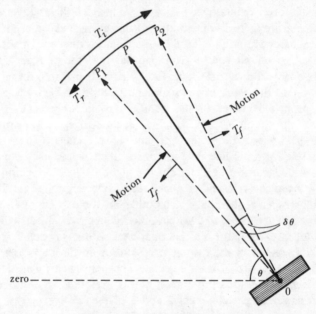

Figure 13.1   Effect of friction

spring stiffness is K, and since T_f will always operate to resist motion,† the condition for equilibrium is:

$$T_i = K(\theta - \delta\theta) + T_f$$

that is,

$$\delta\theta = (T_f/K) + \theta - (T_i/K)$$
$$= (T_f/K) \tag{13.1}$$

since $T_i = K\theta$.

Thus the angular error is proportional to the friction torque, and inversely proportional to the spring stiffness. In other words, the error is proportional to the friction torque and to the sensitivity of the movement, since the sensitivity is given by θ/T_i, and $\theta/T_i = 1/K$. A similar result would be obtained

† To simplify the argument which follows, differences between kinetic and static friction have been ignored.

if the input torque were reduced slowly from a high value, the movement then coming to rest at the position OP_2.

From the above discussion, it might appear that friction errors are not in fact random, but well defined. This is true only if the conditions of application of the input signal are closely controlled. In normal use, an observer seeing the pointer in the position OP does not know the direction of the friction torque acting on it, nor does he know whether or not the maximum friction torque is in fact being exerted. Suppose the pointer is in its correct position P with an input torque T_i acting on it. Under these circumstances, there will be no friction torque, since there is no tendency to move. Any change in the input torque will result in friction torque being developed, and no motion will ensue until the change in input torque is sufficient to overcome the maximum value T_f. Movement of the pointer will in fact commence when the value of T_i is that corresponding to one of the positions P_1 and P_2. Thus, an observer seeing the pointer in the position P knows only that it may represent a true reading somewhere between P_1 and P_2, and has no means of knowing what that true reading is, unless he has been able to control the input. Under normal circumstances, the error is therefore truly random, within the angular limits of $\pm \delta\theta$. The range of values of the measured variable corresponding to $2\,\delta\theta$ is often referred to as the *dead zone* of the instrument. It may not be entirely due to friction. Often elastic elements used in instruments, such as bellows units, exhibit hysteresis characteristics which produce effects similar to those of friction.

For simplicity, the above discussion of dead zone has been based on friction in a simple indicating instrument. Similar effects are experienced if any other part of the measuring system, such as an electro-mechanical transducer, suffers from friction or hysteresis.

Summary

The relative importance of the static and dynamic characteristics of a measuring system depends on the use to which it is to be put. In many static measuring situations, reproducibility is more important than accuracy.

Errors may be constant or random, and may be caused by the observer, the equipment, or environmental effects.

Friction and hysteresis in the mechanical parts of measuring systems cause a *dead zone*, which increases with increasing sensitivity.

References

1 BS 2643:1955, *Glossary of Terms Relating to the Performance of Measuring Instruments*.
2 BS 3693:1964:Part 1, *The Design of Scales and Indexes*.
3 BS 3693:1969:Part 2, *The Design of Scales and Indexes*.

14. Dynamic performance

A measuring system with inherent static errors will, in general, still experience these errors when subjected to a rapidly changing input. However, if the system is incapable of responding at the required speed, dynamic errors will be introduced which may be far more serious than the static errors.

The main reason for dynamic errors is that virtually all measuring systems contain mechanical moving parts, which are displaced by forces derived from the input signal. Often these moving parts are in the display, though they may also be in the transducer or in signal-conditioning elements. As the forces derived from the input cannot be infinite, the displacement takes place with a finite acceleration, as determined by Newton's second law. Thus, if an instantaneous change of input occurs, there cannot be a corresponding change in the response; it must lag behind in some way which can be determined mathematically if sufficient data are available. This type of lag may be described as being due to *mechanical inertia*. Similar lags may arise from other causes—e.g., in temperature measurements, delay inevitably occurs in the response of transducers because of their own thermal capacities, and of the thermal capacity and thermal resistance of any protective material with which they are surrounded. This effect is sometimes referred to as *thermal inertia*.

An instantaneous change in the input is in fact impossible in practice, though measurements sometimes have to be made of variables which change in a manner which is very nearly instantaneous. At lower rates of change, lag problems still arise, but become progressively less significant as the rate of change of the measured variable decreases. There is consequently a problem in assessing the likely magnitude of dynamic errors, since in general the rate of change of the measured variable is not known before the measurement is made.

14.1 Test inputs

It is necessary to have criteria for judging the suitability of a particular measuring system for dynamic measurements, and for comparing the merits of alternative equipments. The criteria conventionally employed are the responses to certain specified input signals. Three types of signal have become established for this purpose: the *step*, or instantaneous change of input; the *ramp*, or steadily increasing input; and the *sinusoidal* input. These three forms of input are represented graphically in Fig. 14.1.

It is possible to predict theoretically what the response of a particular system to these inputs will be. However, before treating the problem mathematically, it is worth considering what type of response would be expected from experience. Suppose a conventional moving-coil ammeter were used, and the three types of signal represented in Fig. 14.1 were applied to it in turn.

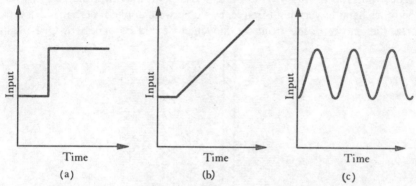

Figure 14.1 Standard test inputs: (a) step; (b) ramp; (c) sinusoid

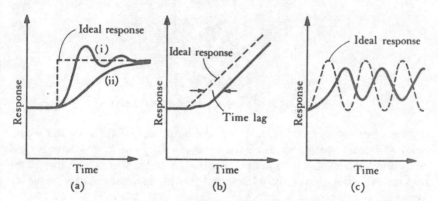

Figure 14.2 Responses to standard inputs

On applying the step, the instrument pointer will not instantaneously take up the true measured value. It requires a finite time to reach this value, and may first overshoot it, possibly making a number of swings before finally settling down. Thus the response of the meter to a step input is likely to take one of the two forms illustrated in Fig. 14.2a.

The response of the meter to a ramp input is less easy to predict, partly because ramp signals are not commonly encountered in practice. In fact the response is of the form shown in Fig. 14.2b, i.e., a parallel ramp lagging behind the input ramp. The magnitude of this lag depends both on the characteristics of the meter movement and on the rate of change of the input.

Similarly, the response to a sinusoidal input depends on its rate of change—i.e., on its frequency. It is again possible to predict the general nature of the response. Consider again a moving-coil meter, but with a centre zero, so that it is capable of measuring current in either direction. If a very low-frequency signal were applied—with, say, a frequency of one cycle per hour—the movement would follow this without difficulty, and with no appreciable lag. If, on the other hand, a very high-frequency signal were applied, perhaps of several kHz, then no response from the movement could be expected. One might

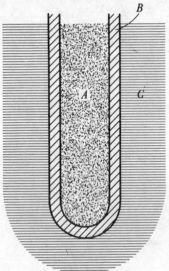

Figure 14.3 Temperature-sensitive element

deduce from these considerations that the amplitude of the response would steadily decrease with increasing frequency. This is not always true, as will be seen in Section 14.2.5. As in the other two cases, there is a lag between the response and the input (Fig. 14.2c), and this lag increases as the frequency increases.

14.2 Analytical approach to system response

The theoretical responses of measuring systems may be calculated from their equations of motion, provided the constants which occur in these equations can be evaluated with sufficient accuracy. The dynamic behaviour of most systems or parts of systems can be represented, at least approximately, by first-order or second-order differential equations.

14.2.1 First-order system. A simple temperature transducer provides a convenient example of a system element which can be represented by a first-order differential equation. Consider the element illustrated in Fig.14.3, which could be the bulb of a mercury-in-steel thermometer. If the sensitive material A (and hence the indicated temperature) is to respond correctly to a change in the temperature of the material C, it must itself experience the same change; this can be achieved only if the necessary heat is conducted through the container B to bring the temperature of A to the new level.

Suppose a step change θ_i occurs in the temperature of the surrounding material. A relationship is required giving the resulting change, θ_o, in the temperature of the material A, at any time t after making the step change. Heat will be conducted through B at a rate determined by the temperature difference across it, its thermal conductivity, and its physical dimensions; the temperature rise of material A will also depend on these factors, plus its own mass and specific heat. However, all these quantities, except the temperature difference, remain constant. The rate of change of θ_o is therefore given by

$$\frac{d\theta_o}{dt} = k(\theta_i - \theta_o)$$

where k is a constant for the system, or

$$\frac{d\theta_o}{(\theta_i - \theta_o)} = k\,dt$$

that is,

$$\log_e (\theta_i - \theta_o) = -kt + C$$

The value of the integration constant C may be found by using the condition that $\theta_o = 0$ when $t = 0$, the equation eventually reducing to

$$\theta_o = \theta_i (1 - e^{-kt}). \tag{14.1}$$

This response is illustrated in Fig. 14.4a. Since, theoretically, θ_o never reaches the value θ_i, some criterion is required by which the speed of this type of response can be specified. The criterion which is almost universally employed is the *time constant*, defined as the time to reach 63·2 per cent of the true value. The choice of 63·2 per cent has a theoretical basis and is mathematically convenient, since the time constant is numerically equal to $1/k$, k being the constant in eq. (14.1). In practical terms, the time constant is the time which would be required to reach the true value if the response continued at its initial rate (Fig. 14.4b). If the initial rate of change of θ_o were continued, the response would follow the path OP. The time to reach P would be represented by OQ, which therefore represents the time constant. In fact after this time θ_o will have reached only the value represented by QS, which may be shown to be 63·2 per cent of θ_i.

Electrical temperature transducers (thermocouples and resistance thermometers) may not follow eq. (14.1) exactly; if a protective sheath is used, heat transfer has to take place through two or more media in series, since the sensitive element seldom makes good thermal contact with the sheath. The time constant criterion—defined as the time to reach 63·2 per cent of the full response—is nevertheless often used for these transducers.

The time constants of some sheathed temperature transducers may well be of the order of 20s if the sheaths are made from refractory material. Such poor response can completely invalidate measurements of rapidly changing temperatures.

The problem of heat transfer considered here is mathematically identical to that of an electrical capacitor being charged through a resistor from a voltage step input. (The use of this circuit as a timing device is discussed in

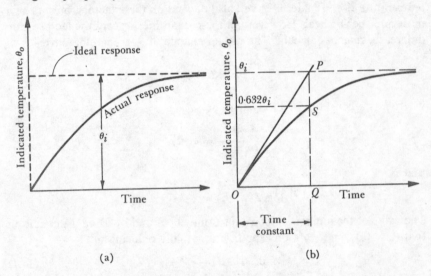

(a)   (b)

Figure 14.4   First-order response

section 11.1.2.) In this case, the voltage developed across the capacitor corresponds to θ_o in eq. (14.1). For this reason, first-order lags are sometimes referred to as RC (resistance–capacitance) lags, the time constant in this case being in fact numerically equal to RC. The term *exponential lag* is also used.

The behaviour of a first-order system is well defined by stating only its time constant in response to a step input. No consideration will be given here to the responses of a first-order system to other forms of input. (The response to a sinusoidal input is in fact similar to that of an over-damped second-order system, discussed below.)

14.2.2   Second-order system. In section 14.1, the moving-coil meter was taken as an example in discussing the expected responses of a measuring system to the standard forms of test input. The nature of the forces acting on a movement of this kind is similar to that of the forces acting on most analogue display instruments. A general system will therefore be considered, in which an input torque T_i is measured by 'balancing' it against a resisting torque T_r. Friction torque, which was considered in section 13.2 will be ignored, on the assumption that it is small in comparison with the other torques exerted on the movement. However, it will be seen that it is essential to apply a *damping torque* to the system. Unlike friction, damping is introduced deliberately, to improve dynamic response. The essential feature of damping torque is that it is proportional to *velocity* (angular velocity in the case considered here); it is thus inoperative when the system is at rest, and does not affect static accuracy.

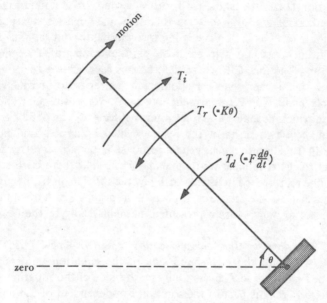

Figure 14.5 **Torques on meter movement**

Damping may be introduced in practice by arranging for all or part of a mechanism to be immersed in a suitable fluid, since the viscous forces acting on a body moving through a fluid are proportional to the velocity of the body. For electrical movements, damping may also be obtained by electrical means (section 5.1.4).

The damping torque T_d may therefore be expressed as $F(d\theta_o/dt)$, where θ_o is the deflection of the movement, and F is a constant for a particular system called the *damping coefficient*. Similarly, the resisting torque T_r is usually proportional to θ_o (it is often produced by a mechanical spring) and may be written as $K\theta_o$, K being constant. The dynamic behaviour of the system is then determined by the equation

net torque = (polar moment of inertia) × (angular acceleration).

229

From Fig. 14.5, it can be seen that this equation may be written:

$$T_i - K\theta_o - F\frac{d\theta}{dt} = J\frac{d^2\theta_o}{dt^2}$$

or

$$\left(D^2 + \frac{F}{J}D + \frac{K}{J}\right)\theta_o = \frac{T_i}{J} \tag{14.2}$$

using the conventional D operator—i.e., putting D in place of d/dt, and D^2 in place of d^2/dt^2.

Equation (14.2) is a standard form of second-order differential equation. The method of solution may be found in mathematical textbooks of the appropriate level or in books dealing with mechanical vibrations (e.g., ref. 1). The solution consists of two parts–the particular integral (P.I.) and the complementary function (C.F.). The C.F. always represents a decaying transient function—i.e., it represents a response which after a certain time will become negligibly small. The P.I. represents the *steady-state* or regular pattern of the response which becomes apparent after the decay of the C.F. The difference between these two parts of the response may be appreciated by reference to Fig. 14.2a. Here the *steady-state* response is the constant reading corresponding to the true measured value (assuming that there is no static error); this will be represented mathematically by the P.I. The initial departures from this true reading—i.e., those early parts of the graphs which do not correspond to the ideal response—are represented mathematically by the C.F.

14.2.3 Transient solution (complementary function). The C.F. is the solution of eq. (14.2) with the right-hand side of the equation put equal to zero. Since the input torque T_i occurs only on this side of the equation, this means that the *form* of this part of the solution is independent of the type of input. (This does not mean that the C.F.s for all inputs are identical; the C.F. always contains two arbitrary constants which must be evaluated by using the known physical conditions of the problem, after the P.I. has been found.)

The general solution for the C.F. of eq. (14.2) is:

$$\theta_o = A_1 e^{\alpha t} + A_2 e^{\beta t}, \tag{14.3}$$

where A_1 and A_2 are the arbitrary constants and

$$\alpha = -\frac{F}{2J} + \left[\frac{F^2}{4J^2} - \frac{K}{J}\right]^{\frac{1}{2}}$$

$$\beta = -\frac{F}{2J} - \left[\frac{F^2}{4J^2} - \frac{K}{J}\right]^{\frac{1}{2}}$$

Some appreciation of the practical meaning of this solution may be obtained from inspection of the expressions for α and β. Note that the quantity in the brackets may have positive or negative values. If it is negative, the solution is 'imaginary', and is rearranged into the form given in eq. (14.4); if it is positive, it is always numerically less than $F/2J$, so that the value of both α and β must in fact be negative. Thus each term of the solution, for positive values of $(F^2/4J^2 - K/J)$, represents a decaying exponential curve, since the numerical values of both α and β increase with t. Note that the condition that $(F^2/4J^2 - K/J)$ should be positive reduces to $F^2 > 4JK$.

When the indices of eq. (14.3) contain imaginary parts—i.e., when $F^2 < 4JK$, the solution may be written in the form:

$$\theta_o = Ce^{-(F/2J)t} \cos\left[\sqrt{\frac{K}{J} - \frac{F^2}{4J^2}} \cdot t - \phi\right] \qquad (14.4)$$

C and ϕ now being the arbitrary constants. It can be seen by inspection of eq. (14.4) that it represents a sinusoidal function of frequency

$$[1/2\pi]\ [K/J - F^2/4J^2]^{\frac{1}{2}}$$

and that, because the index of e becomes more negative as t increases, the amplitude of the wave finally decays to zero.

14.2.4 *Complete solution—step input.* Unlike the C.F., the P.I. is dependent on the form of the input. It is therefore necessary to specify the type of input in order to obtain the complete solution to the equation. Step and sinusoidal inputs will be considered here; ramp inputs, though used to some extent in the related field of servomechanisms, are used relatively rarely for measuring systems, and will not be discussed further.

For the step-input $T_i = S$ (S being constant), the P.I. is equal to S/K. Physically, this expresses the fact that the final reading is the same as would be obtained if the torque S had been applied under 'static' conditions. It is convenient to use the symbol θ_i in place of S/K—i.e., θ_i represents the 'correct' response to the input torque T_i.

It was stated in section 14.2.3 that the C.F. takes one of two possible forms, depending on whether F^2 is greater or less than $4JK$. Consider first the case for which $F^2 > 4JK$. Adding the P.I. for a step input to the C.F. of eq. (14.2) gives the complete solution

$$\theta_o = \theta_i + A_1 e^{\alpha t} + A_2 e^{\beta t} \qquad (14.5)$$

In a particular practical case, the constants A_1 and A_2 have to be evaluated using the known conditions that when $t = 0$, both θ_o and $d\theta_o/dt$ are also 0, since a system having mass cannot acquire an instantaneous velocity.

If this is done for a system provided with variable damping—i.e., with K and J constant, but F variable —a series of response curves of the type shown in Fig. 14.6 will be obtained. It will be noted that as the value of F is decreased, the speed of response increases. The fastest response represented by eq. (14.5) is that corresponding to $F^2 = 4JK$; this particular response is referred to as being *critically damped*, and the corresponding value of F, which will be denoted by F_0, is called the critical damping coefficient.

It is customary to express other degrees of damping in terms of the *damping ratio*, c, defined by

$$F = cF_0 = c\sqrt{4JK}. \tag{14.6}$$

The advantage of working in terms of c rather than F is that it allows generalization of the results, so that conclusions can be drawn which will be relevant to *any* measuring system governed by an equation of the same form as eq. (14.2). To complete the generalization, it is necessary to introduce

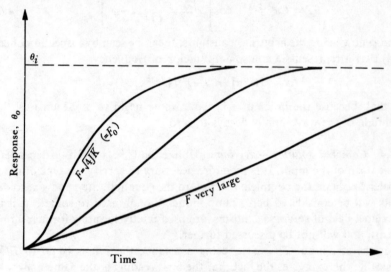

Figure 14.6   Overdamped step responses

another quantity, ω_n, the *undamped angular natural frequency* of the system.

To clarify the meaning of ω_n, consider the case of the oscillatory response to a step input, represented by the P.I. $= \theta_i$ and the C.F. of eq. (14.4). The complete solution is then

$$\theta_o = \theta_i + Ce^{-(F/2J)t} \cos\left[\sqrt{\frac{K}{J}-\frac{F^2}{4J^2}}\cdot t - \phi\right] \tag{14.7}$$

For an undamped system, $F = 0$, so this reduces to

$$\theta_o = \theta_i + C\cos\left(\sqrt{K/J}.\,t - \phi\right) \tag{14.8}$$

Using the initial conditions $\theta_o = 0$, $t = 0$ and $d\theta_o/dt = 0$, $t = 0$ gives $C = -\theta_i$ and $\phi = 0$, so that (14.8) may be written

$$\theta_o = \theta_i\left(1 - \cos\sqrt{K/J}.\,t\right) \tag{14.9}$$

Equation (14.9) represents a sinusoidal response with mean value and

232

amplitude both equal to θ_i. The point of particular interest here is the angular frequency of this sinusoidal response, ω_n, which by inspection is $\sqrt{K/J}$ (i.e., the actual frequency f_n is $\sqrt{K/J}/2\pi$, since in general $\omega = 2\pi f$).

Using eq. (14.6) and this value of ω_n, the two coefficients on the left-hand side of eq. (14.2) (F/J and K/J respectively) may be expressed in terms of c and ω_n. Also, since in this case $T_i = K\theta_i$, the right-hand side becomes $K\theta_i/J$. The result of expressing the coefficients on both sides in terms of c and ω_n is then

$$D^2\theta_o + 2c\omega_n D\theta_o + \omega_n{}^2\theta_o = \omega_n{}^2\theta_i \qquad (14.10)$$

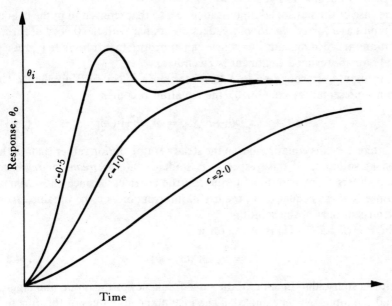

Figure 14.7   Effect of damping ratio on step responses

This is a general equation which may be applied to any system in which the resisting force or torque is proportional to θ_o and the damping force or torque is proportional to $d\theta_o/dt$. In particular, it can be applied to various transducers, such as those based on strain gauges and piezo-electric crystals.

At first sight, it might appear that the two newly introduced quantities, c and ω_n, are somewhat abstract and difficult to evaluate. In practice it is usually easier to determine these quantities, by suitable dynamic tests, than it would be to determine F, K, and J.

For the remainder of this discussion of dynamic performance, the generalized eq. (14.10) will be used. Firstly, it is instructive to reconsider the step-function responses of Fig. 14.6, expressing the damping in terms of c rather than F, and including a curve for a value of $c < 1$. This has been done in Fig. 14.7. If it is assumed that the requirement in the case of a step input is that the final value should be reached in the minimum time, it can be seen that a value of $c<1$ is desirable, though this will necessarily allow some overshoot. In most measuring systems there is no serious objection to overshoot.

14.2.5 Complete solution—sinusoidal input. In practice, sinusoidal test inputs are more widely used than step inputs. Suitable variable-frequency electrical sine-wave generators are readily available to provide the input signals, and if a non-electrical signal is required, the problem of conversion is usually not too difficult—e.g., commercial equipment is available to convert electrical to pneumatic signals.

The case of the sinusoidal input is identical to that referred to in the field of mechanics as a *forced vibration*. Readers unfamiliar with the theory of forced vibrations are recommended to consult an appropriate text book (e.g., ref. 1), as only an abbreviated treatment is given here.

If an input corresponding to a 'true' response $\bar{\theta}_i \sin \omega t$ is applied to the system represented by eq. (14.10), the equation becomes

$$D^2\theta_o + 2c\omega_n D\theta_o + \omega_n^2\theta_o = \omega_n^2\bar{\theta}_i \sin \omega t \qquad (14.11)$$

The interest in this equation lies in the steady-state solution rather than in the transient solution. In this respect sinusoidal-input (or *frequency-response*) testing differs from step-input testing; in the latter case, since the ultimate response is always equal to θ_i, the useful information is to be obtained from the transient part of the solution.

The P.I. of eq. (14.11) is of the form

$$\theta_o = \bar{\theta}_o \sin (\omega t - \psi) \qquad (14.12)$$

i.e., it is a sinusoidal function of the same frequency as the input, and lagging behind the input by some angle ψ. The instantaneous values of this function are of little interest—the useful data are the amplitude $\bar{\theta}_o$ and the angle of lag ψ. Ideally $\bar{\theta}_o$ would be equal to $\bar{\theta}_i$, and ψ would be zero. It is not possible to realize both of these conditions in practice, except at very low frequencies (theoretically only at zero frequency).

The conventional way of showing the variations of $\bar{\theta}_o$ is to plot the amplitude ratio $\bar{\theta}_o/\bar{\theta}_i$ against frequency; the results may again be generalized if, instead of plotting against the true frequency, the frequency ratio ω/ω_n is used. If this ratio is denoted by u, the following results may be derived from the P.I. of eq. (14.11):

$$\frac{\bar{\theta}_o}{\bar{\theta}_i} = \frac{1}{[(1-u^2)^2 + 4c^2u^2]^{\frac{1}{2}}} \qquad (14.13)$$

$$\psi = \tan^{-1}\left[\frac{2cu}{1-u^2}\right] \qquad (14.14)$$

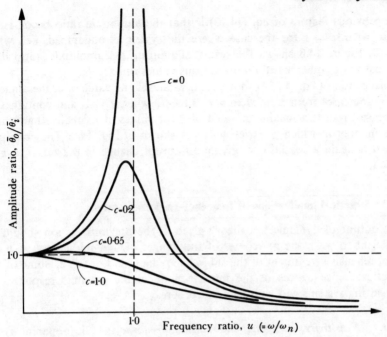

Figure 14.8   Relation between amplitude ratio and frequency

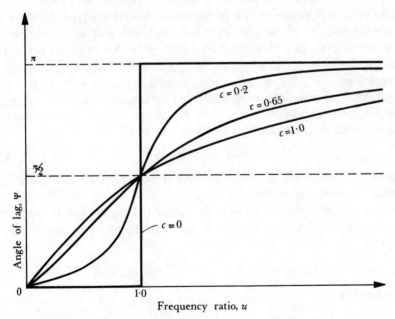

Figure 14.9   Relation between phase lag and frequency

One obvious feature of eq. (14.13) is that the amplitude ratio becomes infinite when $u = 1$ for the case where the system is undamped, i.e., when $c = 0$. Figure 14.8 shows the result of plotting the amplitude ratio θ_o/θ_i against the frequency ratio u for various values of c.

Inspection of eq. (14.14) shows that, whatever the value of c, the angle of lag ψ increases from zero when $u = 0$ to $\pi/2$ when $u = 1$, and continues to increase towards a maximum value of π for values of u greater than unity. The manner in which ψ varies with c is shown in Fig. 14.9. The condition $c = 0$ is again a special one, giving an abrupt change in ψ from 0 to π at $u = 1$.

14.3 Practical implications of frequency-response results

The outline of dynamic test theory given in the previous section should be sufficient to warn the newcomer of the danger of dynamic errors. A more comprehensive treatment of the subject may be found in ref. 2. Some of the practical consequences of the imperfections in the dynamic responses of measuring systems will be briefly noted here.

14.3.1 Sensitivity, damping, and natural frequency. It is apparent from Fig. 14.8 that, for any particular damping ratio, the range of frequencies over which the amplitude ratio θ_o/θ_i remains acceptably near unity increases as the value of ω_n increases. A high value of ω_n is therefore generally desirable. Unfortunately, a high value of ω_n is not compatible with high sensitivity.

Consider first the undamped case. Equation (14.9) shows that in this case the angular natural frequency, ω_n, is $\sqrt{K/J}$. But sensitivity is defined as output/input, or θ_i/T_i in the case considered here, where T_i is the steady applied torque which produces an output deflection θ_i. As $T_i = K\theta_i$, sensitivity is inversely proportional to K. If J is constant, ω_n is therefore inversely proportional to the square root of sensitivity, or

$$\text{sensitivity} \propto 1/\omega_n^2 \qquad (14.15)$$

There is consequently a design problem if both high sensitivity and high natural frequency are called for.

For a damped system, eq. (14.7) shows that the angular natural frequency, ω_d, is $\sqrt{K/J - F^2/4J^2}$. Using the same substitutions as in section 14.2.4, namely,

$$\omega_n = \sqrt{K/J} \quad \text{and} \quad c = F/\sqrt{4JK}$$

this becomes

$$\omega_d = \omega_n\sqrt{1-c^2} \qquad (14.16)$$

Thus, the value of ω_d decreases as c increases. The conflict between sensitivity

236

and natural frequency remains, as in the undamped case, though the simple relationship (14.15) no longer holds.

14.3.2 Optimum damping. The best value of the damping factor c depends to some extent on the manner in which the measured value varies. In the general measuring situation, this is not known in advance; it is therefore customary to set c to a value which gives both good step response and 'flat'

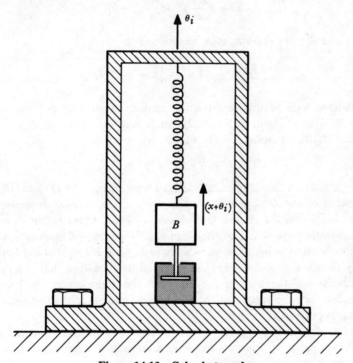

Figure 14.10   Seismic transducer

frequency response. Assuming that step response is required to give the fastest 'settling time'—i.e., the least time between the application of the step and the indication of a steady value—the optimum value of c is about 0·65. The frequency response with this value of c is then acceptably flat up to about 60 per cent of the undamped natural frequency f_n (Fig. 14.8).

14.3.3 Seismic transducer (displacement mode). Mention was made in section 11.6.2 of the use of seismic transducers for measurements of vibration amplitude. The dynamics of seismic transducers are almost identical to those of the generalized second-order system discussed in section 14.2; some slight differences arise because the measured output is proportional to the displacement of the mass M (Fig. 11.12) *relative* to the body of the transducer, rather than to its absolute displacement in space. Suppose the input displacement (i.e., body movement) is θ_i, and the displacement of the mass relative to the body is x, upward movement being regarded as positive (Fig. 14.10). If K is the spring stiffness and F the damping coefficient, the spring and damping forces acting on the mass will be $-xK$ and $-F\,dx/dt$ respectively. Since the absolute displacement of the mass is $(\theta_i + x)$, the equation of motion is

$$-Kx - F\frac{dx}{dt} = M\frac{d^2}{dt}(x + \theta_i)$$

which, using the D notation, may be reduced to

$$\left(D^2 + \frac{F}{M}D + \frac{M}{K}\right)x = -D^2\theta_i \qquad (14.17)$$

The left-hand side of this equation is mathematically identical to that of eq. (14.2). Using arguments exactly analogous to those used to derive equation (14.10), equation (14.17) may be written

$$(D^2 + 2c\omega_n D + \omega_n^2)x = -D^2\theta_i \qquad (14.18)$$

It will be noted that the significant difference between eqs. (14.18) and (14.10) is the presence of the D^2 operator on the right-hand side. Now suppose, as is often the case, that the seismic transducer is used for measurements of sinusoidal vibrations. θ_i is then of the form $\bar{\theta}_i \sin \omega t$, and $-D^2\theta_i$ is $\omega^2\bar{\theta}_i \sin \omega t$. When this term is substituted for the right-hand side, eq. (14.18) becomes virtually identical to eq. (14.11). The only differences are that the relative linear displacement x has replaced θ_o, and the right-hand side has been multiplied by u^2, the square of the frequency ratio, which is constant for a particular input signal.

Reference to a suitable text on forced vibrations indicates that the phase lag of the output x with respect to the input θ_i is as given in eq. (14.14), and that the amplitude ratio is given by

$$\frac{\bar{x}}{\bar{\theta}_i} = \frac{u^2}{[(1-u^2)^2 + 4\,c^2u^2]^{\frac{1}{2}}} = \frac{1}{[(1/u^2 - 1)^2 + 4\,c^2/u^2]^{\frac{1}{2}}} \qquad (14.19)$$

Inspection of eq. (14.19) shows that if u is very large, the amplitude ratio is approximately equal to unity, irrespective of the value of c; also, from eq. (14.14), it can be seen that the tangent of the angle of lag becomes very small and negative as u becomes large—i.e., the lag approaches 180°. These results confirm the statements made in section 11.6.2, namely that, for high values of u, the mass is effectively a reference fixed in space. (The displacement of the mass in space at any instant is the vector sum of x and θ_i; since $\psi \simeq 180°$, and $x \simeq \theta_i$, the peak values of x and θ_i occur virtually simultaneously, but in opposite senses.) An output proportional to the relative displacement x may therefore be used as a measure of θ_i.

238

The results above were obtained on the assumption that u was 'very large'. For the optimum value of c (about 0·65) errors are in fact scarcely significant if $u > 2$, and for $u > 10$, errors are negligible for most purposes, irrespective of the value of c. It will be apparent that the general usefulness of the seismic transducer as a displacement measuring device is increased as ω_n is decreased, since this permits its use over a wider range of frequencies. Comparison of eqs. (14.17) and (14.2) shows that, by analogy with eq. (14.8), the undamped angular natural frequency of the seismic transducer is given by $\omega_n = \sqrt{K/M}$. The value of ω_n may therefore be decreased by reducing the spring stiffness K and/or increasing the mass M. There are practical objections to increasing M in many applications—e.g., the mass of the transducer, being added to that of the vibrating body, may be sufficient to modify the nature of the vibration appreciably.

14.3.4 *Seismic transducer (acceleration mode)*.

It was stated in section 11.6.2 that the seismic transducer may be used to measure acceleration, the requirement in this respect for vibration applications being a *high* value of ω_n. A brief justification of this statement is given below.

Again considering the case of the sinusoidal input, if $\theta_i = \bar{\theta}_i \sin \omega t$, the acceleration is $-\omega^2 \bar{\theta} \sin \omega t$, and the *maximum* acceleration is $\pm \omega^2 \bar{\theta}_i$. Now eq. (14.19) may be rewritten

$$\bar{x} = \frac{\omega^2 \bar{\theta}_i}{\omega_n^2 [(1-u^2)^2 + 4c^2 u^2]^{\frac{1}{2}}}$$

or

$$\frac{\bar{x}}{\omega^2 \bar{\theta}_i} = \frac{1}{\omega_n^2} \frac{1}{[(1-u^2)^2 + 4c^2 u^2]^{\frac{1}{2}}} \tag{14.20}$$

For the device to work satisfactorily as an acceleration transducer, a relationship of the type $\bar{x} = k\omega^2 \bar{\theta}_i$ is required, k being constant. The response represented by (14.20) will therefore be satisfactory if the right-hand side of the equation is constant.

Comparing eq. (14.20) with eq. (14.13), the right-hand sides of the two equations are in fact identical, apart from the multiplying factor $1/\omega_n^2$ in eq. (14.20). This factor is constant for a given transducer. Hence, the condition that the right-hand side of eq. (14.20) should be constant is that the right-hand side of eq. (14.13) should be constant.

This quantity has already been plotted against u in Fig. 14.8, and the conditions under which it may be regarded as effectively constant (actually equal to unity) have already been discussed in connection with the dynamic performance of the general second-order system. The conditions for satisfactory frequency response of the seismic accelerometer are therefore the same as those for the general second-order system. In the optimum-damping case, the condition is that the input frequency should not exceed about 60 per cent of the natural frequency of the transducer. Thus the general usefulness of the

239

seismic transducer as an accelerometer may be increased by increasing its natural frequency, assuming that the corresponding reduction in sensitivity can be tolerated (section 14.3.1).

For a seismic accelerometer in which a significant displacement of the mass occurs, as in strain-gauge types, it is possible to design the transducer for optimum damping, and this is customarily done. In piezo accelerometers, it is not feasible to build in the required damping, because of the extremely small displacement of the mass: only the inherent damping of the crystal, corresponding to a damping factor of about 0·2, can be exploited. The restriction this imposes on the useful frequency range can be seen from Fig. 14.8; it applies equally to other piezo devices, such as pressure transducers, which can be represented by eq. (14.10). It is generally considered that piezo transducers of all types can be used satisfactorily only up to about one fifth of their natural frequencies.

As it has been emphasized that the mass displacement in a piezo transducer is small, it might be questioned whether the analysis above, showing displacement to be proportional to acceleration, would be relevant to piezo accelerometers. However, it will be recalled that it is the *strain* in the piezo crystal which produces the charge, and this strain is in fact proportional to the displacement of the mass relative to the case.

14.3.5 Interpreting frequency-response data.
The importance to the average user of an understanding of dynamic testing lies mainly in the necessity of interpreting manufacturers' data when assessing equipment for a particular application. Quoted data is usually based on frequency response tests, and is often limited to the frequency range over which the equipment is said to have a flat frequency response. In certain cases, where the damping may be adjusted by the user, the value of the undamped natural frequency may also be given. This will usually be given as f_n, the frequency in Hz, rather than as the angular frequency ω_n which has been used in the analysis above.

The term 'flat frequency response' refers to a diagram in which the amplitude ratio is plotted against frequency, as in Fig. 14.11. This is basically similar to Fig. 14.8 except that it is plotted to a base of true frequency, f, rather than the frequency ratio u. The curve shown represents a system with a damping ratio of about 0·6.

If it is required to make quantitive measurements at various frequencies using the system represented by Fig. 14.11, it can be done with acceptable accuracy only if the amplitude ratio remains close to unity, i.e. if the graph remains approximately flat. No value of c will in fact give a truly flat response. A decision must therefore be made regarding the acceptable departure of the amplitude ratio from unity. The range over which the response is said to be flat depends on this decision. If the lines *AA* and *BB* (Fig. 14.11) represent the acceptable tolerance, the nominally flat range will obviously be less than if the lines *CC* and *DD* had been chosen.

If, therefore, a range of frequencies for a flat frequency response is specified, it is meaningful only if the tolerance band is given. The most straightforward method of doing this is to give it as a percentage—e.g., to make a statement of the type 'frequency response flat 0–200 Hz within ± 2 per cent'. This is in fact the method normally employed for mechanical systems. For electronic equipment, however, it is common practice to express the departures from the ideal response in terms of *decibels*. The relationship between two values V_1 and V_2 of any variable may be expressed as $20 \log_{10} (V_1/V_2)$ decibels. This apparently arbitrary definition originated in the field of telecommunications, where there are better reasons for using it than can be found in the field of measurements. Thus, in a specification for a piece of

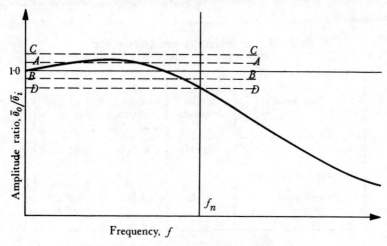

Figure 14.11   Typical frequency-response curve

electronic equipment, a statement such as 'frequency response better than 3 dB down (or -3 dB) at 10 kHz' might occur. In terms of the symbols used earlier in this chapter this means that, at 10 kHz, $20 \log_{10} \bar{\theta}_o/\bar{\theta}_i$ is numerically less than 3.

14.4   Typical frequency-response data

Having discussed dynamic response in general terms, a few typical figures relating to equipment described in earlier chapters will now be given for the purpose of comparison.

14.4.1   *Transducers.* Transducer responses do not necessarily follow eq.
(14.2). Some, like the majority of temperature transducers, respond in an approximately 'first-order' manner as described in section 14.2.1. However, most transducers in which displacement takes place against an 'elastic'

restraining force may be described fairly accurately by eq. (14.2), or by eq. (14.17) in the case of seismic devices.

Pressure transducers represent a typical case. The problem of obtaining adequate dynamic response in pressure-measuring systems has become very apparent in the testing of reciprocating engines. Traditionally, the engine-indicator used for slow-speed steam and gas engines was a spring-loaded piston driving a pen through a mechanical linkage. The dynamic response of this system would be completely inadequate for modern high-speed engines, for which transducers based on strain gauges or piezo crystals are employed. The relative merits of these devices were discussed in section 8.6. Some typical dynamic performance figures are given in Table 14.1. As a contrast, a representative 'static' measuring device—a mercury manometer—has been included in the table.

Table 14.1 Dynamic characteristics of some typical pressure transducers

Transducer	Undamped natural frequency	Flat frequency response (± 2 per cent)	Damping
Piezo	200 kHz	40 kHz	Inherent ($c \simeq 0{\cdot}2$)
Diaphragm–strain gauge	50 kHz	30 kHz	Optimum ($c \simeq 0{\cdot}65$)
Mercury manometer	1 Hz	0·6 Hz	Optimum ($c \simeq 0{\cdot}65$)

14.4.2 Displays. If full benefit is to be obtained from the high-speed characteristics of a transducer, the response of the display must be comparably fast.

The ultimate in high-speed displays is the oscilloscope (section 5.3), which is sufficiently fast to respond satisfactorily to any mechanically generated signals. (Oscilloscopes do have frequency-response limitations, but these are unlikely to restrict their use for measuring mechanical phenomena.) The main disadvantage of the oscilloscope is that it does not readily provide a permanent record. Where records of rapidly changing variables are required, u.v. recorders (section 5.1.3) are commonly used. Being electro-mechanical, u.v. recorders have frequency limitations which have to be considered in dynamic measuring applications. Further, the damping of u.v. galvanometers for dynamic applications must be arranged for optimum response (section 5.1.4).

It was shown in section 14.3.1 that the requirements for good frequency response and high sensitivity in a second-order system, such as a galvanometer movement, are in conflict. Makers of u.v. recorders therefore offer a range of interchangeable galvanometers, so that an optimum combination of sensitivity and frequency response can be chosen for a particular application. Some typical figures showing how the undamped natural frequency varies with sensitivity are shown in Table 14.2. The figures in the table do not follow the relationship predicted in section 14.3.1 exactly, because the relationship (14.15) was derived on the assumption that J, the polar moment of inertia, remained constant. In practice, J does not remain constant for a range of galvanometers, since physical dimensions, the number of turns, and the gauge of the wire may be varied.

Some typical comparative frequency response figures for three common electrical display instruments are given in Table 14.3. As in Table 14.1, the third example, the commercial milliammeter, is a 'static' type of instrument, included as a contrast with the other two 'dynamic' instruments.

Table 14.2 Typical sensitivity and undamped natural-frequency figures for u.v. galvanometers

Natural frequency (Hz)	100	1000	5000
Sensitivity mm/mA	2000	10	0·7

Table 14.3 Frequency responses of displays

Display	Undamped natural frequency	Flat frequency-response range	Damping
Oscilloscope	—	0–3 MHz (-3 dB)	—
U.V. recorder	1000 Hz	0–600 Hz (± 2 per cent)	$c = 0·65$
0–10 mA meter	2 Hz	0–1 Hz (± 2 per cent)	As found

Summary

When measuring systems are subjected to rapidly changing inputs, dynamic errors may occur. The main cause of these errors is mechanical inertia, or thermal inertia in the case of temperature transducers.

The response of a simple temperature transducer to a step input follows an exponential curve. Speed of response is defined by the time constant—the time to reach 63·2 per cent of the true response. This type of response is referred to as *first order*, since it can be represented by a first-order differential equation.

Systems in which mechanical displacement occurs can usually be represented with reasonable accuracy by second-order differential equations, and are consequently known as *second order* systems. The dynamic responses of such systems may be tested conveniently by step or sinusoidal inputs. The responses to these inputs depend on how much damping is applied. If heavily damped, the step response of a second-order system is similar to that of a first-order system; if lightly damped, the response overshoots the true value and oscillates about it before finally settling down. The response is said to be critically damped if a further reduction in the damping coefficient would produce an oscillatory response. The ratio of the actual damping coefficient to the critical damping coefficient is called the damping ratio.

The response of a second-order system to a sinusoidal input is a sinusoidal output. In general, the amplitude of the output differs from the amplitude of the ideal output, and lags behind it. The ratio of actual amplitude to ideal amplitude at a particular frequency provides a useful criterion for judging dynamic performance. The value of this ratio depends on the damping ratio. A damping ratio of about 0·65 gives an amplitude ratio close to unity at frequencies up to 60 per cent of the undamped natural frequency. Equipment specifications quote the frequency range over which the amplitude ratio remains within a stated tolerance of unity.

The high natural frequency required for good frequency response can be obtained only at the expense of sensitivity. The sensitivity of a system having a given moving mass (or polar moment of inertia, if the displacement is angular) is roughly proportional to the reciprocal of the square of the undamped natural frequency.

The mathematical analysis of the responses of seismic transducers shows that, for use in the displacement mode, the transducer should have a natural frequency well below that of the input vibration. In this mode, the natural-frequency requirement for the seismic transducer differs from that of the general second-order measuring system. When used in the acceleration mode, the requirement is as for the general system, namely that the natural frequency should be well above the input frequency.

References

1 G. D. Redford, J. G. Rimmer, and D. Titherington, *Mechanical Technology*, Macmillan, 1969.
2 Eric B. Pearson, *Technology of Instrumentation*, The English Universities Press, 1957.

Appendix

Conversion factors

(Most of the factors given below are for the conversion of Imperial units to SI units.)

Length	1 ft	$= 304\cdot8$ mm
	1 in	$= 25\cdot4$ mm
Mass	1 lb	$= 0\cdot4536$ kg
Density	1 lb/ft^3	$= 16\cdot02$ kg/m^3
Pressure	1 lbf/in^2	$= 6\cdot895$ kN/m^2
	1 mmH$_2$O	$\equiv 9\cdot81$ N/m^2*
	1 mmHg	$\equiv 133\cdot0$ N/m^2*
Volume	1 ft^3	$= 0\cdot02832$ m^3
	1 gal (UK)	$= 0\cdot004546$ m^3 $(= 4\cdot546$ dm^3, or *litres*)
Viscosity	1 poise	$= 0\cdot1$ Ns/m^2
Temperature	°C	$= \frac{5}{9}$ (°F $- 32$)
Force	1 lbf	$= 4\cdot448$ N
Torque	1 lbf ft	$= 1\cdot356$ Nm
Energy and work	1 ft lbf	$= 1\cdot356$ J
Power	1 h.p.	$= 745\cdot7$ W

* Dependent on the value of the gravitational acceleration g.

PRINTED IN GREAT BRITAIN
BY ALDEN AND MOWBRAY LTD
AT THE ALDEN PRESS, OXFORD

Index